D0041065

The Last Marlin

VIKING
75 years

FRED WAITZKIN

The Last Marlin
THE STORY OF A FAMILY AT SEA

VIKING

VIKING
Published by the Penguin Group
Penguin Putnam Inc., 375 Hudson Street,
New York, New York 10014, U.S.A.
Penguin Books Ltd, 27 Wrights Lane, London W8 5TZ, England
Penguin Books Australia Ltd, Ringwood, Victoria, Australia
Penguin Books Canada Ltd, 10 Alcorn Avenue,
Toronto, Ontario, Canada M4V 3B2
Penguin Books (N.Z.) Ltd, 182–190 Wairau Road,
Auckland 10, New Zealand

Penguin Books Ltd, Registered Offices:
Harmondsworth, Middlesex, England

First published in 2000 by Viking Penguin,
a member of Penguin Putnam Inc.

1 3 5 7 9 10 8 6 4 2

Names and other descriptive details of several individuals represented in this
book have been altered.

LIBRARY OF CONGRESS CATALOGING-IN-PUBLICATION DATA
Waitzkin, Fred
The last marlin / Fred Waitzkin.
p. cm.
ISBN 0-670-88261-5
1. Waitzkin, Fred. 2. Fishing. 3. Marlin fishing. I. Title
SH20.W38 A3 2000
799.1'6—dc21   99-046887

This book is printed on acid-free paper.

Printed in the United States of America
Set in Stempel Garamond
Designed by Lorelle Graffeo

For Stella and Abe

. *Acknowledgments* .

I COULDN'T HAVE WRITTEN THIS BOOK WITHOUT BONNIE. SHE HAS been a creative and tireless collaborator. Every time I got confused or bogged down, she pointed the direction. Bonnie fixed my sentences. She encouraged and inspired my writing days.

So much thanks to Margaret Johns, for her support over the years. For readings, advice and pep talks I am indebted to Patty Bryan, Mike Bryan, Paulette Chernoff, Tom Chernoff, Steve Hanks, Lynn Mullins, Jeff Newman, Paul Pines, Charles Russell, Steve Salinger, Joe Spieler, Josh Waitzkin and my smart savvy Katya Waitzkin.

When I began writing this book, I believed, I suppose naively, that I remembered my life. I quickly learned that I recalled moments, like buoys in the ocean. But often there was a problem getting from one marker to the next. Conversations with my mother were indispensable. Not only did she remember scenes but her sense of color and juxtaposition and her deep emotion brought me back to my childhood and adolescence. Also I am indebted to Celia Blum, Leon Conn, Betty Holiday, Chet Mudick, Leatrice Rose, Joe Stefanelli and Laurie Ziman for sharing memories. Howie Blum helped me recall the sounds and smells of the plant, and Dad's rage, largesse and humor sitting at his desk above the small Lee Products shop.

Much gratitude for my agent, Binky Urban, who has urged me to write about my father for more than a dozen years and encouraged me through the drafts.

Wendy Wolf, my editor at Viking, did smart careful work, made tough suggestions, nudged me and became a pal.

After reading an early draft of this book, Barbara Grossman said to me that for perhaps the first time, she was moved to admire her own father's business life. That meant a lot.

. Contents .

PART I
EARLY FISHING

. Family Values .

WHEN I BEGAN VISITING BIMINI AS A TEENAGER, I PASSED LONG days in the white fiberglass fighting chair on my father's boat trolling for marlin off the pines north of the island. Even back then fishing for me was a combination of action and fantasy. With long stretches to burn between strikes, I learned to love daydreaming on the ocean. While I stared at the baits and listened to the throbbing diesels, I thought of *Sexy Mama* dancing topless to the thumping beat of conga drums at the Calypso Club halfway between Alicetown and Porgy Bay. I was a drummer myself and imagined her shaking her chest to my beat. I tried to seduce her with passionate slaps and rolls and then I slowed the rhythm until her movements were earthy and we were both dripping sweat. She wouldn't let me touch her. I drummed on the armrest of the fighting chair until her shapely legs and full coffee-colored breasts faded in my mind to office buildings in midtown Manhattan, new high-risers sheathed in plate glass and glimmering with thousands of fluorescent lighting fixtures—I loved thinking about fluorescents. My dad was a lighting fixture salesman, and we were always talking about his newest deals and the finer points of selling. In the fifties there was no one in New York City landing more big fluorescent lighting jobs than my dad.

I kept an eye on the big mackerel and bonefish baits skipping through the white water behind the boat and frequently I bounced up in the chair and pointed astern. But the dorsal fin and long sickle tail sliding off a wave or coming up behind a distant outrigger bait was usually an illusion. The wash of wake and waves churned up legions of record-breaking blue marlin and accolades I would receive on the dock at the Bimini Big Game Club or I could see myself modestly describing my latest eight-hundred-pound catch to envious fifteen-year-old buddies on Long Island.

Then half-asleep I would glimpse a long brown shape beneath the surface forty yards astern streaking toward me and suddenly a massive head coming out right behind the boat, swinging at the mackerel. This was no fantasy. Again the marlin lifted itself out, grabbed the bait, crashed back in, throwing water like a depth charge. I struck with the big rod, my shoulders wrenched forward by a violent lurching weight, bracing against the footrest, and then after the fish's long first run, I reeled until my right arm burned, slowly lifting the rod with my back and legs, winding on the downswing, pumping and winding while the boat backed down into the sea and I was drenched in blue water. I could hear my father's deep cough and feel his tension and excitement behind me. "Look at him jump," I could hear him say. "Look at him jump." After an hour or two of lifting and cranking, this immense beast of my dreams was alongside and we were actually pulling him on board Dad's Ebb Tide.

The value of this curious semi-somnolent blood sport was confirmed to me by its association with Ernest Hemingway, who was, of course, my favorite writer and who, I believed, understood and enjoyed life better than anyone else. In the thirties, when Bimini was anointed sportfishing capital of the world, Hemingway lived on the island, writing and trolling for marlin and bluefin tuna. There were vast numbers of marauding sharks offshore, so many that when a large fish was hooked and slowed by the drag of the reel, it was forced to confront an impossible gauntlet of ten- and twelve-foot killers. When the marlin or tuna was finally cranked to the boat, the pioneer angler cursed his bad luck, for the trophy fish was now backbone and a dead head.

When I first came to the island there were still tremendous numbers of sharks. I was appalled and fascinated that these powerful hunters appeared in the Gulf Stream whenever a game fish was wounded. We even watched hammerheads and tiger sharks finning along the white bathing *beach or slowly moving through the clear water of the Bimini harbor. I could hardly wait to step off the boat in the late afternoon to begin preparing my rigs. In a few hours I would be chumming the water off the Game Club's dark and rickety east dock while my father sat in the bar sipping a Scotch. I caught some big sharks from that dock. One moonless night I hooked one that started leaping—I could hear the heavy thud each time the shark slammed into the calm water. Suddenly it turned back in my direction and the shark rammed the shaky piling right beneath my feet. I was impelled to drop the line and run for my life, but I wanted Dad to be proud of me. I heaved on the thick line wishing he would bring his drink out here and take a look. I actually got the eight-footer onto the dock, a female blacktip, and a dozen little ones wriggled out of her. They squirmed at my feet, and in the confusion of the moment with the mother bucking and snapping at my legs, I didn't know whether I wanted to kick the baby sharks into the water or to crush them with my shoes.*

At the Compleat Angler Hotel, where Hemingway resided much of his time on Bimini, you can see photographs of the writer holding his Tommy gun beside gargantuan dead sharks. Such was his strength and prowess as an angler that he landed the first unmutilated bluefin tuna brought to the Bimini dock. On my first trips to the island I studied photographs of boatloads of large marlin and wahoo he had landed. I thought of the waters off Bimini as Hemingway's Garden of Plenty, a gorgeous blue world landscaped with tuna, marlin, broadbill, shark, kingfish, wahoo, cero mackerel, grouper. It was a child's vision of immutability. Hemingway's smile from the flying bridge of the Pilar *promised limitless catches, thrilling times ahead. Bimini was a place where you could pull in fish forever, where you could troll and never grow old, where your father would never die.*

As a boy I was confused that fishing was a source of tension in our home. I believed that if we kept trolling plentiful waters, Mom and Dad would get along while we made great catches, our family would prosper and endure; but Mother wasn't interested in dropping a line or even coming on the boat. Dad was the fisherman. She considered it boorish and brutal, a big waste of time except when she could work themes and colors of the ocean into her strange art. I kept thinking that Mom would come around. Only today at seventy-eight, when she remembers my father Abe and my brother Bill, does Mother refer to the family sport with a trace of warmth. For Stella, decline has always conferred a measure of distinction.

Mother says that I was conceived in a house across the road from Revere Beach at the north end of Boston, where my parents lived for two months during the first year of their marriage in a cozy, bright room with a view of the ocean. Stella was twenty and had plans to write a great novel. She wanted to be by the sea, to listen to the surf as she had summers with her family in Far Rockaway. As a teenage girl Stella had been romantic and rebellious and had bridled against the provincial outlook and materialism of her immigrant parents. My mother's father was the founder of Globe Lighting, a large fixture manufacturing plant in Brooklyn. It was important for him to show the neighbors his success. He drove a Cadillac and painted the wood in his home with gold leaf, put in taffeta drapes and Persian rugs trying to re-create Versailles. Stella was embarrassed to invite her friends over. Isadore Rosenblatt was a forceful businessman and a patriarch with a master plan for all members of his family, including his eldest daughter. But his merchant dreams were insufferable to my mother, who yearned to be an actress or a writer, something more exotic than the telephone operator job her father had in mind as her springboard into the lighting industry.

Stella met Abe for the first time when the young manufacturers' rep from Boston stopped by the Globe factory wearing his trench coat and felt hat. There was something mysterious and dashing about this young man. "I was struck by your father's hypnotic eyes. I would talk to him about Emerson, Thoreau, Dickens, and he would smile and nod. I believed that he loved these writers," she says tartly.

We are sitting on the raised deck of her small Cape Cod home with a view of the woods at dusk. I've been visiting her for a few days, pressing her to tell me about Abe and Bill, and she has grown tired of it. "I don't share your interest in nostalgia," she declares, the past suddenly between us like an alien land. She is right. I am easily seduced by memories, comforted. Mother would prefer to begin each day with a fresh slate, like a new being. Speaking with her about our lives has been fitful; I ask her questions, she is moved to describe past events, then she becomes angry or emotional, and I resolve to leave her alone. But soon Mother can't resist telling me something more.

"Abe promised to take me away from New York, that we would make our own lives in New England. He could convince you of anything."

My father's desire for the water was a quality Stella found attractive initially, because it played against his salesman lifestyle and materialist cravings. One day in Revere Beach Abe came across a dory in bad shape. He bought it for next to nothing. This first boat was a humble beginning for a passion that would be passed on in curious variations to his children and my children. That winter Abe worked on the little dory, sanded, painted, reinforced the stern for a little engine. But most important, he cut a hole in the center of the open boat, built up a little throne to sit on, a toilet. All my father's relatives were amazed that no water came in the hole. Even as a young man Abe had terrible intestinal problems, cramps, diarrhea. His eyes would bulge from the pain, but he wouldn't say a word about it. The summer before I was born, Abe and Stella rode up and down the Charles River in his dory. Abe loved the boat. It was medicine for his physical pain, a retreat from tension and his abiding anger. Stella cannot recall why he gave up the dory after one summer, and there is no photograph of the double ender, which saddens me. Abe didn't own another boat for ten years.

Mother realized that the marriage was a mistake from the start. She was humiliated and angry each time my father brandished her pedigree to impress his customers. Globe was one of the giants in the lighting industry, and the little New England distributors Abe cultivated from Bangor to Manchester danced on their toes in the presence of Izzy Rosenblatt's daughter. One time Abe introduced Stella to a customer and the man inquired unctuously, "So how is your father?" Stella answered, "Fine, how is yours?" which made Abe furious. My mother has always been one to clobber her foes with words, to dazzle with hyperbole and fiction. They must have been something in the early years: my father, who believed in convention and connections, who charmed with his smile, intimidated with his big green eyes; Mother spinning tales, lashing out without regret, shocking his customers and the Boston relatives. "There was an atmosphere around his friends and family: what a coup, Abe has married the boss's daughter. It was disgusting to me."

She believed that my father decided to give her a baby only to quell her restlessness and disappointment, to keep her trapped. One of his salesman buddies had counseled him, give her a handful of babies, she'll stop complaining. Nonetheless, Abe surprised her with his caring touch as a father and she began to enjoy the life they were making together. Babies—my dad's salesman buddy had been right on target.

Even as a young mother Stella was resolved to make her own career. Borrowing Abe's assertiveness she went to Filene's basement and sold them on the idea of a radio program, *Beauty Is Yours*. Her weekly show began with the song "A pretty girl is like a melody . . ." Stella disseminated beauty tips over the air: the best cream to use if your skin is oily, how to dress if you are underweight, choosing the perfect scarf for a pudgy face. She became the beauty sage of New England, each week answering scores of letters from adoring fans. But the show was a fiction. Stella knew next to nothing about women's beauty products, she has never cared about such things. Over the years my mother has amused herself creating false personas, re-creating reality. She is impatient with prosaic distinctions between truths and lies.

During the early years of the marriage my father began his own little manufacturing business, Lee Products, specializing in wiring troughs and electrical boxes. He sold his electrical enclosures throughout New England. But my father didn't make a hit in Boston, didn't earn any real money. Dad was not suited to be an inside guy. Abe knew that he could sell, but his little shop did not have the capability to manufacture big jobs and Dad lacked the patience to acquire more machines and hire more men, methodically to build his business. It was his style to stay out late wining and dining customers and to sleep late. Abe was frustrated, impatient to make a big success. And often he was sick, doubled over in pain, as if fights with his dad, with whom he did not get along, and competition in the electrical business took a direct physical toll on his frail body. My first memory of my father was from the lawn of a hospital. I was two years old, standing beside my mother, who was pointing to a window two or three stories above. Dad was in the window wearing a bathrobe, waving.

Soon after my brother was born my father moved the family to New York and took over the sales division of my grandfather's business. This was his dream, to test his selling prowess in the big leagues, to be in a position to sell thousands of costly recessed fluorescents instead of dozens of chunky panel boxes. By all accounts my father became a tremendous success, the top commercial lighting man in the New York area. He sold the lighting for the United Nations buildings, Aqueduct Race Track, the Seagram Building, the Socony Building, Time-Life, many others. At dusk, when the Manhattan skyline began to sparkle with lights, it was my dad's work— that's how I saw it.

For my mother the move to New York was high treason and she suspected that for some time her father and mine had been plotting their business association behind her back. "Abe never discussed anything. He just did it," she says. "I was in California when he bought the house in Great Neck. No discussion. Can you imagine just buying the house without my being there? I hated Great Neck. I hated the house. It was an insult. I hid in the closet when a busybody neighbor came to visit with her husband. She came many times. I could hear her calling through the window, 'You can't keep hiding from us. We're your neighbors.'"

When I was ten or eleven my father purchased Babe Ruth's boat from the slugger's widow. I recall going to her apartment in the Bronx with my father to give her the check and to get the title. She was dressed in a bathrobe and stunk badly of alcohol. Garbage was piled in the kitchen. There was no cheering, no more home runs in her life. The Babe had been gone for many years.

The twenty-three-foot speedboat was narrow-beamed with a varnished mahogany finish like fine furniture. "A work of art, a sculpture," Mother said when Abe showed it to her. It was fast—that's what I liked. It had a big inboard that growled at idle speed, issuing a challenge. In the Long Island Sound we took on all comers and rarely lost. One time in the Babe Ruth boat, that's what we called it, we cruised up the Hudson River past the building on the Upper West Side where my mother's parents lived. My father pointed to a balcony on the seventeenth floor, two tiny people sitting in chairs. My father waved exuberantly. I can still see the smile on his face—he was on top. Mother sunned herself and appeared not to notice her parents.

During the first winter my father sanded the boat down to raw wood and then, after filling little cracks with putty, brushed on a half-dozen coats of varnish. Sometimes I patted the smooth hull like a horse's neck. I couldn't believe that it was ours. I wanted to help with the work but Dad became impatient when I sanded against the grain or put too much varnish on the brush so that it dripped. Mostly I watched him work. It was a pleasure watching him stroke on the varnish or tinker with the big engine. My dad was a terrific craftsman and mechanic.

When we went to work on the boat the following winter, Dad discovered dry rot. He pushed a screwdriver through the pretty hull to show me. It was like the boat had cancer. I kept insisting he could fix it, but he shook his head. "We're gonna get rid of it," he said. I couldn't believe that he would get rid of it. I still dream about the Babe Ruth boat.

Dad would often stay out until ten or eleven entertaining his customers. I waited impatiently until I heard the sound of his Buick turning onto the driveway. Then I would run to the hall so that I could give him a hug when he opened the door. Dad explained to me that his customers, his "contacts," as he sometimes referred to them, were his true friends. Perhaps he noticed some flicker of incomprehension on my face for he insisted that I would understand this someday. By now Dad was known in the trade from Bangor to Miami, and whenever he arrived in his Buick for an appointment, he never had to wait. His chin quivered a little when he described how he was received. This made me feel very proud. Once or twice a year he returned to New England to make calls on his old customers and sold some boxes and troughs for his little Boston business, which was now run by his brother-in-law and his father. Although he was making big money in New York, Abe seemed to know that someday he would need these old contacts. This was a form of insurance.

When I was eleven I once traveled with him from Boston to New Hampshire making calls for Lee Products. His customer would usually come into the outer office to greet my father, put a hand on his back, ask how he had been feeling. My father would receive these greetings with a devoted smile, would refer to a recent episode in the hospital as "a rough time." One of them whispered to me that my old man was a great fighter, other men would have given up. I smiled but a shudder went through me. Many nights I had sat at the top of the stairs listening to his moaning. In our home there was often talk of Dad getting sick or doing better, going into the hospital or making a terrific recovery. I worried constantly that I would lose him. But with his customers Dad used his health as a lever—he opened hearts with his courage or his neediness, whatever it took.

I waited in the outer office with a secretary while Dad went in and made his pitch. The longer the meeting took, the better. I wanted it to last forever. I could wait. My father was selling. In the car I would ask him, Did you make a killing? I was thirsty for every detail. As we drove to the next distributor he would tell me about how many troughs and boxes of various sizes and gauge metals he had sold. All of this was so important. After this trip I told my mother that I wanted to be a salesman. She became very upset and called the life of a salesman banal. We argued bitterly. I insisted that I wanted to do what my father did.

Our next boat was a Richardson, a cabin cruiser. My mother actually urged my father to buy this twenty-seven-footer, entranced by the cerulean blue of its hull. On weekends my seven-year-old brother and I would fish for sea bass and porgies off the buoy in front of Sands Point. My brother held his rod with great seriousness, he wanted to catch more than I did. Usually we caught begals, a ratty little fish, flipped them back over. My father always looked so happy when we reeled them in. Occasionally a small boat would come around selling ice cream Popsicles, what a treat. My mother would sit on the bow sunbathing. She had no interest in fish.

During the second summer we took the Richardson all the way to Montauk. There were big seas in the Long Island Sound, towering rollers. Mother watched Dad with admiration as he steered us through the waves. It was so unusual for her to look at him this way. We tied up at the Montauk Yacht Club alongside pricey Wheelers, Huckinses and Ryboviches, run by captains and mates for owners like Bob Maytag, the washing machine magnate, and Denny Phipps, who would soon become president of the New York Thoroughbred Racing Association.

These were the kinds of boats my father yearned to own, stallions of the sea that could power through twelve-foot breakers searching for broadbill swordfish, makos and giant tuna off Block Island or No Mans Land, an island south of Martha's Vineyard. "Someday," he told me. I figured one or two more killings and we would have her.

At the Montauk Yacht Club, everything was larger than life. In the late afternoon grand boats bristling with near unbendable rods and golden reels pulled up to the dock with eight- and nine-hundred-pound tuna and makos—fish that were stupefying, out of this world. I couldn't imagine landing such giants. I peppered captains and mates with questions about where they'd trolled, what baits they'd used. They dismissed me as a pest. In the evening I wandered the endless winding wood-paneled halls of the hotel, which were studded with photographs of record game fish. Even the practical jokes had a mythic quality. One afternoon an enormous kid, known for his angling prowess with tuna, tied my brother by his feet and hung him from the tall scaffold where they weighed in fish. I found Bill hanging there like a forty-pound white marlin. When I lowered him down, he was furious but wouldn't discuss it.

In the evenings, in the crew bar, captains and mates ate thick steaks and traded stories of fierce battles with colossal fish on distant oceans. They fished off Panama for striped marlin, traveled to Chile hunting for thousand-pound broadbill. One story in particular stayed with me. An owner sent his forty-foot boat, manned by the Cosello brothers, an experienced, fearless crew, to Peru to fish for fifteen-hundred-pound black marlin in the Humboldt Current. One afternoon the brothers went out fishing and never returned. It was believed that the boat had been dragged under by a giant squid, a hundred-footer. One of the mates in the crew's bar wore a large white shark tooth on a gold chain and spoke of mammoth blue marlin in the Gulf Stream off an island called Bimini. The past winter his boat had battled a world-record-sized blue marlin off Bimini, but before they could put it in the boat the fish was mutilated by sharks. I was determined to go to these distant places and battle giant fish.

In the Richardson we fished off Montauk Point for bluefish. When one hit, it felt like it would pull your arms off. My mother always rooted for the blues to get off our lines, which infuriated me. I recall Dad cleaning them while they wiggled and the smell when Mom fried fish as we trolled our wire lines. Stella learned to brace herself against the seas and how to cook in a tiny galley, but all the while she knew she should be someplace else.

By the time my dad bought the Richardson, my mother had started spending time painting in her studio, which they built onto the end of the Great Neck house. During our summer fishing trips to Montauk she drove to East Hampton to work with Willem de Kooning, who was borrowing Robert Motherwell's studio. During the school year she traveled regularly to the city to study with the legendary teacher of abstract painting Hans Hofmann, and to attend the lectures of Meyer Schapiro at Columbia. When I came home from school the walls of the house were shaking with the irreverent solos of Thelonious Monk and Charlie Parker on the hi-fi. I hated this music but she told me to keep listening, that I would come to love it. She read aloud passages from Jack Kerouac's *On the Road.* I found them strange and stirring. Mother attended parties in the city where Negro drummers pounded out Afro-Cuban rhythms and smoked dope, homosexuals held hands and kissed. When she told me about these escapades I felt humiliated. My parents lived in different worlds.

I fished despite my mother. How could she find it so distasteful? When my dad was away on business she brought painter friends such as Malcolm Morley and Louise Nevelson to the house. Mother and I would sometimes drive to Port Washington to visit her best friend, Betty Holiday, a painter and photographer. Betty lived sinfully with a young lover. Although she was a beautiful woman with blond hair below her waist, her huge self-portraits were haunted by madness. Life-sized sketches of nudes hung on her bright studio wall, the hips and thighs of Betty's women dissolving into lusty abstract motion, tantalizing. While I tried to glance casually at the nudes, Mother and Betty spoke rapidly about art, how to get more deeply into the work. Painting was everything. My father didn't approve of Betty. I felt that coming to visit her was an act of betrayal.

On the way home I made my mother stop for lunch at Dad's favorite seafood restaurant. The walls were covered with aged fish mounts and photographs of striped bass and bluefish. Then before driving back to Great Neck I insisted that we stop at the bait store to buy a box of sandworms; I always double-checked to make sure the box had a clump of seaweed to keep the worms fresh and moist.

I often fished by myself off the floating dock at the Great Neck Estates Park. One time in the early spring I caught a three-foot eel, kept it squirming at my feet for an hour until my father came for me and I could show it off to him. Occasionally I would attempt to entice my brother Bill into fishing with me, but usually he would say no.

Even as a child, Bill preferred his own company. He loved to walk along the water's edge, skipping rocks into Manhasset Bay or kicking over horseshoe crabs and skates that were rotting in the slime. When I offered to come with him, he turned me down. I could never get him to play ball or to go bowling. He spent time alone with his dinosaur collection, studied books on sharks and sea turtles. He loved Mother's rock garden in the backyard. When Mom blew up the engine in her old Morris Minor, they planted the rusty car in the garden, placed rocks and shrubs around it. Flowers were soon growing out of its windows and trunk. Bill was intrigued by his mother's unusual sensibility; only she could really touch him. It annoyed Bill when her friend Betty visited in the afternoon and the two women sat for hours in the studio talking about painting, not noticing the darkening light. One evening when Betty left to drive home she discovered a big pile of rocks on the hood of her car.

Bill's only friend was a next-door neighbor, Ezra. Sometimes they would go off for hours, and more than once they were brought back by the police for breaking windows with arrows or shooting them into bags of cement piled in front of half-built homes. While the officer explained things to Mother, Bill's expression was unrepentant, fierce. One afternoon four or five children stood on the street in front of our house pelting rocks at Bill, who stood his ground on the driveway flinging rocks back at them. When I rushed outside to help him the kids ran off and Bill became angry, lectured that he didn't need my help. I would try to persuade Bill to sleep in my room. No thanks. Should we play together with your dinosaur collection? Not today. I loved Bill and kept trying. Bill's taste always tended toward the extravagant and bizarre. And so it was not altogether surprising that months before his eighth birthday he showed genuine enthusiasm for my great fishing scheme. While I read fishing magazines and developed my plan, he faithfully kept the secret for an entire winter.

My mother was planning to spend the next summer in Provincetown on Cape Cod painting with Hans Hofmann in his outdoor studio. I had learned that during July and August giant tuna, the most powerful of all game fish, proliferated off Race Point on the west end of Provincetown. I am talking about big tuna. During their annual spring migration up the coast, the bluefins grew huge dining on bluefish off Hatteras, North Carolina, and menhaden in New Jersey's mudhole and the Nebraska shoals south of Rhode Island. When they arrived at Race Point to gorge themselves on mackerel and blues in the rip, many of them had reached eight or nine hundred pounds. Bill and I intended to catch one from a small boat. It would be like bringing down a rhino with a slingshot. We would be the talk of the crew bar at the Montauk Yacht Club.

During the winter I collected gear, large hooks, three nylon handlines. I wanted to catch a bluefin the way the old man had fought the marlin in Hemingway's book—I wanted to feel the fish in my hands. I liked the idea of suffering while the fish was suffering, one of my favorite parts of *The Old Man and the Sea*. When it died two hundred feet below, I wanted to pull my eight-hundred-pounder up with my arms without the leverage of a big rod braced in a fighting chair.

Finally it was summer. We celebrated my twelfth birthday with Mother in Provincetown. It wasn't hard to convince her to rent us a small outboard for an afternoon's cruise in the shallow bay; she was thinking about her painting. That summer Hans Hofmann was in the habit of taking Mother's paintings and ripping them in half, then putting the bottom on the top. I didn't understand this. Maybe she was learning how to paint upside down. The man at the boat rental warning us, "Don't take this skiff out into the ocean. She's not fit for the ocean." I nodded okay. Why would we want to go out there?

I had purchased a half-dozen large squid at a fish market. Gunning the engine, I left the shallow bay and headed east, keeping the skiff about a hundred yards off the beach. The wind was in our faces, and there was a three-foot chop on the ocean. Bill looked into the seas with a resolute expression. After a few minutes he was soaked. Over the years, whenever I could get him to come with me, he was first-rate, a real fisherman, no complaining no matter how rough the sea or bad the fishing. That day it took us about an hour to get to Race Point. I hadn't realized it was so far. The boat was an old fourteen-footer and each time we came off a wave the flimsy bottom shuddered and water seeped in along the seams. Bill bailed with a can.

Finally, ahead of us, I saw the rip, a breaker six or eight feet tall that stretched down the beach for half a mile. From that little boat it looked like a tidal wave. The idea was to keep the bait beneath the curl of the wave, at the edge of the white water. That was what they said in the magazine. The giants would be milling there, feeding on mackerel and blues. There were probably hundreds of them right beneath the white water, some over a thousand pounds. My heart was beating in my ears. The big moment was here. I rigged one of the squid onto a hook and played out the handline. And then I began to worry. What would happen if we got a strike? The beast would hit like a truck. How would I stop it? What if I couldn't? Just holding the handline with the pull of the trolled squid through the ocean was tiring my arm. What if a tuna hit and the line got twisted on my hand? But now, looking astern, preparing myself for the strike, I had lost track of the towering rip. Too late to turn off, we were right into it. Before I could shout to Bill we were clobbered by a ton of wave, sputtering, flooded, the gas can was floating in my lap, life preservers over the side. Somehow, Bill had stayed in the boat and was crouched in the bow holding the gunwale with two hands. But we were sinking. All my planning. I never imagined this. Nothing else to do. I turned the bow to the beach and gunned the engine. Bill couldn't swim. What would happen to my brother if we went down? The motor screamed but the logy boat barely inched ahead. We were mostly underwater when I felt the bow plow into the sand.

Bill and I sat on the beach, some distance apart, and watched the boat turning over and over in the big surf, her flimsy bottom coming apart from the sides. Eventually a Coast Guard officer came up to us on the beach. "What were you kids doing out there?" the man asked me incredulously. My mother was about fifty yards behind him, climbing down a sand dune. She was waving a white handkerchief in the breeze as though we were all playing a scene in a Fellini movie.

Grimly I went back to flounder and eel fishing off the dock in Great Neck. Mostly I fished alone. I was biding my time. All my friends were studying hard for their Bar Mitzvahs. I tried to study but each week I lost my books. Rabbi Guttman got red in the face fighting back his anger with me. I was thinking incessantly about fish. The water in the Long Island Sound was turgid and rank, nothing like what Hemingway described off Cuba, but still there were working birds, and occasionally small fish broke the surface. Each little flounder was a victory. I fished to spite my mother, couldn't stand the way she painted, nothing was recognizable or lyrical. Thick lines of dark colors obscured traces of warmth and form. She was patronizing about my taste in art, which made me furious. She showed me the work of Jackson Pollock, which she greatly admired. I didn't like his painting either.

Occasionally I trolled lures for striped bass in Manhasset Bay. The water was polluted; there were signs posted that swimming was dangerous. Old-timers used to say that they once caught thirty-pound bass here, but the fish had disappeared from this end of the Sound years ago when the water became rank. But one afternoon I caught a five-pounder. My fingers trembled as I tried to take the treble hooks out without breaking its delicate lips. It was a lovely-looking fish, black stripes with a greenish cast in between, wonderfully white flesh when it was cleaned. We broiled my bass that night for dinner. It tasted of diesel fuel. I have never enjoyed eating striped bass since.

When I was thirteen we flew to Miami and went out on a party boat for kingfish. When these forty-pounders hit and made their runs in the green water, they left a bubbly wake like a torpedo. I decided that kingfish were my favorites. That same winter my mother dragged me kicking and screaming to the Philip-Fort Dance Studio on West 44th Street in Manhattan, a seedy-looking place that smelled of sweat. But there was a funky piano paced by the wild rhythms of three black drummers. I had never heard such music. It was seductive and pulled me in. I couldn't get this place out of my mind. Soon I became a regular at the dance studio. I would leave Saturday services in synagogue filled with the strains of mourning—though he was alive, I believed that the Kaddish was for my father—and take the Long Island Rail Road into Manhattan for my weekly conga drumming lesson that was held in a tiny back room crammed with a half-dozen of us pounding away. I was good at drumming, the best in my class. Occasionally I was invited to drum in the front room overlooking the China Bowl restaurant. Black girls in leotards would curl and leap to my white Jewish-boy rhythms. One night one of them kissed me on the lips, held her body against mine. I ran back down Seventh Avenue to Penn Station, rushed home to Great Neck in a sweat, tried not to think about it. I fished for Olatunji and for my father and for Ernest Hemingway. I dreamed of catching kingfish off Miami and of the black girl, though I avoided her at the studio. What a fool I was. She was so beautiful.

. De Kooning or the Blues .

THE SUMMER I TURNED FIFTEEN MY FATHER CHARTERED A BOAT
out of Frank Tuma's dock in Montauk. I had dreamed of this day. We
were going after broadbill swordfish, the fastest of all game fish, a
seventy-mile-per-hour sprinter with freight-train-pulling power. We
had to run twenty miles out before even starting to look for swordfish. It was rough and foggy. All day the captain, a tall, rough-talking
John Wayne type, rode the swaying tuna tower searching for working birds, fins and telltale color changes beneath the cold slate-colored
ocean. As Dad was too weak to pull on a three- or four-hundred-
pounder, I was the angler. I sat in the fighting chair, waiting, wet from
spray and fog. Mom and Bill sat behind me on the engine box, whispering and giggling. They were in their own world.

The captain eventually allowed me to join him on the lurching
tower platform. He predicted that we would find a swordfish late in
the afternoon, which seemed far-fetched. How could he possibly
know this? While he scanned the ocean he held me transfixed with
stories told with an edge of menace: a few years before, a thousand-
pound mako had ripped off half the stern of his boat, they had had to
bail furiously to make it back to Montauk. One time, when he was
night fishing off Islamorada, a hooked sailfish, attracted by the light,

had leaped aboard and speared his lady angler through the chest, killed her. The captain had learned a lesson from this: when night fishing he would try to keep his cockpit light off.

If we found a broadbill, he told me, we would let it eat the bait for a full minute, maybe longer. Broadbills have soft mouths. If you hook one in the mouth, the hook almost always pulls out. We wanted it hooked deep in the belly. I nodded, deep in the belly. All the while he glared at the water. Hours passed, no fish. I worried that the day would end. When would I ever get another chance like this? Soon I would be back on the Great Neck Estates floating dock dropping down sandworms for eels.

A half hour before we had to turn back, the man tensed, focused on a far-off patch of ocean. He hissed for me to go down, get into the chair. I couldn't see a thing and told him so. When he turned toward me I thought he was going to throw me off the tower.

From below I could see that he was tracking something, like a hunter in the woods, the boat just idling ahead. Fifteen or twenty minutes later, behind the boat, I spotted a tall fin clipping the rough sea like a ragged stick. I was harnessed now to a heavy rod and reel, which was in free spool so the fish would feel no pressure when it mouthed the bait. The boat was dead in the water. The mate spoke to me in hushed tones as though I would soon endure the greatest test of a lifetime. I was very nervous. How had the captain known we would find one in the late afternoon?

Line began jerking off my huge reel. The mate reminded me to let him eat for a minute. Soon the fish was running with it and in no time a couple of hundred yards were off the spool. I was afraid that I would lose it all. It was like the moment in the movies when they say not to fire until you can see the whites of their eyes. I recall the mate telling me to strike, and then I hefted up the pole maybe a foot and came up against a wall of resistance. I tried again to set the hook. I remember only fragments of the fight. The captain charged after the streaking jumping fish, the engine roared, the captain and mate cursed, yelled orders back and forth. The mate helped me lift the rod and wind the reel and said that I was doing a great job.

Eventually the fish tired and I could see him close beneath the waves, long as a skiff and colored radiant purple, who could even imagine capturing such a creature? With each pump of the rod and wind of the reel I pulled him two feet closer. I remember Mother clenching her fist and closing her eyes, praying for my swordfish to get off the line. I screamed at her to stop doing this. About forty-five minutes after we hooked it, the eleven-foot fish was stone-cold dead on the deck and quickly turned black; the captain was smiling broadly and shaking my hand.

It was hard to find our way back in the fog. A half-dozen boats stayed close to us as though sharing a piece of our glory. Three hours later we weighed in the 309-pounder at Tuma's dock while Yul Brynner and Eli Wallach stood by gaping with jealousy—they had been skunked that afternoon. My mother gave me a big hug. I remember this because it was so unusual. Mother had become afraid of the passion she felt for her sons after reading in a psychology text that kissing and hugging little boys might create Oedipal problems later, but she bent to the fervor of the hour. Maybe for a moment or two she wondered if she had been wrong about fishing.

Nonetheless, subsequent fishing trips were marred by Mother's reluctance to come out in the boat. At the last minute she would persuade us to take her to Frank Motherwell's studio in East Hampton where de Kooning was painting and also working with a few students. The twenty-mile drive often meant that we would miss the tide. We would be arriving at the Point in the Richardson after the other boats had already filled their boxes with blues and the fishing had turned slack. During dinners at the club we would be talking about the action off the point or a big mako or broadbill that had been landed by one of the forty-footers, and Mother would interrupt the flow with something de Kooning had said about her watercolors. She confided to me that he was a giant, he had eyes that penetrated your soul. Her adulation rankled me. I am sure that her distaste for my fishing life spurred me on.

I wanted to be great, but the path was not always easy. One afternoon, without mentioning it to the owner, my brother and I borrowed a skiff that was tied up at the Yacht Club's small boat dock. There were ten- and fifteen-pound fluke running just outside the Montauk jetties, locals called them "doormats." I had asked a pretty girl to come along with us, and a friend, Jon Lehman. I wanted to show them what a real fisherman could do. After catching my broadbill I was swelling with fishing pride and impatient to take my place in

the inner circle of Montauk captains. But it was rougher than I anticipated in the bay and soon our overloaded boat was taking waves over
the side. I cursed the little boat and kept pushing for the jetties. I was
determined to show this lovely girl how to catch doormats. It was
amazing to me how quickly the boat filled with bay water. I watched
us sink in disbelief. Seconds after the engine sputtered to a stop, the
boat flipped over. We were holding on to the slippery bottom for life,
waving at runabouts that were planing in the distance. When no one
turned our way Jon and the girl swam to shore for help. Bill still
couldn't swim and a few times he lost his grip and paddled weakly
while I tried to keep a hand on him. Once again, near to drowning, my
brother stuck out his jaw and seemed prepared to accept his fate.
Death was never the concern to Bill that it has been for me.

Even before a cruiser came alongside and hauled us from the chilly
water, I was wrestling with my shortcomings as a skipper. My father
drank all night in the crew's bar and accepted consolation from the
captains and mates I admired so much. This was a terrible humiliation. Mother was as oblivious to this newest sea disaster as she had
been to the last one. But other than her disinterest there was no retreat from the gossip of boat stealing and bad seamanship.

One afternoon Mother was folding sheets in the Laundromat in East
Hampton when de Kooning came in with Jackson Pollock. By way
of introduction de Kooning told Pollock that she was a painter,
spending time in Montauk fishing with her family, and Pollock invited her to come by his home. Stella drove to Springs and found
Pollock drinking beer in his barn in the early afternoon. She was surprised that he wasn't working. If she didn't paint for even one day,
Mother was afflicted by guilt.

Stella had brought a gift of some bluefish we had caught the day
before off the point and Pollock was delighted. "Why don't you
bring your boat to Springs and we'll do some fishing," he suggested.
Oh great, she thought, Jackson Pollock and Abe hip to hip in the
stern jigging for blues.

Pollock showed her his recent drip paintings on large sheets of
glass and then they talked for hours about the New York art scene.
He was concerned what New York artists were saying about his
work and pressed Stella for opinions and information.

In the fifties New York artists were often jealous about rising reputations and who was getting credit for various stylistic break-throughs. Hans Hofmann claimed that he was the first to use the drip method. Others said that it was Pollock. The critic Harold Rosenberg had recently been extolling de Kooning as the greatest painter of the day and others were saying that Pollock's run as an in-novator was over. His rise had been meteoric but now he felt sup-planted and was depressed and drinking much of the time. When Mother mentioned these issues to me I became angry. Who cares who dripped paint first or whether Kline's black lines were more im-portant than de Kooning's tortured women? She spoke of de Koo-ning and Pollock like gods. I kept thinking that my mother was temporarily sidetracked and waited impatiently for her return to normalcy. I knew that she could paint realistically if she wanted to. I tried to reason with her about her art and she laughed at me. I couldn't imagine why she persisted in this awful style.

I felt bad for my father. How could he put up with abstract paint-ing and Mother's oddball friends? Her rebelliousness was galling. Why was she so oblivious to his success? He was selling more com-mercial lighting than any other five salesmen in the city. He hob-nobbed with electrical distributors like Maxi Kamins, Sauli Schniderman and Harry Fischbach—the giants of the industry. Dad was lighting the sky with recessed fluorescents. Some of them were manufactured with his own invention called the "miracle hinge." When he walked into posh midtown restaurants Dad didn't even need to order: maître d's knew his favorite dishes. I was so proud of him. When he was away selling in Cleveland or Detroit, I would smell the shoes in his closet, the sheets on his bed.

From time to time Mother hinted that she would leave him. She would remark gravely, "I want you to be prepared." I thought that she was saying this just to torture me—that the problems were be-tween her and me. It was my job to argue with her, to appease her. Dad was above this strife, selling. We were so close to getting the forty-footer.

Mother wouldn't mention divorce for a month or two and I would become convinced that it had gone away. She was content to paint in her studio. She played the records of George Shearing and Cal Tjader, urged me to drum along on my congas. She brought me

Tito Puente records. I beat along on the *timbales*, which made her happy. I rapped out rhythms on the cowbell while she danced in the living room in her leotard. Her earthy dancing made me uneasy but I went along with it. She gave me Camus to read, urged me to write stories like him. I agreed, but secretly I knew that I would be a salesman, Mother would stay married, we would get the forty-footer.

. Bimini Sweet Bimini .

UNLESS MY MEMORY DECEIVES ME THE FINE DOCKS AND SHADED *cottages at the Big Game Club have hardly changed. At night the surface of the original kidney-shaped pool still shimmers with lights; palm trees rustle in the breeze, and the sea-scented air fills me with longing as it did when I first came here. As a teenager on Bimini I would notice prim and proper secretaries from Miami and Orlando bound off the Chalk's seaplane hungry for piña coladas, the mandatory prelude to the weekend hunt for black lovers. On Sunday afternoon before the last flight out, the white ladies strolled the waterfront with their muscled conch fishermen as though love had forever conquered social convention. I glance at the pool now and recall sultry nights spanning four decades watching nude ladies frolic in the shallow water. On this tiny island even the most conventional folk feel the license to throw off their clothes. One late night I was drawn to the pool by the howling of island dogs. As I sat spellbound in the shadows I watched a federal prosecutor who'd been a player in a big obscenity trial fornicate with his girlfriend in the shallow end as she sipped tequila and threw back her lovely neck and said in a southern drawl, "To kill ya."*

On Bimini time slows down, becomes layered and thick. It's hard to connect the moments to specific years. Take a skiff ride from the Game

Club up to Porgy Bay, running between the broken stakes that mark the green inside channel, past little mountains of ancient conch shells, past Ansil Saunders's wooden boat ramp, then head north beside the baseball field where Jackson Ellis hit his Homeric blast, bonefish flats spreading east and south for miles. The channel veers close to shore beside the dump, somehow aromatic when they burn Bimini garbage, the smoke marking the direction of the wind and determining which way the off-shore boats will head in the morning. The channel passes the power plant, the A&A liquor supply where I once stopped to give Isaac three plump strawberry groupers in return for a half-dozen lobster tails. Now the route isn't marked, but I can find my way by sticking to the green water that runs deep right up against the flats; past Charlie Rolle's cinder-block factory, out of business because Charlie's blocks were too sandy (homes built with these blocks might crumble in a big blow); recalling a time when the island was overrun with howling, emaciated dogs and a guy in Porgy Bay carried a half-dozen of them out in his skiff along with six of Charlie's blocks, tied a block with a length of rope to a front leg of each of the dogs, and pushed them over one at a time as though he were set-ting channel markers. The dogs bloated and with their genitals engorged and bobbing up and down like buoys in the current, they marked this part of the channel for weeks (for some reason the sharks left them alone); next we come alongside Charlie's little rental cottages in Porgy Bay. I had loaned him the money to finish building one of them twenty-five years ago, and in return he had let me live there for three summers when I was fishing for marlin with my wife Bonnie out of a twenty-foot open boat and Minnie Davis was taking care of our son Josh. We ride past the decrepit dock and little cottage where Craig Tenant lived on the thirty-two-foot Pacemaker he ran for Judy Hammond. He became my closest friend. Craig had traveled to Bimini seeking adventure and a new lease on life. His exploits, along with those of a few other expatriates liv-ing in rustic Porgy Bay, would change the character of Bimini to this day; although, cruising north from the Game Club along the inside channel, the island looks remarkably as it did in the home movie my dad shot run-ning up this lovely waterway in a skiff when I was fifteen.

"It was Abe's dream to pull up at a fancy marina with a big boat," says my mother. "He wanted to make a statement: Do you know who I am? I'm not some jerk. I'm Abe Waitzkin. I once said to him, 'Abe, you're so tense. I think you should pump gas for a living.' I thought pumping gas was sexy. But Abe became furious and told his sister Celia what I'd said. 'She wants me to be a gas station attendant. Abe Waitzkin!'" After so many years living alone in her house on Martha's Vineyard Island, making sculpture, Stella remains angry with Abe. She can't give it up or doesn't want to. When she lashes into him I become a kid again, feeling the need to defend my father. "Abe is so conventional," she used to say to me, "a lighting fixture salesman . . ."

What did my mother know about the art of selling? She never listened to him, didn't care. I listened. He was as much a master of timing and mood as George Shearing or Dizzy Gillespie. He knew when to cool it or exactly the moment to tighten the screws. He would call a contractor on the phone and speak softly about illness in the man's family, fishing for cod off the Boston lightship, or the deer that grazed on the contractor's wooded back lawn in New Jersey. A sweet deal was hanging in the air, but Dad wouldn't touch it. Not yet. Sitting next to him I would ache—why doesn't he pull the trigger? Dad might even sound offended by the crassness of selling panel boxes. We'll fish together in the islands, he'd romance his customer. . . . How is your daughter? . . . Terrible what that guy did to her . . . Prick bastard . . . Don't worry, we'll all go out in the boat. . . . There was always a subliminal dialogue and both men listened like hounds. Businessmen positioning themselves while musing about their declining sex drives or the terrible fire at the Cocoanut Grove that had killed Abe's cousin. Before hanging up the receiver Dad ruefully accepted a fifty-thousand-dollar job for Lee Products, work to keep the Boston shop busy for three months. Beautiful. He waited until he could see the whites of their eyes.

Abe's warmth and friendship were legend in the trade. Wives played second fiddle as Dad wined and dined his buddies, hatching grand plans for high-risers in Chicago and fishing trips in Puerto Rico. When the water was calm he guided tough guys to unexpected moments of empathy and caring. More than his lighting fixtures, more than Globe or Lee, my father became his own product. Along with profit, camaraderie was the payoff for a big order faithfully executed with Abe. I watched in awe, loaned him to his contractors and union guys for a night or a week. Even while I yearned for my father to come home to go fishing or to watch me play softball, I loved imagining his dinners in distant nightclubs with Maxi Kamins, who was Danny Kaye's brother, and Sauli Schniderman, or their fierce joy sitting at the fights in Philadelphia; there were legendary moments, such as the night that the great light-heavyweight champ, Harold Johnson, was drugged and lost to the plodding Julio Mederos. Dad was there ringside making a deal with Billy Blieman. Unable to sleep in my bed, I watched him walking through airports with his brief-case fat with orders. He was coming home to me.

Mutual trust is the key to selling, Dad told me. The pact between business friends was sacred, and unless someone gave him a real screwing Dad was faithful as a monk. He worried about his buddies. He brought home their concerns and was pained when a successful salesman or manufacturer was down on his luck. Dad rarely turned down a friend who needed a favor, loaned money even when he was short. But his specialty was health, and in this regard he always came through. The biggest contractors in the lighting industry came to Dad with their medical problems. Abe had connections with the top stomach guys at a distinguished research hospital in Boston that he warmly referred to as "the Clinic." Dad frequently invited surgeons from the Clinic out in his boat. The doctors fell in love with Abe. They found it exciting to talk with him about business deals.

Probably because he had survived many close calls himself, it seemed to his customers, as it did to me, Dad had inside information about life and death. He frequently booked friends into the Clinic, for surgery, mostly abdominal operations. When Abe picked up the phone and called the hospital, there was no waiting time for major surgery. One time he told me that even the British prime minister, Anthony Eden, had to wait his turn for a stomach operation at the Clinic while Dad and his customers were always moved promptly to the top of the list. Dad had a way of talking about major surgery as though it was only slightly less onerous than time spent in resorts like the Ocean Reef Club in Key Largo, where he liked to entertain his customers. Most contractors seemed to have stomach problems, and Dad had it down to routine: It's not so rough, I can recall him saying on the phone. He calmed them, pointed out that he had been through much worse, and booked them into the Clinic. Years later several of Dad's customers complained of losing feet of intestine, or in one instance a stomach, when it wasn't necessary. I don't know if this is true or not. What is clear, without question, is that Dad eased their fears. They believed in him and he landed the orders.

But occasionally contractors said no to Dad, and then the change in him was fast and stunning. Abe's face blistered with rage as if he'd been pelted by deceit and betrayal, his thin arms and legs gained strength from some desperate source. He forced his spindly frame through the closing door. He vented fury with spittle on his lip, choked on his cigarette smoke, spit into a handkerchief, came up running. Who could face down this emaciated man with huge damning eyes? Defeat was no option. He knew the vulnerabilities of his customers, his buddies, after all, and, if it came to that, Abe Waitzkin's revenge would be unfettered by remorse.

Perhaps even more than reprisal, I think it was Dad's style that won losing games. Abe recognized that power could be gleaned from a weakened body—this frail vessel pushed by a whirlwind of fury to be on top, to close the deal. At any second Abe might tear apart, literally split a gut. But he held the pedal to the floor, always took the dare. Dad had no fear of imploding, of vessels bursting his brain, of dying. But more to the point, he knew how to use illness and the specter of his demise—whatever it took. When Dad finally wrote up the order, his ravished customer was so relieved to be free of Abe's tension and blackmail, for life to continue as before. They called him "Transfusion" in the trade because of his chicken-bone arms and legs, his near-to-death bearing. Imagine, "Transfusion." The name humiliated my mother, but Dad grinned, rolled and clicked the false teeth in his mouth.

The winter after my first swordfish, we flew to Miami. "Abe heard about this little island, Bimini, from one of his gangster friends," says Mother. "He would have been happy to keep going to the Fontainebleau in Miami. He didn't like blacks. He said they smelled, except for Dizzy Gillespie. One time at a club Dizzy stopped by Abe's table. After this, Abe called Dizzy his friend." Whenever Mother referred to Dad's friends in the business as gangsters, I became enraged. This aspersion impugned his art. She insinuated that Dad landed so many big deals for Globe Lighting because he arranged kickbacks to electrical contractors or bribed city commissioners or union big shots. She was only guessing. She would say anything against him. But in this instance the haggard man who told us about Bimini had recently come out of jail for some unexplained offense.

In Miami we visited the man's lighting fixture plant. It was boarded up, with weeds growing between cracks in the cement in the parking lot and loading bays. There were three or four abandoned forklifts with tires melted by the sun. This sorry state must have been related to his jail time. While we walked through the hot, empty factory, Dad and I agreed wordlessly that this was a shame, a tragedy. The plant must have been 125,000 square feet. I could almost hear the crack of spot welders, the crunch of the ten-thousand-pound automated shear that had once bent ten-foot sheets of eighteen-gauge steel like cardboard. Cut into the floor there was an empty concrete pool littered with debris. Such a waste. I knew the sharp pungent smell of the degreasing tank when it bubbled with cleaning solvent. I had grown up around the sights and smells of factories, and to me they were the good earth. I took pride in my knowledge of the names and proper placement of heavy machines. Dad and I had often talked about the best layout for a plant, moving presses and lathes in our heads like rooks and knights in a chess variation. I envisioned big commercial jobs rolling toward the loading bays, belted bunches of fixtures on forklifts, the enamel still sweet-smelling and warm from the oven. Oddly enough, Mother also enjoyed the acrid smell of a lighting fixture plant. She paused to admire the huge conveyor-belted oven that had once been used to bake white and gray enamel on eight-footers. She observed that the oven would be perfect for melting glass into sculpture. The man had smiled sadly at this and mopped his brow with a handkerchief.

Later, we relaxed with the manufacturer on his hundred-foot yacht that had also fallen into neglect. In the salon the varnish had blistered and there was a dank, moldy smell like unwashed sheets. He and his wife lived on board. She was in a bathrobe, sipped her drink, occasionally mumbled something. He paid no attention to her.

While they drank Scotch, the manufacturer confided to Dad that he had to "get back on his feet." Abe was supportive, threw an arm across the man's shoulder. They began to talk about the lighting business, trading guys they knew who had closed deals for Lightolier, Neo-Ray or Ruby-Philite. I loved this shoptalk; just the names of these great firms gave me goose bumps. Behind all their palaver was the fact that Dad ran the commercial division of Globe. In the industry "Globe" was a name that filled men with awe. Dad assured the haggard man that soon he would have his welders and presses operating again. Who knows, maybe he could subcontract a deal for Globe. The possibility of doing business with my grandfather's company hit this battered man like adrenaline. Next thing he was speaking about getting new batteries for his yacht, varnishing the mahogany, taking her to the Bahamas.

We stood on the foredeck of the hundred-footer, tied up on the intracoastal directly across from the Fontainebleau Hotel. The new hotel's galaxy of shining windows lit the Miami night with glamour and promise. It was a monument to my father's dreams. Dad was smiling, feeling great. The strains of a poolside rumba band carried our way on a soft breeze and seemed to suffuse my mother, who closed her eyes and moved her shoulders to the beat. The next morning we took our first trip to Bimini.

We stayed at the Big Game Club in one of the original cottages on the north end, near the old Lerner Marine Laboratory. From our porch we watched large hammerheads and tiger sharks circling in dockside pens. Mother immediately began painting watercolors of pelicans on the pilings. Her colors were softer than in New York, but I could not find any pelicans in them. Bill loved these paintings. With a little rod he dropped his line for grunts and snappers. Stella didn't mind his colorful little fish. She considered them ethereal and otherworldly, connected to his unusual fantasy life and love for ancient creatures.

Mother complicated my more conventional big game fantasies by pointing out the stunning women wearing tight pants and stiletto heels who appeared magically on the island each afternoon with the seaplane from Miami. In the evening they walked slowly down the dock, gift-wrapped and thrilling, languorously swinging their hips, seeming to select yachts to board like chocolates from a box. Mother was amused by my gaping adolescent sexuality and Great Neck values. One day she introduced me to a gangly man in a cowboy shirt and hat whom she met outside the Compleat Angler Hotel. He was a past bull-wrestling champion of the United States. His ribs and

shoulder were broken, and he was on the island recovering for a
month before returning to the rodeo circuit. When she felt that I was
duly impressed, she mentioned that he was sharing a room in the
Compleat Angler with his boyfriend.

Mother was always on the lookout for Bohemian life choices,
ragged edges, blotches on pretty faces. She loved all floundering
souls. She would call reprobates and underachievers "great artists,"
which was confusing to me. Most merchants and professionals, in her
view, were losers. Mother took pleasure in Bimini's underside, the
whores, the drunks. She was captivated by the rusting refrigerators
and propane tanks that were unceremoniously dumped on the North
Beach by the diaphanous blue water, called them "sculpture." When I
objected, she said that I was blind and ordered me to look again.

Mother noticed that Bimini had an appeal that was only tangential
to big game fishing. This spit of sand attracted celebrities who were
down on their luck, healing or in hiding. Just being on this staging
area for big fish hunts conferred a measure of cultured machismo. It
was like visiting Pamplona before the feria, swimming in Hemingway's prose without reading a sentence. On Bimini in 1958 one was
surrounded by the unassailable purpose and art of angling without
needing to pull on a seven-hundred-pounder.

While Mom painted her abstract pelicans, Mike Wallace walked the
King's Highway with a fierce expression, plotting his next exposé.
His style of journalism was brand-new, shocking, no one was quite
sure whether it was a new art form or a heightened expression of mal-
ice. Sammy Davis, Jr., was holed up at Brown's Hotel recovering from
exhaustion and some form of substance abuse. Sammy sat at the bar,
sad smile, played with his cigarette smoke, stared quizzically at the
photographs on the wall. All of them were more or less the same: a
man dressed in a gaudy Hawaiian shirt, big cigar in his mouth, holding a heavy bent butt rod with a Fin-Nor reel, standing alongside one
or two large blue marlin hanging by the tail from a scaffold. A few
years before, this man, Axel Witchfeld, had spent the month of August on Bimini and had caught at least one blue marlin for thirty-one
consecutive days. To me, this was like hitting seventy homers in a season. Occasionally I still wonder what Sammy thought about all the
big dead fish. He sat there day after day with this sad but grateful expression, soaking in atmosphere like a weak man sipping soup.

That was the first year that Julian Brown, my friend Ozzie's older brother, began running the hotel for his dad, Harcourt Brown. Julian was back from the Olympics, where he had run the four-forty for the Bahamas, coming in fourth. He had missed a medal by an expanded chest. It seemed like such a terrible loss to me, but handsome, quick-witted Julian was looking ahead to great success in his life. One evening he confided to my dad that Sammy could barely walk, his liver was real bad. Maybe he would die. This was sobering news; in Vegas a few years earlier Sammy had stopped by Abe's table for a drink. On Bimini, perhaps because of my father's concern, Sammy's weakened state seemed earthshaking, like war against Israel.

By then Dad had already made a lasting mark on the island. One morning, on the spur of the moment, I had invited our handsome young bonefish guide, Ansil Saunders, to have breakfast with us at the Game Club. I had no idea that blacks were not permitted to eat in the dining room, which was festively decorated with larger-than-life portraits of locals cracking conch, cleaning turtles and hanging laundry in the breeze. When the waiter refused to seat us, my father was incensed. How could this short sweaty Negro say no to Abe Waitzkin? My father, who never had the patience or interest to focus on social or political questions, could not accept being crossed. He stormed into the kitchen demanding that we eat our eggs there. But in the kitchen there was no place to sit and the counters were greasy; Dad's eyes were bulging; what to do? The cook and waiter were flummoxed: Abe was bullying them with the same withering wide-eyed stare that buckled the confidence of union tough guys. We were all led back into the dining room and served.

After that memorable breakfast we went bonefishing and Ansil demonstrated his wondrous art. We caught six fish that morning, including a nine-pounder that ran like a torpedo. While he poled across the flats and stalked a quarry that was invisible to me, Ansil described his life on the shallow water.

As a teenager he had fallen in love with the flats. He spent long days in a skiff above this terrain of translucent water over expanses of grass and stretches of white sand, telltale currents, ripples and weed lines, half-beached hammerheads, tailing permit, skittish barracuda, leaping leopard rays and diving seabirds. Ansil followed mysterious trails through forests of mangroves and cold underground currents said to have medicinal value, cool deep pools thick with snapper, the trails opening onto miles of flats, looking through glare on the water for little clouds of mud hiding grubbing bonefish, their clusters of tails breaking the surface like mangrove shoots. As a young man he discovered that he could sense bonefish before he could see them, and then in the distance he could pick them out so far away that other young Bimini men believed he was imagining bonefish. Drifting on his little weather-beaten skiff with his arms folded, he became Lord of the Shallows. His minyan swam here and there with rush and purpose on this grassy potholed plain that was magnified and made hallucinogenic by a lens of slow-moving water.

Ansil had studied the wind and tide and took meticulous notes on the habits of his quarry. He learned where the schools scattered when the tide began to ebb, where they congregated on the spring tide; when the wind blew out of the north he knew the deep spots to find them along the mangroves. He discovered that there was reason and rhythm to the arrival and mysterious disappearance of the great schools.

A year or two after our first trip to the island, Ted Williams said that Ansil was the only man he knew who had eyes better than his own; Ansil could see bonefish in water muddied by wind and current; he could find them in the late afternoon when the sun was lying on the water and he was staring into a blinding sheet of glare, could see or sense these gray ghostly fish on cold, sunless days in March when there was a roaring wind out of the northeast and the other guides didn't leave the dock. Visitors to Bimini began referring to Ansil as the greatest fisherman in the world.

Following our breakthrough meal, Ansil Saunders began having his breakfast once or twice a month in the Big Game dining room. No one ever tried to stop him. The Red Sea had parted. My father had gained the reputation on Bimini for being a great freedom fighter. Fifteen years later, during Ansil's tenure as Bimini's mayor, he would give a speech before Prime Minister Pindling and the Bahamian Parliament in Nassau in which he recalled breaking the color line at the Big Game Fishing Club with the help of a courageous idealist, Abe Waitzkin.

Of course Sammy Davis didn't die in 1958. He was back in Vegas a week later, hoofing and crooning with Frankie and Dino. Everyone got well on Bimini. This was my early impression. My father would sometimes arrive on the island barely able to move and after a week trolling in the Stream he was ready to sell, "a new man" was his phrase. On the wall of the Compleat Angler Hotel and Bar there was a motto: The days that a man spends on the sea fishing are not subtracted from his allotted time. I wondered if this might actually be true. Legend, superstition and fact mixed easily in this watery place where men pulled larger-than-life creatures from the depths.

One fine morning during the first Bimini trip, Dad chartered a sportfishing boat out of the Game Club. The captain was a freckled man, Bill Verity, the lover of Sexy Mama, who danced topless at the Calypso Club. There were two mates, David, a tall, handsome man with a bad speech impediment, and Eric Sawyer, a short, ruddy-skinned Bahamian, Bimini's foremost blue water skipper, who happened to be between captain jobs. He had been Hemingway's captain twenty-five years earlier.

"Hemingway was very strong, you couldn't beat him as an angler," recalled Eric. "And he knew a lot. He taught me the Cuban style of rigging baits. We were never much successful with the drift fishing they did in Cuba, too many sharks over here. But we caught many marlin trolling."

For me this was the real Bimini, not the whores and celebrities or even the bonefish flats. I had dreamed of this day, blistering morning sun, diesels throbbing, dragging baits across Hemingway's blue ocean. As we trolled the swells, I imagined canyons below crowded with huge feeding fish. I was in the chair, in the big leagues only a few years behind immortals like Tommy Gifford, Kip Farrington, George A. Lyon, Axel Witchfeld and Hemingway himself, men who had refined the techniques of big game fishing and landed many world records right here off the north end of Bimini. Not to mention Eric, who had once catered to Hemingway and now adjusted my back harness and treated me like a big deal.

"Some days I'd tell Hemingway, we're gonna hook a blue off Picket Rock at four-thirty," he said. "Come four-thirty, there he was, long and brown, moving like a tiger behind the bait. I have a knack, can't explain it. It's a feeling I have about finding fish. I know when and where to look. It is like when you go to sleep and dream the answer to a question. Hemingway would treat my predictions like a joke, he never believed me even though I showed him many times. 'Eric, it's just a coincidence,' he'd say." Even at forty Eric did not make conventional distinctions between the supernatural and the here and now. As he grew older, and less sensitive to doubting Toms, he more frequently reported miraculous events: deceased friends reappearing on Bimini to give him messages and advice; dreaming at night about lost treasure from a sixteenth-century galleon and then actually finding it in the mangroves of South Bimini. I am tempted to say that great saltwater skippers have an unusual capacity for fantasy and that finding gigantic fish requires a visionary side. But in truth, some of the very best skippers in the world could not be more literal and logical in their approach to finding game fish.

It was afternoon now. As Verity searched for working birds, David, second mate, rigged mullets and sang to the blue cloudless sky: "Bimini, sweet Bimini, drop your line in the water and catch a blue marlin—one, two, three." There were many verses celebrating the great catches and limitless bounty of Bimini's waters. In all the island bars and restaurants guitarists joyfully crooned these lyrics of perennial conquest—they still do today—but David was a natural blues singer and his rendition pricked my fishing optimism and left me with uncertainty and yearning. Over time I would learn that wondering and musing are, at least for me, at the center of marlin fishing. But at fifteen I was not looking for spiritual depths. I wanted a big fish in the boat, I wanted trophies and glory, fame; and David's song brought me back down to earth. We had not caught a blue marlin one, two, three, and from where I sat it did not seem likely we would. I could not imagine how a blue marlin could find my mullets and mackerel in all the acres of breaking foamy seas. "The big ones come up late in the afternoon," Eric mentioned to calm me, "when the water begins to cool."

As we worked north into head seas, I started each time a school of baby flying fish broke from the crest of a wave, imagining a ten-footer racing up at the school from below. Dad was standing behind me enjoying his sea legs. Soon he began talking about business. As a fisherman I have always needed quiet to concentrate, to ready myself. But talking about fixtures with my father was irresistible.

Dad was about to close the Aqueduct Race Track deal. I had little enthusiasm for this job and told him so. It was smaller than some of the others and I felt that it was a waste of his time. He would need to spend many hours poring over blueprints deciding which little fixtures belonged in nooks and crannies. I favored the chunky rectangular buildings that in the late fifties and early sixties were springing up in major cities. The new generation of skyscrapers, with thick, tinted floor-to-ceiling windows, required nearly unbroken miles of recessed fluorescents. From the street you could see them lighting labyrinthine mazes of halls and offices.

Dad assured me that although it was more spread out, Aqueduct Race Track would be a good job, more than a million dollars in lighting. There were offices, restaurants, barns, tack rooms, training facilities, bathrooms. I remained dubious and Dad seemed to consider my restraint. Big buildings were going up all over the country. All of them would require thousands of units of lighting. It was only a question of Dad having the time and health to fly from city to city closing deals. As we fished, we felt the greatness of our plans. Together we would light the cities and troll big baits for marlin.

Mother and Bill were the other team. I was in the fighting chair, Bill sitting on one of the engine boxes, occasionally looking at me, fuming. He didn't care about fluorescents. He was biding his time, brooding about his own fishing life, which he would not discuss with me. He dreamed of catching twenty-foot sharks—smashing my father with his great catches. He was already studying books about the *Carcharodon megalodon.* He believed that somewhere in the dark depths of the ocean there still existed a few of the prehistoric hundred-foot killing machines feeding on giant squid. I read this theory in one of his school notebooks. It was clear that Bill shared his mother's taste for hyperbole and drama. He was always reshaping the past or implementing extravagant or absurd fantasies.

As Dad and I talked and watched the baits, David, the second mate, guzzled beer and sang a medley of Bahamian favorites and jazz classics. Although the mate could not speak three words without stuttering into silence, his singing was fluid and arresting. Mother could not take her eyes off him. It made me very uneasy. "He's beautiful," she whispered. I hissed at her to stop looking at him.

Despite David's heavy drinking and heedless flirtations with white women that often resulted in beatings from captains and husbands, the mate was invited to sing at all the bars and restaurants, including the Game Club. "He has the timing of Nat King Cole," said my mother. By the end of the evening you could usually find him passed out in his vomit by the side of the road. I was appalled by his drunkenness, but Mother seemed to connect David's depravity to art. She found David exciting and was disgusted by the insipidness of our lighting fixture dreams.

By four in the afternoon, the crew was slack from the sun and no action, already thinking about night plans. The ocean was calm. Bill and Mom were asleep when a fish grabbed the trolled mackerel. The fight of my first blue marlin was fast and violent. As the fish greyhounded on the surface the boat backed down furiously, shuddering, water crashing over the transom. My father shouted, "Look at him jump." I was bent over the reel, cranking. I couldn't see a thing. When Verity couldn't gain ground backing down, he spun the boat on its heels and chased the marlin while I fought him off the side. Eric coached me to save my back by absorbing the power of the fish in my hips and thighs. While the fish sprinted and circled, Dad's job was to turn the chair so that the rod directly faced the fish, but he kept forgetting to do it. Whenever we hooked up he was prematurely celebrating the catch or too tense to be helpful. Oddly, his timing was never good as a fisherman.

After half an hour the two-hundred-pounder was close, and Eric began pulling on the wire leader that was connected to the end of my line. When the marlin felt the wash of the props, he went crazy. He leaped into the air only a few feet from our faces, crashed down, leaped again, his bill pointed our way while the boat gunned ahead to keep the fish out of our laps. After a minute of this infighting, Eric was able to get a flying gaff into his shoulder. Then Eric and David pulled him over the gunwale. On the deck the ten-footer tapped a little with his long tail and then grew quiet.

Following the short run to the Bimini harbor, I was once again the toast of the dock. Ansil Saunders was there admiring my marlin. Cameras clicked while Verity and Sawyer shook my hand. But they had done more than I had. It was at this point in my fishing career that I began thinking that I would like to be the one finding the fish like Bill Verity or Ansil Saunders. The angler just cranked the reel. It was the guide who performed the magic.

A few years ago Jackson Ellis began referring to Ansil Saunders as the Michael Jordan of bonefishing and the name caught on. At sixty-seven, when a bonefisherman should have lost his extraordinary vision and his strength for poling across the flats, Ansil Saunders remained incontestably the top fisherman on Bimini.

On most days Ansil outfished the other guides; he had more knowledge and could see better. But more than his many tournament victories and record fish, what was most compelling about Ansil was his restraint. Each morning he would smell the wind and find bonefish, sometimes a large feeding school that remained calm while the skiff drew closer. A small man, Ansil poled his skiff without apparent effort and with hardly a whisper of sound. Sometimes he entered the school itself, an almost gaudy show of hunting stealth, so that the boat was surrounded by hundreds of grubbing, tailing bonefish. You could practically lean over and fondle them with your hand. Other times he would spot a single large fish a long way off, and he would lean hard on the pole, planning his course to intercept the bonefish in fifteen or twenty minutes. If you were a new client, without prior example of his remarkable eyes, you might well decide that he was conning you about the eight-pounder slowly swimming across the grassy bottom a quarter mile away.

Typically, first thing in the morning, Ansil would position his clients to catch one or two bonefish and then after a flurry of action and high fives, he seemed to withdraw from the hunt; he would begin talking, probing the minds of his charters. He was insatiable for knowledge and had received his college education through a lifetime of conversations with charters. He learned to make political speeches from Adam Clayton Powell in the sixties and eventually was elected Mayor of Bimini. He would talk the trade of his clients, occasionally stand, cast, politely disagree, net a fish, take the hook out with a single sure twist and put it back over the side or, if it was a nice one, place it on the deck under a white cloth. He ate a sandwich, talking, thinking, developing his ideas about the world, barely fishing, and yet finding bonefish every hour or two.

If you chartered him regularly it became clear that Ansil could produce fish whenever he wanted. Stretches of time without action were largely a function of his management, and perhaps an aspect of his greater genius. For Ansil, finding fish had relatively little to do with the *wiles and vagaries of bonefish; he had conquered such technical questions long ago; rather he was guided by his own whim and aesthetic and the knowledge that catching too many could as easily tarnish a fine day as too few, cheapen and demystify the endeavor. Ansil caught just enough to keep his charters happy, to keep the conversations going. His clients left the flats musing about his ideas perhaps even more than bonefish. Ansil's sense of the big world was more stirring for being articulated while drifting across this shallow universe that he understood so well in a skiff he had made with his own hands.*

There were times each year when Ansil abandoned understatement and crushed the dreams of other bonefish guides, particularly Bonefish Cordell, who was a great fisherman in his own right and believed that someday he would be recognized as Bimini's greatest. Beginning in the sixties wealthy businessmen from the states began sponsoring annual Bimini bonefishing tournaments, each of them lasting two or three days. Now, of course, everyone recognized Ansil's prowess; but still, fishing is fishing, there are elements of luck, and so the guides and their charters began each of these events with great anticipation and hope. Except for a stretch of years when he retired from the flats, Ansil won every single one of these bonefish competitions. Incredibly, in each of the twenty or so events, Ansil not only won, but he boated more bonefish than the sum of fish landed by all the other guides combined—he had never once failed to accomplish this unlikely feat.

It was following one of his recent victories that Ansil wrote a letter to Michael Jordan, describing his own career, his astonishing record in the Bimini bonefish tournaments and that people were beginning to refer to him as the Michael Jordan of the flats, the nickname bestowed by Jackson Ellis. Ansil invited the legend of the court to come down to Bimini to fish the flats with him and compare notes about artistry and the nature of competition. All the Bimini bonefish guides knew about Ansil's letter and they looked forward to Michael's appearance in Bimini and this rare meeting between legends. It was unexpected and disturbing when the great Jordan failed to respond to Ansil's letter.

. *Globe* .

THE GLOBE LIGHTING SHOWROOM ON WEST 40TH STREET IN MAN-
hattan was where salesmen for the residential line brought their customers. In the front offices attractive secretaries with long painted
nails typed swiftly and answered the phones with a chilliness that
bordered on disdain. When the principals of Globe, my grandfather
Isadore Rosenblatt, known as I.R., or his son Alfred, visited the
showroom, the girls sat a little straighter, typed even faster. The Globe
secretaries were to me paragons of enticing but unattainable woman-
hood.

Spreading uptown from the offices were room after room of lighting fixtures, hundreds of models from which Globe customers could
select: there were lamps of assorted designs and heights, chandeliers
of all prices and sizes dripping with imported crystal, dining room
fixtures that traveled up and down on enclosed pulleys, vanity lighting for bathrooms and dressing nooks in modest or bolder designs,
hypermodern models anticipating the space age, austere designs mir-
roring Protestant values, fixtures in the style of the thirties with
richly colored leaded glass, kitchen fixtures and outdoor lighting, a
large children's line, fixtures that were spoofs on fixtures, sleek models with the cold chrome look of money favored by the bourgeoisie

in Shaker Heights and Great Neck. There was lighting in the showroom for nearly everyone.

Globe had risen to the top of the industry through the canny
marketing and design work of my immigrant grandfather, who as a
young man recognized that attractive moderate-priced lighting fixtures would have a limitless market in this new country.

In 1911, at the age of fifteen, Isadore Rosenblatt had come to the
United States with no knowledge of English and only a few dollars
in his pocket. His first meals in this country were potato soup and
bread at Ratner's on Second Avenue for fifteen cents, and when he
ran out of money one of the waiters fed him for free. Izzy found a
job as a laborer in an automobile factory. Soon he had a second job
and was working sixteen hours a day. He married his first cousin
Sadie, who had come to the States shortly before him and was working as a seamstress. In several years he had saved enough to bring
over his parents, brothers and sisters from Austria, which he always
referred as the "old country." In 1921 he and a few men began assembling very rudimentary fixtures in a dingy loft on the Lower East
Side. This was the first Globe factory and the modest beginning of
my grandfather's American dream.

Thirty-five years later, communities across the United States were
reading, eating and sharing family hours illuminated by my grandfather's designs. Globe had become the lighting of choice in high-rise
apartments as well as in Levittown and other prefab communities.
Customers buying their kitchen and bathroom lighting from Sears,
Roebuck would not have seen it on the label, but they were buying
Globe. By the fifties Globe was developing a European market; my
grandfather felt enormous pride shipping his newest line to brighten
the bleak war-devastated old country.

Once a week I.R. swept into the showroom for a couple of hours,
his stylish gray overcoat chilly and smelling of his new Cadillac. He
waved hello to the full-bodied receptionist who tittered and called
him I.R. He liked being greeted by the accountants, salesmen and
secretaries but it was my impression that he made these appearances
on 40th Street mainly for morale, like a general visiting troops sta-
tioned abroad. He preferred to stay at the factory, which was the guts
of the company.

As my father did not sell Globe's residential line, he almost never appeared at the showroom. Whenever I came, it was with my mother or one of my uncles, Chet or Alfred. Chet Mudick, another Globe salesman, was married to Mother's beautiful sister Thelma, who also worked for the company. They lived twenty minutes from us in Roslyn with their son and daughter in a dream house with tennis courts and a swimming pool nestled into a tiny landscaped forest. What a memorable couple they were. Both of them smart and sexy and riding the high life with Globe's cachet and power. My handsome, athletic uncle would stop for me in his new white Thunderbird and we would drive into the city talking basketball or the trade. Chet wanted to make it clear that he was a big-time salesman and would refer familiarly to Dad's contacts such as Sauli Schniderman or Maxi Kamins. I liked to think of Dad operating in a league of his own, and though I loved Chet, his competitiveness with Dad put me on edge.

Other times I drove into Manhattan with Uncle Alfred, I.R.'s son, a gentle man with a passion for bebop jazz. Alfred was being groomed to take over the company someday; this was Grandpa's fervent dream. However, by the time I started visiting Globe, Alfred, in his thirties, had deteriorating vision and a bad heart. He slept in his Great Neck house, around the corner from ours, with oxygen canisters beside his bed. Grandpa brought Alfred to the top doctors, put his wealth and resolve to war against his son's disease, but still the loaded question, who would someday take the helm of the great company, hung in the air during the years of my adolescence.

I had my showroom routine: after a few hellos I would walk dutifully from the office into the nearest display area, flip on eighteen or twenty switches, notice what was coming on and then turn them off and sullenly move to the next room. After four or five rooms and maybe a hundred switches, I would give up the exercise. My father sold commercial lighting; the residential side of Globe did not engage my imagination. In the showroom there were no eight- and ten-footers to make an office building come alive in the night, no luminated ceilings with intricate lens designs that dipped down with Dad's miracle hinge. The fixtures here were tacky, like the knick-knacks that came in cereal boxes.

When I wasn't flipping switches, I passed time in the showroom with impure thoughts about the Globe secretaries. Where did the company find such women? All of them had willowy legs and big breasts, or so it seemed to me. I was surprised and stirred whenever one of them compromised her daunting efficiency to butter her lips and powder her nose in front of a pocket mirror or slowly crossed her legs or adjusted her girdle on the lingering walk to the bathroom. The Globe girls were oblivious to my notice.

One day Mother mentioned casually that Grandpa came to the showroom for companionship. When I was slow to understand, she added, as though it should have been obvious, that his marriage to Sadie was unhappy and incomplete. How could this be true? Whenever I visited my grandparents in their apartment on West 73rd Street they were sitting on their seventeenth-floor balcony looking out at the Hudson River, Grandma's legs covered by a knitted shawl; or they were on the living room sofa watching *This Is Your Life* on television—the show always made Grandpa emotional. How many times had I watched Grandma carefully lighten her meatballs and stuffed derma with bread crumbs, so the meal wouldn't be too heavy and gassy for Grandpa. This news threw me into turmoil. Mother even mentioned which of the secretaries was the object of Grandpa's affection, but I could not conceive of this office dynamo taking off her clothes and allowing him to touch her on his green leather sofa. I didn't believe my mother. As usual, her boldest declarations seemed crafted to throw me off balance, to attack my deepest-held assumptions.

Mother hated Globe. To her, the showroom was a humiliation, a glitzy advertisement for wealth and success, and for reasons that I did not understand, moneyed success was to her equivalent to abject failure. Whenever possible Mother tried to pretend that she was a pauper, a rag lady. She would come to the showroom wearing a shirt that was torn and smeared with oil paint or black tights with runs. She would arrive at the fancy Bar Mitzvah of one of I.R.'s nephews smelling of turpentine. Over the years her slovenly dress was a source of humiliation to I.R. But Mother believed that being the heir to the Globe fortune damned her as a serious artist. It made her furious to have this legacy around her neck. One of Grandma's tiny sisters, Rose, was a Communist who disavowed the evils of capitalism on a soapbox on 14th Street in Manhattan. Occasionally Mother would join Rose on the street, or at least she would tell her father that she had. Another sister, Dora, was also a Communist, though less strident. Once or twice Mother met Dora at "black and white parties" and danced with Negroes to assert her open-mindedness. When she announced this to her father, I.R. turned red in the face.

But capitalism was not my mother's battle. That was old and picked-over material and Mother valued originality above dogma. She positioned herself against the status quo, hallowed traditions, social norms, banal success, bourgeois dreams, humdrum realities, wherever she found them. In Great Neck she cultivated a tiny legion of followers and kindred spirits, mostly painters and failed actors, showered them with little starbursts of revelations. For a time one of her closest friends was Gus, a corner grocer. Though Gus had no formal education Mother could sense from his eyes and the delicate turn of his head that he was a great aesthete. Gus became her primary cause. Over a period of months she urged him to give up the store and devote his life to painting or acting. Though caught in the sway of Mother's charisma, Gus hesitated. How would he support his family, his new baby? They arrived at a compromise. Gus would close the grocery, open an art supply store and paint through the night. Within months the new store went under and Gus, broke and exhausted from lack of sleep, was gone from Great Neck, driving an Entenmann's delivery truck. Mother hardly noticed his downfall. She spoke of the great contribution he might have made as an abstract painter.

I.R. and his daughter were pursuing irreconcilable dreams. My grandfather envisioned Globe as a kingdom. He pleaded with his daughter to dress in a manner appropriate to her station as heiress to Globe. When strangers asked my mother about her father, she referred to him as a designer, a gifted artist, a glassblower, an inventor—anything but a manufacturer. Even adulterer was preferable to entrepreneur. At the least it would be passionate and wicked. Mother burst my head with her outrageous ideas. But maybe it was true. Visiting the showroom I observed that Grandpa's door was closed for a long time while he was in there with his long-legged secretary. I sighed deeply.

This gossip about Grandpa instilled in me a new urgency, even a responsibility, but I did not know how to proceed. I hated the showroom but now I felt pressure to come. I looked at the girls differently.

They were fair game. I tried to imagine them on the sofa with me. I snapped off their girdles and brassieres, felt their luscious wetness with my hands. Then I no longer knew what to do. Two or three times I even tried to engage a showroom girl in conversation. I was received with boredom or irritation, which made me worry about my pimples and kinky hair that bird-nested no matter how hard I brushed. After my feeble attempts I fell back into sullen malaise about the showroom. I leaned on the fact that Dad rarely made visits here. The showroom was not a place for serious business.

The Globe plant in Maspeth was a different story. It was huge, a half-million square feet on two floors, and designed to mirror the essence of modernity. With its sleek lines and enduring construction of concrete and brick, the factory proclaimed that Globe would do its part designing and manufacturing the lighting of America for centuries. I have a reel of film shot in the fifties showing my grandfather smiling at his factory. The Maspeth plant was the embodiment of I.R.'s dream.

As a teenager I savored the size and texture of the factory. I was thrilled by the roar of a thousand big machines cutting heavy metal, stamping, bending, punching, welding, lifting, hauling. When lighting fixtures are reduced to discrete parts, it is not entirely obvious which will go into commercial or residential models. I would pretend that all of this activity was the fulfillment of my dad's work; the giant maw of the shipping bay was pouring out fixtures for Dad's high-risers.

Globe was too much to absorb in a single day, in three days. Usually I would spend an entire visit in one of the many departments, nearly all of which were managed by Grandpa's brothers and cousins. One day I devoted myself to the intricacies of the block-long paint-spraying department, which Grandpa had designed himself. A spinning wheel threw electrically charged paint onto eight-footers that rolled past hanging from hooks on an overhead conveyor before going into the oven. At other times the imported glass for lenses rested on top of molds that were also Grandpa's invention. After a trip through the oven the glass had melted into the shapes Grandpa had shrewdly designed for fickle American buyers. I.R.'s technology for melting glass allowed him rapidly to modify a large line of fixtures, giving him an advantage over other manufacturers.

On another day I would visit the shipping department, strolling past rows and rows of benches where a hundred men and women twisted wires, mounted ballasts, sockets and starters into metal housings and tightened the nuts down with screeching electric screwdrivers. The next time I visited they might be assembling the framework of my dad's miracle hinge. The workers gave me a glance and then returned to their jobs and conversations. I was Abe's son, I.R.'s grandson, someday this operation, or a big chunk of it, would be mine. I felt like a prince.

Usually I took a break to have a grilled ham and cheese with one of Grandpa's brothers in the factory luncheonette that was run by I.R.'s sister Anna. Often I ate with Sammy, who owned a truck and made deliveries for I.R. He was a serious bowler and I would ask him to tell me again about his greatest game, the 299. Sam recalled his picture-perfect hook that day, one ball after the next sliding right into the pocket, until, alas, he came in high on the last shot. Sammy always smiled when he described his achievement, but I felt the wrenching sadness of the 299, one pin short of perfection. In the ensuing years Sammy had become a diabetic, his best games were now behind him.

Sometimes my grandfather would stop by, his face flushed with pride that the different generations of his family, his own flesh and blood, were eating and enjoying themselves under his roof. I.R. was not one to mask his emotions, and it was his vision to employ all of his brothers and sisters and children, for the family to share the prosperity of his tremendous achievement. It occurred to me this might be the reason that he became so emotional when watching *This Is Your Life*. He saw Isadore Rosenblatt appearing on the show one day, basking in the adulation of all the little brothers and cousins he had brought over from the old country. Of course he knew that family members envied his wealth, especially the wives of his brothers who seethed that he drove his new Caddy and lived like a king while they played out their years in little apartments on Eastern Parkway. But Grandpa regarded such complaints as foolishness. He had brought them all to America. He was confident that Rose and Dora loved him despite their little rebellions. Grandpa had the perspective of a man acting out his destiny on a very large stage.

Usually, at the end of the day, I would visit him in his wood-paneled

office. He would say to me, "So?" and I would look at him. A pause
hung in the air but we both knew what was coming. "So, mister?"
he repeated. Eventually I told him something about my life. To
whatever I mentioned he responded wryly with "So what?" That
was the signal for us to talk about politics. Grandfather was a liberal
Democrat. He loved Truman and, later, JFK. I was greatly impressed
with his understanding of politics. Occasionally he hinted that his
information came from more direct sources than the newspapers,
and whenever we shared our views of Hubert Humphrey and Lyn-
don Johnson, I felt that our ideas would have a hearing beyond his
office.

In the late afternoon the big circular urinals were crowded with
men pissing, then scrubbing their filthy thick forearms with Borax.
Outside on the street the block swelled with Globe workers. On Fri-
days men held fists of dollars in their hands and I could feel the pulse
of the weekend. Globe would be there on Monday. Five hundred
men and women relied on the business acumen of my grandfather
for food, rent, vacations, cars, babies, sundry little dreams. I.R. was
the man for the challenge. He was a daunting figure striding through
the huge factory or waving smartly as he pulled away from the curb
in the new Caddy.

My father was often away from the plant, but he was a presence
nonetheless. While he was off making deals, Dad's faithful secretary
Kate filed the blueprints of all of his office buildings, answered the
phones, typed letters, putting her initials on the lower left corner of
each of them as though it were an honor to be a part of Abe's work.
Kate had a caring manner and a lovely smile to go along with her unwavering fidelity to my father. My uncles and aunts resented Kate
for the secrets she would never divulge. Her sweet good mornings
were an irritation. How did he get so many orders? they wondered
while Kate smiled tenderly and took shorthand as Abe spoke from
Detroit or Cleveland.

Apart from conversations with my grandfather, I avoided the ex-
ecutive offices at the plant. I knew that my father was a subject of
gossip and jealousy. Why should Abe earn more than us, more even
than I.R.? was a favorite dialogue between my uncles and aunt. I
could imagine their fervor complaining to I.R. behind my father's

back. Whenever I showed my face I saw their tight smiles. I returned them in kind. I wanted them all to know where I stood.

Abe was gall in their sides and I relished it. My father, with his emaciated hawk face and gangster hat, was an outsider who had wedged himself into this tight family group. Family members found his style as detestable as his success. He slept late and was rarely inside their clanging, bending, molding, assembling universe. Abe did his business in planes and airports, marinas, nightclubs, ringside, courtside, at the fifty-yard line; even in the hospital, he kept the orders coming in. His large empty office was a reminder of an alien and distasteful power.

"Abe was a sick man but completely remarkable," recalls an old business friend who still marvels at my dad's enigmatic artistry. "When he was in New York he might come into the Globe office for one hour, make a couple of phone calls, close a deal. He didn't need to spend eight hours like other salesmen. That's why they hated him."

Before Abe came into the business, Globe was known internationally for the residential line. Commercial lighting was a relatively small part of the business. My father changed all that. The office building deals were sweet because they were all in one high-rising shell, fifty thousand homes' worth of lighting, a hundred thousand homes within one breathtaking edifice. Huge as the Globe plant was, my father could close more orders than the factory could produce.

Naturally, with all the backbiting and plots against him by the in-laws, Dad did not feel completely devoted to Globe. If they could, they'd cut my balls off, he said of my uncles and aunt. Occasionally Dad made side deals with one of his competitors, like Ruby-Philite. He did not keep this a secret. Dad operated as an independent force within Globe. But more often other companies would come to him. "Other lighting companies would call Abe in as a kind of doctor," recalls Dad's friend. "To close an order that was hung up. Abe would speak with the contractors or union guys. Often, just a phone call from Abe resolved the problem. More complex situations would sometimes require his presence at a meeting or dinner. Abe's involvement always seemed to provide the magic touch, though the actual mechanics of what went on during his meetings and phone calls remained a mystery to most of us."

Despite the ill will Dad liked the security and cachet of Globe behind him and was constantly pressing I.R. to back off on the residential line, to leave more machinery for fluorescents. I.R. dragged his feet. He was dubious. He believed in the line; the line was like wheat for my grandfather. He cherished his catalog with hundreds of models to choose from. He trusted his sense for what designs the American public desired for their bedrooms and dens. He had no feel for Abe's mega-orders and late-night selling. But my father prevailed. How could you ignore million-dollar orders—today they would be ten- or fifteen-million-dollar jobs—one after the next? I.R. agreed reluctantly, because of the numbers. The numbers were staggering. Such grandiosity from a sickly little man. Every office building in America was my father's prey.

But even while the company prospered and grew, I.R. resented Abe. I once heard him ask my mother, Was Abe doing monkey business? Even if it was monkey business, I wondered, how bad could that be? None of the other salesmen could close orders like Abe. All of them together couldn't match his sales. What did it matter if they talked? If they hated him, so what? They couldn't touch him.

. Baiting Fischbach .

ABE'S FATHER, JOE WAITZKIN, WHO LIVED IN CAMBRIDGE, MASSA-chusetts, was acidly critical of his son's lavish spending and murky business style. Where does it all go? Joe railed darkly in his thick Jewish accent. Abe spends the money before he earns it. For all his fancy jobs, one big building after the next, what money does he have to show for it? Joe complained about Abe's profligacy to whoever was around, to me and my mother whenever we visited, to members of his minyan in shul, but mostly to his daughter Celia, living up-stairs with her husband Lennie and their three children in the same three-story house in Cambridge where Dad had been raised. As Abe's fixture sales reached dizzying heights, Joe's invective took on greater urgency, as though his son's way of life were violating the very essence of Judaism. And at the same time, "Pop," as we all called him, extolled I.R. as an American hero. During those years Pop earned his livelihood working in the Lee Products shop in nearby Everett that had been founded by Abe, an irony that did not escape my father.

As a younger man, a recent immigrant, Joe Waitzkin had been am-bitious and hardworking and had accumulated considerable real es-tate in Cambridge. With the Depression he lost everything, and to my father's humiliation, Pop was forced to make a living in a corner grocery store. This big failure left Pop a frustrated and angry man. I recall one afternoon when the Lee shop was in the midst of moving from one location to another. I happened to be standing in the doorway while Lennie and a few workers were dismantling the dingy office. My grandfather began striking the unyielding timbers of the wall with a hammer. He struck blow after blow as though trying to slay an enemy. This went on for what seemed like a long time with Pop sweating and Lennie and the others begging him to stop. He beat the wall until he was doubled over and heaving.

Even during Pop's calmest moments I found it difficult to pierce his simmering rage and religious fervor to have a proper conversation with him. I cannot remember ever seeing my father and his dad together when there wasn't anger. I wonder if Pop ever paused to consider that his own fall from success contributed to his son's unremitting drive to reach the top, to live rich. On the other side Dad complained to me that Joe and Lennie operated the business in Everett like a mom-and-pop store, kept no inventory because of the financial risk and had no plan or ambition to expand. All they wanted from Lee, Dad would say, was a modest weekly income. With all the big deals in New York, Dad had little time to focus on expanding the Everett shop, which employed only six or seven men who labored on out-of-date presses and lathes. Still, the timidity of his family was frustrating to my father, who would have liked to send them large orders from New York contractors he had befriended.

Dad's sister Celia was caught in the middle of warring sensibilities, titillated by her brother's flair and success and yet mindful of both the wrath and reproach of her father and the more conservative business approach of her husband, who ran the Everett shop. Probably because my mother couldn't have cared less about Abe's wheeling and dealing, Dad frequently called Celia in Cambridge with stories about the union guys he courted, what clubs they went to and such. In the Great Neck house, Dad talked on the phone to his sister with the door closed, and it made me jealous that he told Celia secrets he kept from me.

My smart, chesty aunt glowed in Abe's presence and at the names of the great men who never kept him waiting, like Charlie Zweifel, another electrical contractor, not to mention Alan Fischbach himself, who would soon take over the presidency of the enormous Fischbach and Moore. Dad and I often visited Cambridge. As the family sat around the kitchen table chewing salad with Kraft French dressing, Celia chose the best slices of steak for Abe, turned them lovingly on a counter rotisserie until they were perfectly well done, the way her brother enjoyed his meat. She served Abe first, while the rest of us waited for our steak. Later, when the kids were in bed, Celia stayed up until two in the morning eating ice cream and talking with her brother about his newest deals. Between them was the tacit promise that Abe's skyrocketing prosperity would spread north to Cambridge and Everett, the Lee shop would someday swell with Charlie Zweifel and Fischbach deals. There was no need for formal agreements between these two. In a world of sharks Abe trusted his sister completely. Within the pull of their intimacy, I felt like an intruder.

Whenever Celia tilted too far in her brother's direction, her husband, Lennie, became irritated—why was Abe such a big deal? After all, Lennie had also bought a boat, a little lapstrake, and trolled daisy chains of squid off Magnolia on summer weekends. Why do you cook the best pieces of meat for Abe? But then, Celia had ways of making it up to Lennie, and he worshiped her.

One time Dad brought Alan Fischbach to Celia's summer cottage in Magnolia. "Alan loved Abe," recalls Celia. "The day he came I accidentally locked myself out of the house. Alan was very tall, six-feet-four, but he crawled through the bedroom window to unlock the door. The sheets were messy but Alan didn't mind." Celia titters over this incident forty years later, as though the king of England had crawled across her messed-up sheets.

Needless to say, I shared my father's view that Pop's criticism of our spending habits was small-minded. True, Dad was often short of cash, but who lived like him, like us? I adored my father for all the great restaurants and fancy trips, for never settling for less than ringside or box seats behind home plate. And no mistake about it, we were getting ahead, closing in on the forty-footer. Together we searched through boating magazines and debated the pros and cons of Huckinses, Wheelers and Rybovichs—the gold platters of the sportfishing world. Each of Dad's trips edged us closer.

I was incomplete when he was away. I treaded water until he was back and we could count his successes over our breakfast cereal and make our plans. On one trip Dad took a couple of union guys down to Puerto Rico for several days of marlin fishing. For some reason he wouldn't take me along, and I was beside myself when he left. He rarely fished without me and such was our camaraderie on the ocean that it was hard for me to believe he would leave me behind. I paced the halls of Great Neck High wondering about their trolling. For three days I could think of nothing else but Dad's lines slipping through the ocean.

He arrived home at two A.M., after I had fallen asleep. In the morning I could hear him snoring in his bed. I was bitter for not having stayed up for him as I had intended, for having squandered an opportunity to talk about his adventure off San Juan. I could barely contain myself while Dad spent twenty minutes in the bathroom. I knew this time was painful for him as I sometimes heard him moan on the toilet.

Finally we were in the kitchen together. Winnie the maid poured Cream of Wheat into our bowls. "How'd you do?" I tried to ask with a measure of detachment. Dad was beaming. "I caught a marlin." A blue marlin! How had he ever managed it? I didn't think my father had the physical strength to pull on such a fish. I quickly concluded that it must have been a small one, but I didn't make him tell me this. According to Dad's narration, the fight was easy except for the sharks. Soon after he had hooked the marlin three or four big bull sharks circled the boat, attracted by the struggling fish's blood. But the captain knew what to do. He took twenty feet of wire leader and twisted large hooks on both ends. Then he put a mullet on each hook and tossed the rig over. In seconds the baits were grabbed by two large sharks. Dad and the union guys could see the roiling on the surface as the sharks twisted and smashed their tails trying to get free of one another. After throwing over several of these rigs there were no more sharks, and Dad was able to wind in the marlin.

When I was a teenager I knew little about union officials and politicians besides their taste for lavish restaurants and fishing trips. In Miami we dined at the Fontainebleau with a couple of union guys Dad referred to as "lieutenants," real tough guys. But over our steaks the conversation was light, families and vacations. Life was a party. Dad said they were terrific fellas who would do anything for him. My father grinned when he had the bill in his hand and these burly men were left reaching and shaking their heads. Joe Waitzkin never understood that such moments were money in the bank.

"Abe always knew the right person to get on the phone. That was the key," reflects his old friend from the Globe days. "If he didn't know who to call, he found out. With his charisma he was able to befriend public officials as well as labor leaders and contractors. He formed friendships with local union guys as well. Because of his close relationship with all parties he managed to get the inside track on deals all over the country."

One time we were eating blintzes at the St. Moritz Hotel on Central Park South, and Dad introduced me to Carmine De Sapio, who was seated nearby. I knew that he was the boss of Tammany Hall but I didn't know what that meant. I recall Dad saying to me that you couldn't get a sanitation job in New York City without De Sapio's approval. A couple of times I had seen him on television taking the Fifth Amendment before a committee. In the dimly lit restaurant Carmine was wearing sunglasses, as was his habit. His smile was sad, world-weary, and he seemed happy to run into my dad. Another night I joined Dad for dinner at Cavanagh's steak house on 23rd Street with a New York City commissioner who was one of De Sapio's friends. I recall this perfumed man eating large shrimp and whispering intriguing delectables to my old man. Dad had told me the Commissioner was a man of vast and unusual power. He said that if I ever had a big problem in my life, this man could take care of it for me. Having access to unlimited power through the Commissioner made me feel like one of the chosen, but I wondered what such a problem might be and if I would be allowed to ask for help more than once.

Dad said that the key to getting jobs was delicate maneuvering between the unions and the electrical contractors. The locals were often at one another's throats. Being friendly with one official might mean trouble with another. If the unions wouldn't go along with it, no deal with any electrical contractor was worth the piece of paper it was written on. If you didn't have the unions, the men wouldn't wire fixtures into the ceiling, they wouldn't even take them off the trucks.

But then, of course, the unions didn't mean much if you didn't have the contractors. I wasn't sure exactly where the politicians fit into the picture. Dad was vague about his methods and connections, even with me. He would frequently caution, never let the left hand know what the right hand is doing.

Without a doubt, making big deals in the fifties took considerable finesse and stroking. I worried about this relative to my own career as a salesman. When meeting potential customers, Dad had style and confidence, and in his field getting through the door was half the battle. When I met people for the first time, I tended to paw the ground and ponder my escape. When I didn't like someone, which was often the case, I found it difficult to be hearty and convincing. Instead, I grew sullen, which is not good for selling. I worried if I would be able to change.

Fischbach and Moore, Dad said, was the biggest electrical contractor in the country, a bigger operation even than Globe, which taxed my imagination. Before he became friends with Harry and Alan Fischbach, Dad recognized that teaming Globe with Fischbach to light skyscrapers would mean a gold mine for him. But it wasn't that simple. Reps from all over the country were always trying to land Fischbach.

At different times Harry, CEO of the company, and his son Alan visited our house in Great Neck for late breakfast. Both men were tall and suntanned from vacations in Palm Springs. I recall Harry making a few remarks to Mom about recent trail rides in the desert. But for the most part, during their visits, we talked about our Great Neck lives and the Fischbachs said little, giving the impression that they were thinking about more important issues. Even without this kingly reserve, their wealth and impressive height gave father and son an aura of aloofness and vague discomfort, as though our rooms were too low and narrow for proper stretching. As we schmeared cream cheese on bagels, the conversation at these breakfasts faltered and Dad's smile was forced. I recall standing and waving with my father on the front lawn as Alan drove off. Dad mused that he was a brilliant man.

Two or three times we tied up our little boat alongside their yacht, the *Friendly Fisch,* which sometimes moored off Sands Point in the

Long Island Sound. Dad predicted that these rendezvous would be great, but once we were on board the talk drifted to renovations for Alan's house in Westchester, trips to Egypt and Africa. Dad's enthusiasm for these topics made me feel uncomfortable. It seemed ridiculous that no one on board the *Friendly Fisch* was interested in fishing. But Dad became annoyed when once or twice I indicated distaste for these rendezvous. "Get with it," he said, as though I lived on another planet.

"Harry Fischbach visited the Great Neck house because I was there," recalls my mother. "When he came at nine in the morning in his big limousine, it wasn't to talk business with Abe. He had been interested in me for years, before I married Abe, but my father put him off. Abe knew that I had this power over Harry, who was seventy years old at the time. Abe encouraged it.

"Harry was rude from the beginning, stuck up his nose at our house. He called it a 'little development' as though it were a six-room Levittown model. He lived in a fancy mansion somewhere, Westchester, I think. I found his remarks annoying, and, though it sounds ridiculous, I insisted that our house was spacious and attractive. Before breakfast I showed him around.

"We were upstairs in your bedroom when Harry pushed me through the door into the attic. He pulled me close to him and kissed me. I was shocked. He was seventy years old. I wasn't used to such passion. Abe wasn't a passionate man. Harry was breathing like a storm.

"By then Harry's son Alan was running the company. He would sometimes join Abe and me at nightclubs like the Copacabana, which was one of your father's favorites. Alan would put his hand on my leg under the table and I would brush it off. I knew that Abe encouraged this just like with the father. Once we were in a club and I said to Abe in a loud voice, 'Abe, do you know what Alan is doing?' They exchanged this expression, 'What's wrong with Stella?' Like I should have been going along with the program."

It is hard to believe that my mother simply imagined these moments, and yet I am suspicious about her claim that my father was the architect. When she speaks of Abe she refers only to his darker maneuvering. She has no memory of my father's warmth and caring, no interest in what the men did when they were off on their own, their courting before the deal, the sense of promise that marked their finest moments. My aunt Celia insists that Alan Fischbach loved my father, as many men did, and reflects that my mother relished drama beyond reality and that she needed to be the center of attention even in theaters she considered dismal. Since Alan Fischbach is no longer with us, the question of which Waitzkin was the object of the contractor's true affection hangs unresolved. But there is no doubt that my mother abhorred my father's networking. She cringed as he curried the favor of men whom she found banal and vulgar.

For my mother the Great Neck years were a deepening fog. By the time I entered high school there were periods when she could not get out of bed except to drag herself into her studio, where she painted into the night. Her work of this period reflects depression and paranoia and impending disaster. In twisted carnival character faces her subjects suggest betrayal and despair. Stella herself is portrayed as a tragic clown, an observer. Abe is a liar, cheat and chiseler. Her sister-in-law Laurie, Alfred's wife, whom she did not trust, is the black widow, smiling behind dark veils.

When I stared at her canvases as a boy, I could see nothing but unrecognizable forms, most of them dark. Her art was careening away from everything that was identifiable and warm. In her self-portraits the faces were obliterated by swirls and gashes of chaos. In one that she called *Abe* the faintest form of a man appeared to be atomizing, he had almost disappeared. Mother insisted that her work was lifelike, which taxed my view of reality and triggered fights between us. She attacked her canvases with long, vicious strokes. Everything about my mother's work was disturbing and I continued to believe that she painted this way mainly to irritate me and Dad.

There were nights when Mother roused herself from malaise. I watched her seated before her Globe vanity mirror with a dozen radiant bulbs, artfully applying her makeup, then posing this way and that wearing a scarf like a Gypsy to go with a long skirt. This was odd because Mother usually did not care about her appearance. Then she would leave my brother and me with Winnie and drive her sputtering Morris Minor off into the night. Mother's trips to Greenwich Village felt different to me than Dad's sojourns in Cleveland and Detroit. He was doing the family business. Mother was driving to a foreign place that had nothing to do with us.

Many would say that the early and middle fifties comprised the most important period in American art history and surely it was the most electric. Abstract expressionism had taken hold of the New York art scene, blowing aside representational work and the hallowed painting principles of centuries. Painters around New York did their work quickened by a torrent of new possibilities and the belief that breakthroughs of historic proportions were taking place every day in junky lofts around town. Everyone was playing by new rules and anyone with a brush felt as though he were making a lasting contribution. At the Cedar Tavern on East 11th Street, where the best painters in the city spent drinking nights, realistic artists were considered pariahs. When Andy Warhol came by, artist George Spaventa labeled him "Andy Whorehole."

At the Cedar Tavern, painters, sundry intellectuals, celebrities and hangers-on would crowd close to listen and gawk, as though the smoky bar itself conferred something close to art. When Pollock or Kline showed up, someone would make a phone call. More painters and would-bes crowded in to drink, argue, try to bed women, learn something. More painters stood on the street waiting to get inside. "They're all ducks," Bill de Kooning would mutter ironically.

Into this new world came Stella, wide-eyed and beautiful, dressed in her Gypsy outfits or sometimes a designer dress from Loehmann's. These thrilling nights were an escape from suburbia, a big chance. She dove into the Cedar Tavern with flair and confidence; she used Abe as her model, how he would have taken over the room.

Mother became friends with Spaventa and painters Gandy Brodie and Jan Müller. She was introduced to Franz Kline, who often painted for only an hour and then put in a long drinking day at the bar. Kline was the spitting image of the actor Ronald Colman. Mother found him intense, smoldering. "If you like someone you should tell them," Kline whispered to Stella, who was clearly drawn to him. She listened, rapt, while Jan Müller criticized Wolf Kahn for painting pretty pictures, and to Kline and Pollock arguing hotly about the work of Philip Guston. One night Jackson Pollock was blind drunk and yelled at Milton Resnick, "You are an imitator of an imitator." To Mother, who already knew Pollock from East Hampton, the painter's massive physical stature lent weight to his pronouncements and mirrored the epic scope of his work. Pollock got plowed and explained that the subject of his paintings was the sky.

Buying great art was much simpler than landing lighting contracts from Fischbach and Moore. At the Cedar Tavern, Kline, Pollock, de Kooning and others bartered drawings for a few bucks to buy drinks. Mother bought a few, feeling guilty and liberated. Money wasn't a big deal. Kline only wanted enough in his pocket to buy a good steak. It was about the work, not the money. It never occurred to anyone that these bartered paintings would be worth millions in a few years, that drunken signatures scrawled on drawings at the bar would be pored over for authenticity by somber museum curators with fortunes hanging in the balance.

For her entire life Mother had played against the rules of I.R. and Abe without her own defining context. In the family and business world she was known for being rebellious or childish or eccentric. But among the painters at the Cedar Tavern she felt part of a family. The themes in my mother's art were serious, embodying her alienation and the unhappiness of a loveless marriage, but still I think that the central alchemy of this new kind of painting was deeply resonant with my mother's prankster soul. The goal was to wrench intense feeling and meaning from lines and unrecognizable shapes, or, as the critic Clement Greenberg wrote, from "abstractness and absence of assignable definition." Such oxymorons have always been at the core of my mother's humor, as well as her art. It tickled Stella to make paintings that the neighbors could never understand, that left her father speechless. Other artists might visit Jackson Pollock in East Hampton with heavy aesthetic questions; Mother showed up with a box of bloody bluefish.

In a reach of impishness extreme even for her, she talked my father into coming with her to a party at the loft of the painter Wolf Kahn. Abe walked in wearing a long gray coat and one of his gangster hats. Immediately my father knew that something was very wrong. There were Negroes milling around. There was a mattress on the floor. Who would sleep on the floor? he asked Mother suspiciously. There were cockroaches climbing the walls. After a few minutes Wolf Kahn came to my mother and asked, Who is this detective? This was one of the few times she brought Abe into her world.

. *The Ebb Tide* .

DURING MY EARLY TEENAGE YEARS THERE WERE MANY NIGHTS when I sat on top of the stairs and listened to my father moaning in his first-floor bedroom. He was rolled up in a ball with cramps. As the minutes passed, Dad's pain would seem to become more severe and I worried that he would die. Sometimes Bill joined me, but I always felt, during these tense occasions, that it was the drama of the moment more than concern that brought my brother to the top stair. After my worry became intolerable there would be a ring at the front door. Mother opened it and Dr. Nelson walked briskly inside and headed toward my father's bedroom. Fifteen minutes later they walked back to the door, and the doctor spoke to her soothingly. A few times after the doctor's departure I crept to the open door of Dad's bedroom. Now my father was sleeping like a kitten. It was astonishing that the doctor had such power to cure.

Disease became the wolf at my door. Only sickness could smash our fishing plans, kill our happiness. Not just Dad's illnesses and operations. At times I could feel disease burrowing into my body, growing tendrils. Shortly before puberty I began the arduous life's work of monitoring my health. A friend of mine was diagnosed with juvenile diabetes and had to go for shots. For months my concern was diabetes. I noticed that I was drinking a lot of water and my fingers and toes tingled from lack of circulation. Then my focus switched to my appendix. Each night I burrowed my hand deep into the right side of my large intestine until it ached. I would break out into a sweat. I had it, all right. Once or twice I asked Dad to arrange a visit to the Clinic for me as he often had for his buddies in the lighting industry. I didn't understand why he wouldn't take me. When I could no longer stand the tension, I would walk into my mother's studio and urge her to drive me to see Dr. Nelson. Usually she talked me out of it. Eat an apple, she advised. Sometimes I insisted. Even when I was twelve and thirteen my visits to the doctor were close to hysterical. With each examination of my abdomen or testicles or neck glands, I expected the worst, whatever that was. As a young teenager I made a distinction between dying of disease and dying in all other ways. Dying of illness was grotesque, shameful, worse than going to hell. Drowning in the Gulf Stream, for example, or being torn apart by large sharks seemed like a tolerable ending.

At night, in bed, or to be precise, kneeling beside my bed, I prayed with my hands clasped like a Christian child I had seen in a movie. I was desperate and hedged my bets. Please, God, let me live, I would begin. After this opening there were innumerable variations over the years. Don't let me die of polio like Mrs. Newman across the street. I used to say hello to her. I watched them take her away in an ambulance. She was gone a week later. . . . My groin hurts. I don't know what it is. . . . Cure my stomach. I have tremendous gas. I am in the prime of my life. Please save me.

With so much internal drama it is not surprising that school seemed flat and meaningless. On warm days I looked forward to the final bell when I could go fishing at the Great Neck Estates Park. When the weather turned bad, I focused more on drumming and religion. After my Bar Mitzvah I became an Orthodox Jew. Friends of mine attended services at the Reform and Conservative temples, but I regarded them as frauds. I went to the Orthodox synagogue on Saturdays and holidays, and sometimes before school I took my place in the minyan with ten or twelve men, the youngest of whom was fifty years older than me. I rocked and sang doleful melodies as they did. As my own religious education had been only a single year of intermittent study with an impatient tutor, I had no idea what any of the prayers meant, but I believed that if I kept singing them fervently, I would come to understand their meaning and Dad and I would stay healthy. One morning, when Dad was away, I pulled the tangled phylacteries he had not used for years from his sock drawer and began coiling them like dock lines, trying to teach myself how to wind the sacred little boxes and straps around my arms and forehead like the old men in the minyan. For weeks I practiced with the phylacteries. If I could master them, surely it would be proof of my pure devotion.

Maintaining Orthodox Jewish traditions in our home was an uphill battle. Winnie the maid liked to prepare platters of pork chops for the family. I would urge her to use different plates and pots and pans to make my holy dishes, but I was never confident that she listened. During religious holidays I had Winnie order meat from the kosher butcher and then I coached her, reading aloud from a Jewish cookbook. But at the table there was little enthusiasm for this food. Bill simply refused to eat kosher. That was that. Mother was in despair, painting in her studio, and rarely joined us at the table whether it was a holy day or not. As I recited the prayers over bread and wine, Dad was curiously removed. He had given up the synagogue years before and I think that my fervor made him uneasy. One Passover, as Winnie and I laid out a lamb shank and hard-boiled eggs, Dad insisted that we go out for Chinese at Lee Wong in Manhasset. Bill was delighted.

I decided that if I could save my brother, it would not go unnoticed. I urged Bill to come with me to Saturday services, promising him sweets and cakes afterward. Once or twice he came reluctantly. My brother giggled when the yarmulke fell off his frizzy hair. He hadn't tried to keep it in place. He was a breaker of idols like his mom. At my Bar Mitzvah, two years before, while I was struggling miserably to sing my way through the Haftarah, my mother had sat in the roped-off women's section, making faces at me so I would laugh.

Bill's audacity was infuriating. I knew that during the best prayers my brother's mind was on marlin and dinosaurs. He was always drawing stout marlin on his school papers or in the margins of his favorite books. He spent afternoons at work on his *Tyrannosaurus rex*, a nine-footer he was making out of papier-mâché in the garage. It took him months to complete the flesh-gulping creature, which he eventually positioned on the front lawn, braced with ropes from trees. A few days later one of Bill's Siamese cats, Trigger, ran away, and my brother fell into a funk and lost interest in the *Tyrannosaurus*. For a couple of weeks cars stopped to look at the fierce dinosaur looming over Locust Drive. After the first heavy rain the predator's head fell off, and Bill left the rotting remains for weeks on the winter lawn.

Saturday meant religious services and then rushing for the train into Manhattan for conga drumming lessons. The winter before turning sixteen I began studying bongos with Danny Berihanas, who for many years was the drummer for Harry Belafonte. I was good on the congas but I had limitations. My hands were fast, but I wasn't strong enough to pound deeply into the center of the thick skins, and also the weight of the drums was a problem. Whenever I picked up one of these forty-pounders with my two legs and rocked back to get a deeper bass sound I felt a pulling in my groin that alarmed me. As a consequence my conga drumming was flashy but without resonance.

My skin color and kinky hair had made me a curiosity at the dance studio, but despite this, I could tell that Berihanas was impressed by my hand speed and feel for rhythm on the little drums. After a couple of weeks learning the basics, the snaps and flash rolls, other drummers, all of them black, would come into the back room to listen to my solos. Often we would jam, two conga drummers holding down an earthy rhythm while I snapped out variations, and little riffs behind or ahead of the beat. Then I changed gait, slowed to a crawl and played the bongos with the jungle thud of the conga—this became my signature. I held my breath waiting for an invitation to come into the front room to drum for a dance class directed by Alvin Ailey or Talley Beatty. Sometimes I would say no, had to get back to Great Neck, but I was bursting with desire, frightened by my desire. At the head of the class, thunderous drums and a rolling Herbie Hancock piano pulled ideas from inside me. Sweating women pushed the beat and sometimes my fingers surprised me tapping out seductive flirtations. The colored girls shook their chests at me and smiled as they bounded past in black leotards, their nipples like flattened strawberries. My groin ached as I beat the skins.

I bought records and at home I matched myself against the best. I pounded against "Bongo Madness" as it blared from the hi-fi until Dad roared that I was driving him crazy. After a couple of months I knew that I played the bongos as well as Berihanas did. There was no need for more lessons. But now I had to face the troubling question of where Afro-Cuban drumming belonged in my Great Neck life.

Mother and I continued to have our difficulties. Except for my drumming, she seemed to disapprove of nearly everything that I believed in. She taunted me for being bourgeois. She drew her boundaries with a knife. I am here. You are there. That's the way it will be. Get it! If we happened to have a warm moment and I tried to hug her, she pushed me away or averted her face. I guessed that it had to do with being Dad's boy, with preparing for my life as a salesman of lighting fixtures and panel boxes.

Mother gave a weekly painting class to several Great Neck housewives. Although she only earned a few dollars Mother made a big deal about her classes, insisting that her money came from teaching rather than Globe. The students worshiped my mother. They called her a visionary. But I found their fawning pathetic. One of them was Helen Rutt, a tall, frail woman who did timid realistic sketches in charcoal. One evening, after the other women had left, Mother was offering criticism to Helen when I walked through the studio and paused to admire the drawing. When I sagely reflected that I preferred Helen's work to my mother's, Helen put her hand to her mouth, aghast. My mother nodded silently but her face had grown dark and forbidding. I knew that I had crossed a line.

One evening the family drove to Montauk for a few days of bluefishing. Dad and I were impatient to get to the Yacht Club. We had brought along jars of colorful double-hooked pork rinds, yellows, greens and reds, to troll off the point. We were ready for blues. Mother had arranged to spend the next day with Jackson Pollock. Near East Hampton we sat stuck in traffic. Eventually we inched up to an accident, a smashed car was being towed off the road. So that was the problem. The following afternoon, while Dad, Bill and I were jigging for blues, Mother found out that the wrecked car was Pollock's. He was dead. The artist had been riding with his girlfriend, who had survived the accident. Mother was reeling. Pollock's friendship had been a source of energy and confidence, like having a secret stash. After this loss, although Dad was sympathetic (Abe was always tender about illness and dying), she seemed to withdraw even further from the family.

In the fifties a colostomy was an unusual and dangerous procedure. Before going into the hospital for this operation, my dad resolved to install an automatic door opener in the garage of the Great Neck house. Electric garage doors were almost unheard-of then. Dad stood outside in the cold looking at the wiring diagram. He wasn't wearing gloves. I was freezing and wanted to go inside, but I held his tools and didn't say anything. He couldn't get the door to budge. Something must be wrong with the diagram, he decided, with his index finger touching his temple. In a few days he would go into the hospital. He wanted to see it work before he went in. This surgery was going to be a rough one. The doctors had warned Dad that he might not make it. Getting the garage door to open and close seemed crucial. From its leather case he removed the fancy ohmmeter that had been a gift from the head of the electrical union. He began testing wires. Nodded. The wiring diagram was incorrect, he explained. It was remarkable, one wire on the wrong terminal made all the difference. I would never have the ability to determine which wire. After Dad fixed the door, he called his secretary, Kate, on the phone, dictated a note to the company about the diagram. During the next two or three days we watched the door go up and down dozens of times.

Mother took a little room near the hospital in Boston, set up camp for a long vigil. Abe's sister Celia recalls that following the surgery, my mother dressed in black and sat beside his bed for weeks while Abe barely hung on, drifting in and out. True, Abe was a disaster in Stella's life, but the idea of losing him made her hysterical. What would become of the family? What would happen to his workshop in the basement? She obsessed about the workshop. Every time there was a slight change in Abe's condition, Mother made life and death phone calls to his doctors. She sat by his bed and willed him to live. I will try to love you, she incanted. We will stay together. I will try to make your life easy. Sometimes she wailed like a lost soul.

At night in her little room she ate rancid tuna sandwiches and worried about Bill. He never fared well when she was away. Bill had come down with a fever the day she had left for the Clinic in Boston. Whenever Alfred or Laurie came over to check him, my brother became furious and ordered them out of the house. When he was back in school he heaved rocks at the other children. Only Winnie the maid could calm him. Winnie knew about wounded children. On days off she cared for her son, who had returned shell-shocked from the Korean War. Bill and Winnie would sit in front of the TV watching soap operas while Winnie stroked his brow with her cool hand.

Mother would call me at night to report how bad Dad was. It was always terrible news. For me, this was frozen time. There was no world without him. My school day was a haze. I could not taste my food.

One night a nurse shaved my father's body and a doctor told Mother that Dad would not last until morning. Mother pleaded with Abe, You must come back. I need you, Abe. Don't die. Come back, Abe. Come back. After hours of pleading, she could feel him returning. Stella believed that she had saved him. She still does. Who knows? When Dad was conscious he said to her, "Stella, can you lift me? Can you carry me?"

Dad came home from the hospital with a male nurse. For about a month he was weak as a kitten, and it was difficult to believe life would ever return to normal. Mother mentioned that the nurse was a homosexual. I worried he would try to take advantage of Dad while he was so weak. I was completely confused about what they had done to my father at the Clinic. I knew about the bag he wore but I wasn't sure if he still had a rectum or if they had cut off his penis. I never asked and no one ever told me. Whenever the nurse changed my father's bandages I turned away. Even now I cannot bear to think of my father's seeping wounds.

Dad's courage and optimism were beyond my scope of understanding. It was as though his damaged, emaciated body had little importance to him. While the nurse rubbed his spindly calves with powder or changed his dressing, Dad was already on the phone talking expansively to his buddies about buildings on the drawing boards for L.A. and Chicago. He could just barely walk and didn't weigh eighty pounds, but we were scouring the magazines for a boat that would power us through big seas on the way to gigantic marlin.

As soon as Dad was back behind the wheel of the Buick, he bought me a fifteen-foot lapstreak with an electric starting thirty-five-horsepower Johnson outboard engine so I could go trolling for stripers off Sands Point and City Island. I was back to beating on the skins and Dad would walk past in his bathrobe and smirk. Time was rolling again.

We were eating again in slick restaurants. I recall the first time we went back to Chez Something-or-other, a favorite among the union guys and contractors, and the maître d' clumped Dad on the back for surviving and coming there to eat. Dad smiled and we ordered the best dishes from their real French chef, who came out to compliment Dad on his choices. Dad could only eat a few bites of the rich food, but he enjoyed watching me put it away.

Nights were still bad for Dad. Dr. Nelson was again making late visits, but they seemed less ominous. I guessed that he was doing some minor postoperative adjustments. He just has to learn to relax, I heard Dr. Nelson tell my mother. By now the faithful doctor knew that I waited on the top stairs and casually turned to give me a cheerful wave on his way out. But why was Dad so tense at night? In the morning he seemed peaceful enough over hot cereal. He had decided to take his time going back to work. What was the rush? he said. The Globe factory was glutted with his orders. I.R. owed him commissions for a dozen jobs, hundreds of thousands of dollars.

While Dad was still healing we looked at a thirty-five-foot Chris Craft that was up for sale in a marina in Port Washington. She slept six and had a lot of fancy varnish work. But the cockpit was small and her transom was too high above the water to easily reach a fish with a gaff. We glanced at one another and knew this wasn't the fishing boat we had dreamed about.

A few weeks later we heard from someone that there was a boat in Florida we should look at. Dad and I flew to Miami, rented a convertible at the airport and drove to Pompano Beach. The first time I saw the *Ebb Tide* she was drenched in blistering light. The expansive teak cockpit was white from the midday sun. She had a tuna tower and three fighting chairs in the stern. There was a hinged door cut into the transom for pulling aboard huge fish. For maybe ten minutes it was hard to look at her. When my eyes adjusted to the light I saw that she was beamy and high-bowed, built to devour the ocean. She took my breath away.

The forty-footer was owned by a woman named Billy, who talked to Dad with a pained expression. The Broward shipyard had built the boat to Billy's specifications one year before and the *Ebb Tide* had been showcased on the cover of *Motor Boating and Sailing* magazine as the world's finest fishing boat. The woman told Dad all the custom details of the Broward as though she were relishing them for herself. We had heard that she had fallen on bad times and couldn't afford to fill the four-hundred-gallon gas tanks or to pay the monthly dockage. But Billy talked about the sale as though it might not be final, maybe she could buy the *Ebb Tide* back in a year. What do you think? she asked my father. Yeah, of course. Anything. We could talk about it in a year. He was making a deal. Billy tried to appear jaunty but her body English told of a string of big defeats.

Dad came back to New York looking forward to telling Mom about the boat. Somehow he believed the forty-footer would save the marriage. For Dad there was always a way around defeat.

"Abe kept me pinned down for years," says my mother. "He would have an intuition that I was plotting to leave him and then his eyes would open like pools of fear. They were pleading with me. 'Stella, I need you to stay alive.' He submerged me in those eyes. I was paralyzed. Every time I prepared to go, Abe went into the hospital again. I would say to my father and sister, I can't leave Abe because he needs me."

By now I.R. was appalled by his son-in-law, who he believed would do anything to close a deal, even dangle Stella as bait. My grandfather must have felt burdened by his own role in Stella's unhappiness. He had urged her to make this marriage and then had brought Abe back to New York and put him into the business against Stella's wishes.

Mother continued to warn me that she was going to divorce my father. One time she and I argued bitterly. I said to her that she was just being difficult. Ruining things. She was playing a game. I reasoned with her as if she were a child. You are messing things up. It is the same thing you do in your painting. Our fight escalated. You wouldn't dare leave him, I sneered at her. Mother ran into the kitchen and came back with a butcher knife. She held it over my head. I dared her to use it.

Afterward I reflected on my power—that I could provoke such a scene. Then I began to worry that she might actually leave him, just to prove to me that she was capable. At night I would tell Bill about my fears. I believed that if he were my ally, then she could never leave Dad. In his room, while he played with his dinosaurs, I explained how terrible it would be for us. All the fishing would stop, all the great catches. Dad would get rid of the *Ebb Tide* before we ever had a chance to put over our lines. What a preposterous idea. Who would take us to restaurants? What would happen to us? My brother would silently pit his *Tyrannosaurus rex* against his *Stegosaurus,* set his jaw. I could not reach him with my logic. To him, my father was a tyrant who ranted and raved. Bill wanted to live in the Great Neck house with Mother and his cats, spend afternoons in the rock garden. Dad and I could live on a different planet. I sensed it was Bill who could sway the balance. His silence made me feel more desperate than Mother's fury.

By the second half of my sophomore year in high school, Mother was no longer painting. Consumed by rage, she couldn't forgive Abe for breaking his promise and coming to New York, for the humiliation of Great Neck and Globe and the stench of Fischbach. She was obliterating her canvases, one after the next, glopping layers of gray and black paint over years of work. Almost no paintings remain from this period.

I believed that Mother was angry with me. I had been a fool to bait her and criticize her work in front of her student Helen Rutt. In my adolescent myopia I kept trying to imagine ways to expunge divorce from her mind. Their divorce was perversion to me. It would bring terrible shame to the family. Mother would answer me, There is nothing you can do about it, which left me incensed and thwarted. It was my job to block the door. To argue or to distract her until she was back inside the studio. Until she forgot. I had no idea that her sister and father were now calling her daily, urging her to leave Abe. I.R. devised stories that during my father's business trips he was carrying on affairs with other women. Thelma complained to Mother, "You are like a plane with the motor running that can't get off the ground."

The timing of the next events is murky, which is disturbing. I should be able to recall exactly what happened, the important dates, the order of significant moments in our lives. It galls me that I cannot remember the names and addresses of more than a few of the tremendous buildings that Dad filled with fluorescents just forty years ago. My mother and Celia cannot agree on exactly what transpired in Great Neck after Dad purchased the *Ebb Tide*. There is no one else left to ask.

Celia and Lennie began taking frequent trips to Great Neck. Whenever they visited, Stella smiled as though things were great in suburbia. But Abe's sister smelled a rat. She and Dad took precautions. Abe signed over to Celia his fifty percent ownership in Lee Products to keep the Boston shop safe from I.R.'s lawyers. He knew Cele was the one person who would never screw him. In between visits to Great Neck, Abe's sister called him with warnings. I.R. is going to try something. Be careful. Restrain your anger.

My twelve-year-old brother was the only one Stella trusted. Of course Mother should leave Abe. Billy believed that the marriage was degrading, Abe was a lout, didn't appreciate Mother's art. Abe had dragged Bill to the barber, cut off all of his hair. They didn't need him. No more of his anger and outrage. The Great Neck house was Bill's Tara. Bill and Stella would live in the house forever, watch Elizabeth Taylor and Kim Novak movies on TV, eat Winnie's well-done rib roasts.

Mother and Bill grew silent when I came around. I didn't know about I.R. and Thelma's constant nagging. Whenever I felt a shadow pass through I yelled at my mother to be good. I pounded on the drums and prayed for good health. The *Ebb Tide* was idling in Florida waiting for events to sort themselves out. We just had to throw off the dock lines and head for the Bahamas.

Abe's sister recalls that I.R. arranged to have Abe committed into a mental hospital. This was part of his master plan for engineering Stella's divorce and throwing Abe out of the Great Neck house. Mother says this never happened. She insists that he was put into the hospital for drug addiction. For years, when Dr. Nelson had made his late-night visits, he had been giving Dad shots of morphine and he was hooked. When he didn't have the drug, Dad became unstable, even violent. Mother says that she committed Abe herself, there was no other choice, but allows that her father might have been encouraging.

Details. It came down to the same gesture. They had locked him up in a small room. I.R. and Thelma had their hooks into Stella's neck. In the hospital Abe satiated himself on deceit and betrayal. I wonder if I.R. ever considered the price of crossing Abe Waitzkin.

It was two or three weeks before Dad was able to talk himself out of the hospital. He came home in a white rage. Mom was now living upstairs in the attic. I was afraid that he might kill her. We all steered clear of him, moved from room to room like terrified little fish. Don't say a word to him when he is like this, she whispered. Stay in your room. I recall the spittle on my father's chin when I told him not to hurt her. I was shaking and could not meet his stare. He walked away from me without a word.

A few days later Dad drove the Buick Roadmaster into Maspeth to the Globe plant. He walked into his office and saw my uncle seated at his desk, talking business on Abe's phone, swiveling in his chair. Cocksucking, prick bastard. The man had simmered beneath a smile at a hundred business meetings because he couldn't sell like Abe.

Dad was out.

Abe was presented with a deal by Mom's high-priced attorney. Get out of the house. I.R. would retain the considerable money he owed Abe in commissions and in return he would support Stella for the rest of her life. Dad went ballistic. The only way you will get me out of this house is in a pine coffin.

By now I.R. had become the pure and unwavering focus of my father's hatred. Stella was only a pawn in the game. I only want to live long enough to piss on your grandfather's grave, he told me. In the next days, while the lawyers battled over the divorce settlement, Dad grew calmer, even reflective. He was already considering the details of his revenge.

PART II
BETRAYAL

. Shark Fishing .

THEY LOVED MY FATHER ON BIMINI. FORTY YEARS AGO MANNY THE *grocer sold Abe cases of J&B to bring back to Lauderdale on the boat. Local guys hefted crates of booze onto the* Ebb Tide, *which made Dad feel vigorous. He slapped them on the back and paid big tips. Abe was a big roller, happy to pay exorbitant prices—it was show business.*

"What a man your daddy was," Manny says to me each time I visit the island now and tie up my own boat at the Game Club dock. I rarely buy anything from Manny, which confuses and irritates him. We all draw our lines. But at times it feels warm and comforting to become my father and here on Bimini I slip into his skin without thinking. One can feel outraged but at the same time attracted to the vestiges of colonialism on these fine docks. It is a wonderful feeling to walk in the night past broken shanties, waving at natives one has known since childhood, talking about the travails of the Knicks and our kids and how the island has changed over the years or not changed and then to slip past the guard at the Game Club gate, to flip him a neat little wave like my old man, that same guard who barks in a harsh patois at native intruders, to breathe in the night air still heavy with yearning, the toss of palm trees in the colored pool lights, the bobbing of sleek fishing machines at rest. There is a sense that we, the sportfishing elite, are untouchable somehow, sleepy at

*the end of a long day of plunging down big seas, trolling foot-long bone-
fish and swimming mackerel; surely we will be sharing this idyllic scene
forever, these deep blue waters and cool breezes rife with desire, not growing old despite sagging bellies and graying hair, sequestered from the
world's afflictions, sportfishing.*

"Throughout the marriage Abe would go out with his womaniz-
ing friends," recalls Mother, "and when the drinking part of the night
was over he would make his fast exit. Sorry, guys, I love my wife. But
Abe was lying. He didn't care about fidelity or passion. The truth
was that Abe was a sick man and couldn't perform. When I said I was
going to leave him, he began telling his buddies that I was disfigured.
I don't know what he thought. Maybe he was referring to the long
scar from my hysterectomy or that they had shaved me before the operation. That stuck in his mind because he rarely saw me undressed.
He needed to tell them something. Appearance meant so much to
Abe.

"When I told him the divorce was final, Abe sneered at me, 'When
did you get so smart, Stella?'

"'Abe, this is no marriage. We don't talk.'

"'Who would want you, Stella?'"

I.R. was a visionary. Everyone knew this in the electrical business.
He anticipated trends in the American market, appreciated the larger
picture. He knew history, that the ends justify the means. Whether
Abe fooled around with women when he was in Detroit was not the
issue. I.R. loved Stella, and Stella was languishing in a hideous marriage. He became emotional when he thought of his love for his eldest daughter and the future he wanted for her. I.R.'s hands were
clean. He was sweeping with a big broom. Thelma was also mired in
a bad marriage to Chet. Here too I.R. began planting seeds. He
would take care of both of his girls. The family's prosperity was as
rock solid as the huge plant in Maspeth.

When my father refused to leave the Great Neck house, I.R. recognized that this wasn't negotiable. He convinced Stella to let Abe
have the house. Call the lawyer, tell him, Grandpa said. Just get rid of
Abe once and for all. The house is nothing, Stella. I'll buy you better.

You can go to my house in Palm Springs and paint the mountains at sunset.

During the spring of my sophomore year in high school, Bill and I lived with Dad. Mother took a small apartment in Manhattan while she looked for a place for the three of us in Riverdale. "Losing the house would have been too humiliating to him, so he forced us to leave. What kind of man would do such a thing to his family. Abe was a monster."

Dad would lie in bed late into the morning, one bony leg raised to his chest, smoking Luckies. Eventually he went into the bathroom to fix himself up, as he put it. Throughout the house I could smell astringent and the sweet aroma of his bowels. Winnie had been with us for nearly all of the Great Neck years and was now gray and stooped. She folded Dad's socks and placed them neatly into the little compartments in his drawers, cooked well-done briskets and chops, tried to keep things as they had been. The Buick Roadmaster seemed permanently moored in the driveway. Each afternoon Dad fell asleep with a burning cigarette in his hand. I would take it from between his fingers and kiss his leathery cheek. His satin bedcover had fifteen or twenty cigarette holes. Where would we ever find another to match the one on Mom's bed? What was wrong with her? How could she move out when he was recovering from a horrible operation and was out of work?

But then Dad would surprise me, emerge from desolation ready to eat Chinese with his boys. We would drive to Manhasset and he'd tell me not to worry about Mother, she'd come around. Or he'd assure me that I was healthy and if anything did come up, we could take care of it at the Clinic, no big deal. He promised Bill that he would always have his house in Great Neck, he could count on it. Over wor wonton my father was believable as a saint. He could make your heart soar with trust and good times coming. I've always loved that quality.

I.R. celebrated the end of Abe. We dined at Cavanagh's and I found myself sucked into Grandpa's largesse. He is your father, mister. Of course you should love him. Grandpa became emotional over his generosity of spirit. He invited me to order shrimp cocktail. Then we all enjoyed Cavanagh's famous sliced steak with toast bits soaked in gravy. My grandfather smiled at me. I was his eldest grandson, loved politics as he did. He lured me with the chance that someday I would be president of Globe. This was only stroking. Grandpa's vision of the future was his son Alfred, only Alfred. If there was a god in heaven, his boy, his soul mate, would have a proper turn to guide the great factory. But what was the harm in dangling a possibility?

Grandpa presented Mother with a brand-new Chevy station wagon. I recall his big round smile, he'd won. Stella, he was just a salesman, a chiseler. Don't worry about everything, will you. I'll take care of it. But listen to me. These dark paintings are not right. Maybe something more amusing with lighter colors. You need to develop a line, something people can relate to. Change it a little each year. But not too much. You want repeat customers. Please don't argue with me. I know the business. You'll see. We'll make a catalog.

Years before the divorce, as a seven- or eight-year-old, I would sit on the lawn of the Great Neck house and practice making time slow down. I would play with my water-pressurized rocket ship and luxuriate in the minutes I had before the next meal. I tried to savor the smallest particles of time. In the midst of my game a few minutes felt like days and the few outdoor hours that I had left before the next hateful school day stretched on like months. With practice I found that I was able to bring time to a near stop. Many afternoons I rejoiced in an endless expanse of minutes. And when time did happen to shoot ahead a week or a month, it was just a lapse of my concentration, and I fancied that I could even pull time back. In this mindset, bad events also lacked finality. I suspected that big events in life, indeed the very question of living and dying, were subject to revision. Nearly everything could be manipulated by clever decision making and concentration, especially when combined with inside connections. My father had proven this again and again making enormous deals with contractors, getting up off the mat, surviving when everyone said that he would die.

I didn't think of my parents' divorce as irreversible. My outrage toward my mother was tempered by this view. I saw the thick clump of papers prepared by her attorneys but still it seemed as though Stella and Abe were only a whim away from putting happiness back together. Dad even implied that the Commissioner might be able to do something about it. We'll see, he added cryptically. Many years later I am still susceptible to such revisionist thinking, particularly relative to tragedy, which I find difficult to look at straight on. Instead of feeling racking grief I tend to explain how catastrophe might have been averted. Betrayal is only a matter of choice. What if Mother had returned to the house? Why not? She was so quixotic.

In the late spring of my sophomore year, my friend Jon Lehman would come by the Great Neck house to commiserate. Both of us had a precocious sense of shame and propriety. Jon shared the humiliation I felt over Mom moving out, the family breaking apart. He even offered to run away with me and I pondered how effective this blackmail might be. Finally we decided not to because the gesture was too gaudy and embarrassing.

In the house Dad was musing and said little for long stretches. I couldn't reconcile the passion I felt for him with my decision to leave with Mom and Bill. I felt like a traitor. Mother had arranged for me to attend a private school, Barnard School for Boys. They bribed me with sweets. On one phone call the assistant headmaster said that I was a smart boy and owed it to myself to come to Barnard to study literature. The football coach called and asked what position I played. Without thinking, I said quarterback, and he answered, we need a good quarterback here. I couldn't believe my ears. Throwing the pigskin for Barnard School for Boys. That clinched it. I was leaving my father to pursue my football career. It was all-American and guiltless.

I told Jon Lehman about the call from the football coach and that in August I would be attending training camp. Waitzkin, this is crazy, he said. In our friendship Lehman's part was to ease me back from erratic choices and to soften my falls. You can't do this, he cautioned. You're a small, skinny guy. You're afraid of pain. And they could break your back. I argued with him a little but fear and sense took hold. I realized that I would never lace on the pads for Barnard. I was abandoning ship, plain and simple. Leaving Dad. Leaving home. Maybe I was afraid to stay with him.

One evening Mother pulled up in front of the Great Neck house and Bill and I threw our things in the back of the new Chevy. We were like three children, running away. Mother drove at eighty, ninety. I recall a million bugs splattering against the windshield. Bill giggled at his mother's wild spirit, the same as his own and Liz Taylor's. I was guilty to leave Dad this way, fretting in his bed, while Winnie cooked potatoes, cleaned, ran half-empty loads of laundry. But I was absolved by the lure of the night. I urged Mother to drive faster, pushed her. Bill laughed and opened the window. A rush of hot wind. We skidded off the road to avoid hitting a truck, took a deep breath and sped off again, spitting gravel. Bill and Mom were free. I wasn't so sure.

We got to Toronto around midnight, stayed up until four A.M. in a half-empty club listening to Carmen McCrae. I rapped out rhythms on the table. Mother swayed and closed her eyes. While Carmen sang her throaty blues I felt Dad's timing and style, imagined him selling the goods to Charlie Zweifel, I yearned for him. The next morning we turned around and headed to Tanglewood. Exhausted, we lay on the big lawn and listened to the Boston Pops. And then late at night we raced off to Jacob's Pillow to hear Dave Brubeck's soaring runs of improvisational Bach, and then cool Ahmad Jamal came on at two A.M. Mother whispered that Jamal was too tame, like Montovani. I could feel this. I was swelling with the music and the heavy summer air full of lusty promise. We ate good food. I told Bill that we would get a great ride if we played our cards right. Mother and Dad would compete for our favor. Imagine the restaurants Dad would take us to, the fishing trips on the *Ebb Tide*. Divorce wasn't so bad after all. Maybe you were right, babe, I said to my brother. I leaned in Bill's direction, stroked him. It's gonna be great, babe. We sell one another out for tips. I see it again and again. But I could never quite win over my brother.

Sure there were big changes, but there was more continuity in our new lives than I could have imagined. Much of that came from Globe. Everyone in the world knew about Globe, and yet it was ours, massive and providing. The company had given our family the home in Great Neck and now our spacious apartment in Riverdale. It had paid for our boats and vacations in Palm Springs and Miami. More elementally, it gave us power, affected the way we walked, our sense of security in the world. Even I.R.'s son Alfred, with shortness of breath and rosy cheeks prescient with demise, was viewed by many as a lion, the heir. None of us could miss because of Globe. The factory was our safety net, a hedge against stupidity, shortcomings and mistakes.

The grandchildren could afford bad grades. The firm would absolve us all, absorb us into its ample offices and showrooms. Even for my mother Globe was essential, providing the perfect anti-Christ—vile commerce, capitalism—spurring her to paint ever more darkly. Rage and degradation drove her work; in one self-portrait of this period Mother's eyeless mouthless mutilated face and rat tufts of hair are whirling into the abyss. Hans Hofmann asked, Stella, where do you get such ideas? Looking at the pavement, she answered. She never mentioned Globe. It was her shame, her dark secret. Mother wanted to be poor so ardently. But my grandfather patiently explained to her that Globe would always be there for her and the family, providing a comfortable way of life, new cars, status in the community, the best medical insurance. It was his destiny to provide for the family. Even after he was gone things would be okay. The company would endure. With his venerable attorneys Grandpa had written up various trusts, wills and position papers (Mother furiously refused to read them) ensuring our futures and the direction of the company into the next millennium at least. To a boy such grandiosity was easily confused with immortality itself. And though I hated Globe for my father, I still felt ennobled by my blood connection to that great firm.

By now Dad had taken a job selling for Ruby-Philite, one of his former competitors. Ruby was less than half the size of Globe, but it was a nice-looking factory with its own luncheonette and automated spray booths. Ruby seemed like a company ready to make a move. Dad came on board wearing his Richard Widmark hat and razzmatazz smile. He installed his secretary Kate in the biggest office and came in one afternoon with a couple million dollars' worth of business. Abe was back. No other salesman in town could touch him. He brought the works. Restaurants. Prizefights. He was buddies now with Charlie Goldman, who was Rocky Marciano's trainer. How could we miss with the champ in our corner?

Dad confided in me that some of the first orders for Ruby were deals he had closed months earlier for Globe before he had been fired. When I asked how he had managed this magic, he gave me his slow Mafia nod, very theatrical. But why had my grandfather allowed Dad to take back business that was already in I.R.'s shop? Fuck the old bastard, said my father. He pointed his finger down the road.

Dad had arranged to have the *Ebb Tide* delivered to Montauk about a month after Mom moved out of the house. A new guy was running her, someone Dad had met in the greasy breakfast place across from Gosman's dock. Dad could never afford one of the thoroughbred captains who won tournaments for millionaire boat owners at the Montauk Yacht Club and the Bimini Big Game. He would usually hire someone for a day or a week who was on his way down, usually a drunk. Employing a captain was important for Dad, and he trusted these men even if they were sick and reeking from booze. I liked to steer the boat, but when we got to the Yacht Club Dad wanted his skipper on the bridge—maybe he was thinking about my past history at the helm. If the man was sleeping it off down below, Dad would wake him to bring the *Ebb Tide* into her slip. For nearly all the years we owned her, he wouldn't let me bring her in.

Twenty miles east of Montauk Point the *Ebb Tide* was loping across soft pillows of summer ocean. Abe smiled and smoked a Lucky, looked down from the flying bridge at his boys. We were out shark fishing. Bill always wanted to fish for sharks.

My brother loved being offshore. He closed his eyes and soaked up the sun. Bill's Siamese cats slinked into the cockpit. They were alarmed by seagulls and hid beneath the fighting chairs until the coast was clear to make a clamorous dash for the salon. Bill giggled at the chaos of his cats, would not hear of fishing without them, and Dad went along with it. Issues between them were set aside on the boat.

When we fished out of Montauk I was usually in the tower searching for finning swordfish to bait. Out here all of my dreads seemed preposterous. On a clear, calm day I could see for miles and the abundance of big fish was intoxicating. In all directions there were finning sharks and schools of small tunas crashing bait beneath flocks of frenzied birds; often there were killer whales feeding on tuna and giant sunfish with a floppy fin that I would almost always mistake for the dorsal of a broadbill. From time to time I saw a school of giant bluefin tuna, six- and eight-hundred-pounders pushing waves of water like minitankers, heading north for the Cape.

Some afternoons the ocean was littered with kegs churning through the gray water, each of them tethered to a three- or four-hundred-pound swordfish, occasionally an eight-hundred-pounder, harpooned by one of the New Bedford "stick boats." Whenever we came across kegs there were meandering blue sharks around, although for the most part the sharks gave the harpooned swordfish a wide berth. When they got around to it, the stick boats put over dories to retrieve the kegs, which were supposed to tire out the fish, but in fact big swordfish still had a lot of fight left and the men in the dories had their hands full pulling them in.

In these waters white marlin were also common and the stick boats sometimes harpooned these sixty-pounders just for fun. They called them "skilly gillies" and these skinny fish leaped and skittered across the surface, trying to shake off the deadly stick. Some of the sportfishing guys thought that it was a shame the commercial fishermen killed them for nothing. But there were so many marlin back then, no one made an issue of it.

With all of the splendid game fish to choose from, we were heading past the swordfish boats looking for makos. Bill dreamed about sharks.

My baby brother was drawn to peril and pain. There was a game we sometimes played on the *Ebb Tide*. Two guys each take an end of a length of ten- or fifteen-pound-test monofilament line and wrap it around a finger. Both start slowly to pull away. As the pressure increases, the mono begins to cut into the skin. Who could take it longest? Bill played this game against all of Dad's tough captains, and I never saw him give in. With his finger ringed in blood he would keep pulling away. More than once I wrestled his arm forward when I feared that he would sever the finger. But my brother was amused by my fears. Taking chances had become his teenage credo and handling sharks was also part of that.

Bill was mesmerized by stories fishermen told about thousand-pound makos attacking boats or long-dead carcasses on the deck suddenly leaping with open fangs upon a careless fisherman. One old harpooner warned my brother that whenever you stuck a mako, it would turn back upon the line and bite itself free, as if the shark had an ominous intelligence. He told Bill about the severed head of a mako that had made a crippling attack on a friend of his, took the man's hand off. He cautioned us never to put one in the boat without first shooting it in the head with a shotgun.

After running about two hours from Montauk, Bill signaled that we had arrived at the right spot in the Atlantic. In a few moments the droning of the engines gave way to silent rocking and the heat of the afternoon. My world became the sound of my brother ladling cups of chum into the ocean, ground mossbunker, sometimes he mixed it with seawater until he had the consistency just right. From time to time he took a whole fish and sliced off a couple of chunks and threw this into the oily slick. The sun flashed against his blade. By now the cats had grown more bold. The stench of the mossbunker had lured them into the sun-drenched stern. They stood on their hind legs mewing and trying to reach the putrid brew. The slick had drifted way behind the boat, maybe a mile. Soon Bill went into the cooler and took a bottle of rotting chicken blood, poured some of that overboard. Seagulls dove into the mess.

My brother was a witch doctor. A chicken wing, some blood, feathers, mossbunker guts. The proper timing and mixture were essential. He ladled over the foul slop for a great white, but secretly he hoped for a *Carcharodon megalodon*. Bill was dangling his hooks into an ancient ocean. He didn't speak much.

The darkness of the cold water compounded the mystery of our waiting. They were coming, but when? How many? How big? The slick connected us to unlimited bounty, and when fins eventually began working up the slick toward the *Ebb Tide*, it seemed inevitable, a natural law yielding to our call. They were blue sharks, sloppy swimmers, dumb and groping for tidbits of chum. Soon a half-dozen were feeding off the stern. Wow, Dad said, looking over the side at the ten- and twelve-foot brutes that slid beneath the boat and suddenly reappeared from under the transom mouthing chunks of chum and blood.

After ten minutes the blue sharks disappeared. Why? Maybe something had scared them. Something fierce and huge. But there was nothing. Very quiet. Even the birds were gone. The tide had stopped running now and the *Ebb Tide* rested in a fetid pool of blood and rotten mossbunker. The wind was still and there wasn't a ripple on the ocean. Then something grabbed one of the baits. We never saw a fin or swirl in the slick. My brother was on the rod and leaned back heavily to sink the hook. But there was no pressure and it seemed as though the fish had let go. Bill cranked slack line and then after fifteen or twenty seconds the ocean opened behind the *Ebb Tide* and a tremendous mako came out of the water, a projectile of muscle. The tail of the shark was fifteen feet above the surface— I'd never seen any fish jump like that. Hanging above us the six-hundred-pounder flipped over and showed us rows of menacing teeth and a beady eye. Then he crashed back on his side and showered us with water. Bill fought that shark for five hours. Pumped and cranked. Sweated. We could have taken him much faster, but each time the shark came close, instead of backing up to the fish Dad's half-soused captain idled the *Ebb Tide* ahead. He was afraid of that big mako, and so was I. The captain ran away from the shark a dozen times and Bill cursed the skipper and wound the shark back to the boat. By the time we had the mako alongside, I think it had been dead in the water for an hour. For Bill, catching the mako was tainted by our lack of courage.

In the late fifties fishermen went after sharks with a spirit of vengeance and payback. Stories of downed airmen in the Pacific being slaughtered by man-eaters were still fresh and inspired anglers to kill sharks in droves. A few charter skippers such as Frank Mundus made hay inflaming the passion of clients for killing sharks, bringing in boatloads. Mundus, who inspired the captain in Peter Benchley's *Jaws*, ran the *Ebb Tide* for a few days and made a strong impression on Dad, who decided that killing sharks was a form of missionary work.

One fall afternoon we were fishing off Montauk Point with a crony of Mundus's on the bridge. Bill wasn't aboard that chilly day, and for hours there seemed to be no more sharks off Montauk. But once they came, they were thick, really thick. I was ladling the chum into the water and fifteen or twenty two- and three-hundred-pounders were feeding off the stern like dogs. One of Dad's friends was fighting one on a rod, and I never noticed when the captain came off the bridge with a rifle. He opened up on the sharks with a 30.06, shot them in the head, the belly. The white bellies of dying sharks mixed with blood and soon a dozen of them were twisting in the pink froth, biting each other's tails and faces while the captain kept blasting away. When he began firing, I didn't know if the killing was great or horrifying, but eventually with my ears ringing I told the

man to stop shooting. I was surprised and a little embarrassed when
he obeyed me. I turned to my father then and saw his appalled expression, as though I had crossed him in front of his buddies.

My brother had no interest in slaughtering sharks. But he loved to
chum for them and dreamed about three-thousand-pound makos
and the *Carcharodon megalodon.* At the Yacht Club Bill cut open
sharks that had been caught by other boats and left to rot on the
dock, searched their entrails to discover what they had been eating.
The cats licked huge shark livers, mewed, and Bill laughed at them
and rubbed their ears with his bloody hands. He cut the jaws out of
makos and tiger sharks and hung them to dry on pilings where the
gulls swooped in on them. In the shallows near the club, Billy played
with baby sand sharks, rolled them over and patted their white bellies. When he found small sharks on the dock, he sometimes saved
them in jars of formaldehyde that he stored in Riverdale on top of his
bureau beneath his collection of lacquered shark jaws.

One afternoon when Dad was off doing business, Bill and I and a
captain, Cliff North, were crossing from Block Island to Point Judith, Rhode Island. The fog was so thick we could barely see the bow
of the boat from the bridge. Cliff was a top Florida skipper in between jobs who was willing to work cheap for Abe for a short period. But he had never seen fog socked in like this and was spooked.
This was before the days of depth recorders, loran and satellite navigation. We were navigating with a compass and watch. Cliff didn't
know the currents around Block Island. We were lost. Cliff shut her
down, scratched his head and studied the chart. The boat was rolling
in a cross sea and from below she must have looked like the belly of
a wounded whale. "I don't know, Buddy," said Cliff, looking at the
chart. He always called me "Buddy." All of a sudden the twenty-ton
Ebb Tide lifted from the water and began to shake. What the hell?
Something big had us and was turning and ripping. I held on, thinking about the giant squid that pulled the Cosello brothers down in
their forty-footer off the coast of Chile. After ten or fifteen seconds
the *Ebb Tide* sat back on the sea. Fog or no fog we knew we better
get out of there fast. During the trip to Point Judith the wounded
boat vibrated badly and my brother had this ecstatic expression,
which was infuriating to Cliff. He was a very straight guy. The following day we hauled her in the boatyard. There were a dozen bro-

ken teeth sticking into the hull, which was torn up pretty bad where we had been hit. It had been a white shark, maybe two thousand or twenty-five hundred pounds. Bill insisted that we had been attacked by an eighty-foot *Carcharodon megalodon.* He was always hoping, searching the ocean for six-foot dorsal fins.

Dad forgave my exodus from the Great Neck house without a word of reproach. We talked regularly on the phone, met in the city for meals. He told me about new jobs he was working on and memorable dinners at Lüchow's with Maxi Kamins and Charlie Zweifel. I often thought of Abe and the Commissioner sitting in fine dark brown leather chairs eating New York sirloin at the St. Moritz. Sometimes Dad drove me to the new factory and we looked at blueprints of office buildings, showed me where all the fixtures would go. Some would be ceiling-mounted, others stem-mounted. It always seemed like a serious matter which mounting style a contractor would choose for his fluorescents. To me and Kate and Dad it was as though they put up the sleek glassy high-risers to buy our fixtures. I walked through the factory watching new eight-footers come hot off the line. At Ruby there was no distraction with residential lighting. The company was putting on new guys to fill Dad's orders and was becoming a real player in the commercial lighting industry.

Dad was having a little problem with his throat, no big deal, he said. But the hoarseness wouldn't go away. His buddies at the Clinic said it was nothing to worry about but he needed to do a little therapy. A couple of times a month he flew to Boston to have radiation treatment. Once I went with him. The doctors gathered around Abe like he was a treasure. They asked about the boat and the fixture business. Dad smiled thankfully. Without his shirt he looked so needy. Before he took his turn in front of the machine, a big-breasted woman was having her treatment. She seemed confused about why I was there watching. But I was the least of her worries and she smiled briefly and put me out of her mind.

Mother dripped paint and turpentine all over the new parquet floors of our Riverdale apartment. Smears of gray, blue and green from wet canvases on the leather seats of the Chevy, a shame, but she didn't care. She urged me to dress in black, be subterranean, make your own statement. Whatever that meant. Her friends Sam Goodman and Boris Lurie made sculptures of shit. Long turds, small constipated balls of shit, clumps of diarrhea realistically colored and textured. You could practically smell it. Mother threw this great art in my face, dragged me to the gala gallery opening of the Shit Show. She took me to the Five Spot to hear Ornette Coleman. The sax and trumpet played without melody or warmth. They devoured one another. Great theater to her was Beckett and Ionesco. I found these writers intriguing but also frightening. In their sparse upside-down worlds I could not find any place for guys like me and Dad and the contractors we both admired. And what good was all of this great art doing her? In her Riverdale bedroom Mother slept amid stacks of abstract sketches and unpaid bills. Without Abe the details of life overwhelmed her.

I cultivated my conventional side. I went for haircuts, bought black penny loafers and two business suits on Fordham Road in the Bronx. I learned from Dad how to tie a fat double Windsor knot on my tie. I taught the knot to one of my friends and soon all the Barnard boys were wearing the double Windsor. I dedicated myself to getting good grades and prided myself on push-ups. Whenever I visited Dad I reeled off thirty fast ones and then stopped as though I had fifty more in me. Watching me do push-ups seemed to give him vitality. Sometimes he would smack me in the shoulder as though roughhousing would follow. Out of the blue he would ask, What's with your mother? I shrugged. We never had a long conversation about her.

In my Riverdale life I worried about asking girls for dates and fretted that my religious devotion was getting away from me. I worked on my basketball skills. Every day after school I shot for three or four hours on the hoop behind our building with Ronnie Penn, who was star of the varsity. Ronnie liked my shot but said that I had to push myself to be more physical: use your body, Waitz, go to the boards, follow your shot, follow your shot! I counted the days until the start of the season. On the first day of practice I was cut from the Barnard Junior Varsity. Almost forty years later I still feel the need to explain. In the first scrimmage I was guarding David Bloomberg, the leading scorer for the JV. I reached in for the ball and he fell to the court holding his arm. Maybe I fouled him but I don't recall much contact. The next day he came into school wearing a cast and I was off the team.

Mother and Dad warred within me. She bought me a subscription membership to the Living Theater, where I attended curious performances of Judith Malina and Julian Beck. During intermission I stood with folded arms as though deeply into existential thought. Sometimes Mother introduced me to her artist friends as a writer. When we were alone I fumed at her that I had never written a thing and had other career plans. Writing is your destiny, she said smugly, and reminded me that at eleven I had composed a brilliant story called "My Family," in which I documented her fiasco with Gus Verner, the grocer whom Mother tried to transform into an abstract expressionist. I suppose that Mother's steady diatribe on the banality and decadence of suburbia had taken hold because in a few short months Great Neck was sliding into my distant past. I went out to visit Dad less often.

But my brother's pilgrimages to the house were like clockwork. On Friday evenings he would take the Long Island Rail Road to Great Neck and then a taxi to the house. Before knocking on the door Bill would stand on the flagstone path soaking in suburban privilege and glamour. He savored the smell of the newly cut grass, the weeping willow on the front lawn was becoming full and majestic, he noticed the little blocks of Spanish tile that Mother had cemented into the crown of the garage that had been renovated into her studio. He walked to the rock garden, weeded a little beside Mother's Morris Minor, which had no windows and was beginning to rust badly. He giggled. Such a ridiculous car, perfect for Mom.

Dad tried to be patient with Bill. Abe's throat was bothering him from the radiation treatments. He was focused on his bodily needs, the rumbling of his stomach, caring for his colostomy. Dad was impeccable, changed his bag frequently, washing himself with astringents. Many patients who had these operations died of infection because they weren't careful. On these weekends together in the house Dad and Bill were separate planets. Abe didn't know where his son was coming from. He tried to constrain his anger. He smiled.

But there were muted grudges all around. From past years Bill could hear his father yelling at Mom for dripping paint on the carpet

or losing twenty bucks or Dad blasting him for his long hair or not
doing his homework or an awkwardness in the workshop or not
coming to eat on time. When he was little Bill had loved to hide in
the dark basement, fooling with the cats, wouldn't answer when he
was called. There had been evenings he was sent to bed without dinner. Mother or Winnie quietly climbed the stairs, handing delicious
secret meals over the Dutch doors.

The stodgy four-bedroom brick house on Locust Drive had become my brother's temple. Dad promised never to sell it. Bill didn't
want anything more from his father than that. His smile for his father was formal, almost patronizing. What's wrong with this kid?
Dad would swallow his anger, write checks in the den. Bill walked
through the living room luxuriating in the soft celadon wall-to-wall
carpet. He opened and closed the little drawers of the Early American hutch. What furniture. Someday it would all be his. He spun
the center piece of the broad, beautifully finished lazy Susan on
Mother's great round table. This always gave him delight.

Half the time Dad was away on business when Bill visited the
house. He spent lazy afternoons watching TV with Winnie while she
folded laundry. One time Dad came in from the airport, went into
his bedroom for a nap. After an hour and a half he came out wide-
eyed and roaring at Winnie for piling potatoes into his sock drawer.
Winnie's face was blank, uncomprehending. Bill became furious at
Dad for making such a scene over Winnie's little mistake.

I kept up my drumming with Auchee Lee, which may have been an
error. Although he was in high school himself Auchee was already
lead percussionist for the great jazz flutist Herbie Mann. I was good,
but Auchee was a giant, understood the soul of rhythm and built
conga solos that had people flying out of their seats at the Village
Gate. Auchee's lukewarm encouragement for my drumming was
painful. I would respond by describing blue marlin fishing off the
north side of Bimini Island to this little black boy from Ludlow
Street on the Lower East Side. Someday we would go trolling together in the blue water, I promised. He didn't know what to say. I
liked it that my friends knew nothing about marlin.

I considered my arty sojourns with Mom a diversion. I lived for
fishing trips and talking the trade with my father. Dad's smiling face

was on the cover of the *New England Electrical News.* He was salesman of the month! Abe was hot as a pistol, as he put it, landed high-
risers in Cleveland and L.A., each needed more than twenty thousand
fluorescents. I couldn't keep up with the numbers, with our success.
Fixtures were limitless like the giant bluefin and marlin off Bimini
in the spring and summer. Dad owned Fischbach. He owned the
unions. He owned the Commissioner.

We made plans to push farther south into the Bahamas, to troll the
Ebb Tide off Mama Rhoda Rock just south of Chub Cay in the
Tongue of the Ocean. Six-hundred-pound blue marlin were log-
jammed into the Tongue of the Ocean. Schools of hundred-pound
cubera snapper swam off Mama Rhoda. We'd fish for them using live
lobster. We couldn't miss.

Abe took his time with I.R., played with him. Wait, he whispered
hoarsely. I'm gonna bury the old bastard.

. *Sexy Mama* .

"CAN YOU FEEL IT?" I ASKED A MIDDLE-AGED ELECTRICAL CON-tractor who was sitting next to me on the bridge of the *Ebb Tide*. I was seventeen and at the controls six miles north of Bimini. "Feel what?" The overweight New Yorker was seasick and miserable. I was annoyed that I had asked the question. This was my chance and I mustn't be distracted now. The sick man covered his face with his arm. Father's captain was drunk, sleeping it off below. For hours the ocean had been flat, lifeless. But now it was sizzling with breeze and current and something else. Something else. A half-dozen birds off the stern were jittering inches above the water.

Dad was talking with some other business friends in the cockpit. None of them cared about fishing. Dad had hoped to wow his customers with the new boat. I steered a little to the left. I called down, told them to get ready. We had not seen a fish all week, but I could feel that one was there. I was sweating all over, tapped into something I couldn't explain. On the Gulf Stream there were clues everywhere you looked. But you had to notice. The nervousness of the birds was important, a cloud passing in front of the sun, any sea change might bring him up.

My dad's friends were bored with trolling, dubious about my ability as a captain. My father had been laughing at all of their jokes, holding his belly. I worried whenever he did this. Despite the colostomy he was always hurting there.

There was a faint color change in the froth behind the boat, a ribbon of brown cutting across the wake. It settled behind the right rigger bait, a long brown log a couple of feet down. Then he rose a little and clipped the surface with his dorsal. Eventually my father's friends could see his tall tail and dorsal so far apart there might have been two fish. The marlin moved sharply from one side of the bait to another like a big cat ready to pounce. He was enormous, eight or nine hundred pounds, I said later, but I really had no idea. Big. His heavy head lifted halfway out of the waves, swung his blade at the skipping mullet, missed. The men were dumbstruck. The unlikely size of the fish had paralyzed them. Again the marlin came out and missed the bait, threw water all over the ocean. I called from the bridge that someone should pick the rod up and pull the line out of the outrigger clip, feed the bait to the marlin. I was calling directions but no one was listening. The fish swung halfheartedly a few more times at the trolled bait and then lost interest. I could see his long brown shape falling farther and farther behind the boat. Below, my father was standing with a clenched fist. I couldn't tell if he was upset about the fish getting away or was it something in their conversation, was the deal going bad? My father's rage eclipsed all else. Maybe there wasn't going to be a killing. I could still see the marlin fifty yards astern, arcing through the wake, swimming away.

Then an hour later at the dock, Dad looked content sipping his Scotch. The men had come to some agreement, Dad would tell me about it later. I was unbearably curious. But I figured he'd won. A captain came on board. One of the fancy boats was broken down. Maybe an electrical problem. No one on the island knew how to fix it. The captain had come for my father. Abe could barely walk, was feeling dizzy, but he said okay. I carried his ohmmeter and the captain helped Abe board the Rybovich. Dad's friends also came along, sipping their drinks. Abe climbed through the hatch and bent his emaciated body between the bulkhead and the hot engine. He put a finger on his temple. Everyone hushed, Abe would get it going. Soon he was perched on the great diesel engine, pulling wires off, testing circuits with his meter. Then he tapped on a part and a few minutes later I packed the ohmmeter into its case. The crew helped him back to the *Ebb Tide*. They would be trolling for blue marlin in the morning.

The rocking and heat of the afternoon would have been enough to make a teenager horny. But there were often ladies on the *Ebb Tide*. One of Dad's friends owned a big club in Lauderdale. Sometimes he brought three or four waitresses for a weekend. They took off the tops of their bathing suits and walked around the cockpit. Breasts jiggled past my face. I could smell them. I wanted to grab these girls and feel their bosoms on my face, hump them on the fighting chair. One of the girls had enormous dark nipples. She put her hand on my shoulder, asked me about marlin bait. I tried to describe rigging mackerel and bonefish. What were the rules when women walked around topless? I sat in the chair with an erection, smelling her, sweating. She looked at my lap and giggled.

Once I arrived on Bimini and Dad was with a girl only a couple of years older than me. She called Dad "Abe" as if they had known each other for years. She was beautiful, blonde, with a dream figure. When I looked at her I went hazy. Amazingly, while we trolled for marlin she read Dostoyevsky. Tremulously I ventured a few observations about *Notes from the Underground*. She was a recent graduate of Barnard. Imagine that, I also go to a Barnard, I said. She adjusted her scarf at my awkwardness. I was freewheeling with desire but she appeared not to notice. What were the rules about your father's girlfriends?

This beautiful creature held Dad's thin arm as he teetered down the dusty road for a J&B in the late afternoon. The idea of them fucking on the boat at night was astonishing, exciting, horrifying. I wondered if he was embarrassed about his colostomy. It didn't occur to me that he paid for this smart, beautiful girl. At my age I only need to come once a month, Dad told me afterward, as though this explained everything. He had almost no voice left at all. To tell the truth I prefer nurses, he said, soothing himself with a Lucky. They know what to do—no hang-ups. I nodded.

After a day of marlin fishing on the *Ebb Tide* I was rife with desire. I looked forward to the night, when the clubs came alive. When

Dad was snoring in his forward bunk, I climbed out of the rack and headed up the road for the Calypso Club. I was a star at the Calypso, playing conga against a funky island sax, blistering them with riffs I had learned in New York. I wanted to seduce women with my rhythms. While I smiled at island ladies I used my middle finger to make the drum moan like Olatunji. Though my groin ached from strain I lifted the heavy conga with my legs, leaned back and pounded with elbows akimbo. I stuck my elbow in the middle of the skin like Armando Paraza. There was one night when I played like Auchee Lee. My sultry jungle rhythm had black bodies swaying and I sprayed the beat with bursts of flitty slaps. Something special was happening and my rhythm tightened like desire. Everything I had poured out when Sexy Mama came onstage in a cape. She was wild-eyed, threw the cape into the audience and leaped topless through a circle of flames. Then she spread her arms wide and shook her breasts while I punished the skins with rolling slaps, picked up the drum and thrilled them with a thunderous bass that shook the ply-wood walls. They were cheering while she made love to the beat and then looked my way for something new. My drumming hands were alive. Sweating, I slowed the rhythm to a crawl and Sexy Mama did the Bimini grind. I knew that later that night she'd be doing it with Bill Verity, the captain who caught me my first blue marlin.

It made Abe furious when natives told him they had seen Fred drumming at the Calypso. The congas were evil, decadent, black. He was sure the locals all smoked marijuana, tea, as he called it. Abe knew that in Boston Negroes smoked tea, walked around in a fog, they smelled. But on Bimini Abe favored them with his smiles and big tips and they loved him.

I thought incessantly about big black breasts. Walked the island in the afternoon sweating to get a glimpse of breasts. I knew where to look. In the shanties they barely bothered to dress. One lady with big ones cared for her pigs outside a broken shack. I would walk by to look at her. She didn't mind. She bent over so that I could see bet-ter. One day she gestured for me to come in. As I walked across her narrow yard, one of the pigs, incredibly large and filthy, ran at me snorting. I jumped up on her buckling porch. I was scared stiff. I sat on a sofa inside that was torn here and there, with tufts of stuffing coming out. Beams of sunlight poured in from cracks in the wooden walls. She unbuckled my pants, began to knead my penis. Soon she was sucking on it. I was thinking of my father. What would he do to me. Outside I could hear the pigs squealing. Babies were yammering. Maybe hers. What if one of them came inside. Or her husband. After a while she lay down and put me inside her. I went on and on listening to the pigs. I couldn't come. The big woman was heaving like a giant tuna on the deck. She was moaning and her breathing was furious. But I couldn't concentrate. Then she stopped. "Baby, I have to catch my breath." After a minute or two we started again. We went on and on, but I couldn't. "Baby, you come yet?" she asked. "You come yet, honey?" It was hard. I was thinking of my father. What would he do to me. "I don't have all day, honey." A fat black lady with thick lips. My first love.

Something about the rocking ocean and searching for big fish opens a torrent of desire. One captain who fished for giant marlin in remote waters accommodated the inflamed libidos of his male customers by engaging an escort service. At fancy prices he ferried hookers in seaplanes a hundred miles from a home port to a small island where a sumptuous yacht was anchored. The women would be sunbathing nude on the top deck when the sportfishing boat arrived in the late afternoon after the day's trolling for thousand-pounders.

Over the years I have noticed the erotic effect of fishing trips on my friends and guests. Couples become lusty, impatient for the evening. Teenage girls want to fish topless for groupers and yellowtail. They smear sunscreen on their firm breasts and bellies. With arched backs they pull up on their rods, their nipples become hard. They don't mind if other boats cruise by for a look. They are fishing, restraints fall away. I am not sure why.

One time I was crossing the Gulf Stream with two friends on a small boat with a tuna tower. One of my buddies, a conservative and entirely proper man, was taking in the ocean sights from the tower, where he apparently believed that he could not be seen from below. At one point I leaned out over the gunwale to call up to him and saw that he was taking his pleasure while staring at a school of breaking yellowfin. Sex and tuna, go figure.

. *Raw Chicken Parts* .

FOR ALL THE YEARS WE OWNED THE *EBB TIDE* DAD KEPT A SHIP'S log with a blue marlin embossed on the cover. He listed every cruise and troll, each hookup and catch, every fuel fill, oil change, dinged propeller, every fishing trip with his boys, contractors and doctor friends. "Took on 135 gallons in Menemsha. Had a tuna on for 10 minutes off the #4 buoy." Another entry: "Picking up the boys at 4PM. Filled crankcase oil. Nick came over Friday night," referring to his favorite anesthesiologist. "Fished Saturday. Hooked a marlin. It got off. A great day." The world depicted in the ship's log was cozy and pleasant. Beyond the sight of land, pulling daisy chains of squid or running toward distant buoys, there were no treasons or treacheries. As Dad began to lose his voice his entries became increasingly verbose and cheerful, as though life were an endless cruise from hookups to landfalls. Dad's vision of the world, his very essence changed when he boarded the *Ebb Tide*.

Between fishing trips Dad lived with Winnie in the Great Neck house. I think that they both believed that Bill and I would be coming back. Winnie cleaned and cleaned. She had a glazed expression now, like her shell-shocked son. She would ask my father, Where's Fred and Bill? and he would tell her. Where's the cats? Riverdale. Riverdale didn't mean anything to Winnie but she nodded and resumed her chores. When they happened across one another again at the other end of the big house, Winnie would ask, Where's Bill and the cats?

Dad traveled even more. Coming home from La Guardia at two A.M., he'd drop his fat briefcase on the living room floor. I'm beat, he'd say to no one. He shook his head. He was closing deals like crazy but there was no one here to tell. Dad had always made the plans. This wasn't on the agenda.

Winnie was still ordering chickens and flanken from the kosher butcher. Dad didn't care about ordering kosher meat and ate out most of the time anyhow, but Winnie kept placing the orders, big orders for the family. He shook his head, threw out the meat. She cleaned the clean floors, vacuumed. Listened for Bill, her baby. Ordered more meat. She began stuffing the wings, thighs and livers into Dad's drawer beside his carefully folded handkerchiefs. She had decided that raw chicken parts belonged there and wasn't deterred when Dad roared at her to stop. He tried to cajole her, Winnie, get with it, put the chicken in the refridge. But she knew better.

Abe had to let her go.

I barely noticed when Winnie slipped out of my life. I was distracted when Dad called to tell me about the chicken parts and that he was considering selling the house. Why should he live in such a big place by himself? In retrospect, I realize that Dad was testing the water to see if I might offer to move back in with him. But I was having a bad time and his problems didn't register. My stomach had been bothering me for weeks. I couldn't eat, couldn't study. It was burning. This was different from my episodes with diabetes and polio. I was losing weight. Every morning I weighed myself on the scale in Mother's bathroom. I began chewing tablets and swigging chalky liquid. I felt weak and terrified. Withering away. I had bad gas. I had what Dad had. It was perfectly clear. I couldn't sleep at night worrying about the bag I would need to wear. My love life was shot before it began. I couldn't get my mother's attention. She was doing performance art on the city streets with her mangy loser friends and making a movie with Taylor Mead, who would later become a regular in Andy Warhol movies. Mother was now sculpting outsized polyester eggs with strange figures showing from within, eggs from another world, and while Mead filmed, she buried them in excavations for new buildings all over Manhattan. She conceived of this as a protest against war and capitalism.

I was up all night sweating in bed. I was dying alone. If the disease didn't finish me, panic would. Finally I begged my father to take me to the Clinic. This was a grim but necessary step. I knew they would take my stomach or some of my intestines. Typically, top guys in the lighting business had left the Clinic with less than they brought. The doctors had recently taken my uncle Chet's stomach and he was bitter about it.

We flew to Boston on the Eastern shuttle. I recall my aunt Celia the night before my tests grilling well-done steak on the rotisserie. I couldn't eat a bite. She nodded gravely as though she had seen this before. She knew all Dad's big-shot friends who had gone in for surgery. Whenever she mentioned the Clinic, Celia tittered. To her the Clinic was status. On my father's side of the family, because of Abe's connections, illness was an opportunity for going first class.

Once again I watched how the doctors were drawn to my father. While I dressed in a chilly white gown, Dad was smiling like a winner surrounded by a half-dozen doctors. He described his deals and promised them marlin fishing on the *Ebb Tide*. They wanted to make deals like Abe. Before I went in for my tests Dad mentioned that one of the doctors he'd been chatting with was a top brain surgeon. I smiled weakly. We were covered top to bottom.

Soon after swallowing the white liquid I heard one doctor say to another, his esophagus is clear. Thank God for that, I thought, never before having realized that the esophagus was a source of danger. The body is so complicated—death can be sitting in any pocket, curve or straightaway. A couple of hours later I learned that my stomach and intestines were also clear. A nervous stomach, one of them told me, relax.

On the shuttle back to New York, my father was disgusted with me. What a head case. You know what that examination cost! But this did not deter my good spirits. I had a clean bill of health, as Dad would put it. What a feeling. I resolved to be more bold with girls. I was free to pursue love and baseball with my full energy. The Clinic had given me back my future.

I had been cut from every team I ever tried out for. Basketball, track, baseball the year before in Great Neck. I was determined to make the varsity baseball team at Barnard, to get a letter. It was my last chance to make a team, but I knew that Coach Kelly would cut me. He was the one who dropped me from the JV basketball team after Bloomberg fell onto the court holding his arm. My friend Ronnie Penn and I made a plan. He was all-city in baseball as well as basketball. He was a lefty with a wicked curve ball, the best in our conference. An unhittable pitch. Ronnie always threw for the tryouts, and hitters were pleased if they managed to foul off one or two of his pitches. Our plan was simple. Before each curve ball Ronnie would touch the tip of his cap. He would take a little off his fast balls. I would write his next two English papers. It was an insider Abe Waitzkin deal, and it worked to perfection. I stepped up on every curve and punched it into right field. I had no power but made contact with everything Ronnie threw. The coach and starters on the team looked on with amazement as I slapped back grounders and little line drives. I made the varsity. I couldn't wait to call Dad with the news.

From the ship's log: "Alan F. [Fischbach] arrived Lauderdale Friday night. Sat morning we took both boats across the Stream. *The Friendly Fisch* rode beautiful. What a boat! We had lunch at the Game Club. Fished the afternoon. Alan in the chair. We had two strikes by marlin. Switched over to center [fuel] tanks 2PM. Tomorrow morning we plan to leave for Chub at 7AM with both boats. . . ."

Now Dad was alone in the house. Sometimes I thought of him by the stove stirring salami and eggs for himself. He had no buddies in Great Neck. Without the kids at home, selling trips had become more of a push, but his fury toward Grandpa was unabated. It got him through.

Dad was slowly tightening the screws, as he put it. I wonder if he ever discussed his master plan with Alan fishing off Chub Cay or dining after drinks at the Colony Club. Most likely not. I always thought that Alan was simpleminded. Abe led him from one deal to the next. Promised great times. More rendezvous in the Bahamas. Rich people are often unhappy, lost at sea on their sumptuous yachts. My dad brought along a vision of special times, an endless horizon of great fishing trips and good talk. Alan gave Abe all the work Ruby could handle and then Dad suggested which other companies deserved orders. Jobs for SmithCraft, Daybrite, Neo-Ray— that was his friend Leon's company—and sometimes they made side deals. Globe was never on the list. Dad made calls to other contractor buddies, eased them away from Globe. It was easy. Whenever he called the Commissioner Dad pushed his voice and projected a sensibility of terrific times, of glee. Lying in the bedroom of our empty, darkened home, Dad asked about the Commissioner's kids and the wife, about barbecues on the back lawn. Eventually they got to trading favors and Abe said a few words about Globe. The Commissioner took Abe's cues quickly and changed the subject. He liked to keep conversation pleasant. After these important talks Dad couldn't speak for hours. He smoked Luckies to soothe his throat, blew rings into the air.

I'm busting the old man's balls, he told me with his chin quivering a little. His voice was hardly more than a whisper and even at that it hurt him to speak. He knew what was coming and was training me to read his lips. Harassing him a little, he said, forming his words carefully. Nothing terrible, he continued, Maybe a wrench falls into the gears of a costly machine. A Globe truck arrives at a building and the union guys refuse to unload the fixtures. Fuck the old bastard. He can throw his fixtures into the river. Dad's impish smile always made me grin back.

During Abe's years landing office buildings for Globe, Grandpa had allowed the residential side of the business to slip while Globe gradually developed the best plant in the industry for manufacturing ceiling-mounted fluorescents. All of a sudden New York distributors weren't giving Globe salesmen the big jobs. Making the payroll for five hundred workers had become a problem. About the same time that Stella left Abe, Chet and Thelma were divorced and now my uncle was also out of the company. With Abe and Chet gone, I.R. needed his son to take up the slack, but Alfred was a gentle man who had never had a great mind for business. And he wasn't well. Alfred responded to his father's pressure by becoming irritable and distracted.

My father's machinations against Globe proceeded like a game to me, not unlike the ruse Ronnie and I had concocted to make the

Barnard baseball team. While I rooted for Dad and found his wheeling and dealing with Fischbach and the Commissioner heady, at heart I believed that Globe was fundamentally impervious. The huge company was like the ocean itself. It would always be there providing lighting for America while enriching our families.

On Sunday evenings Grandpa took us to dinner at a steak restaurant on 72nd Street where the waitresses wore tiny black outfits and were chosen for their plump rear ends and large bosoms. During these meals Grandpa was cheerful and confident, smiled when the girls leaned over to take his order. One Sunday he showed up triumphantly in a brand-new green Caddy with enormous fins, talked buoyantly about his color catalog. It was clear that Grandpa would soon rebuild his sales force and come out with a smashing new residential line.

Abe Waitzkin's *Ebb Tide* log: "No fishing today off Cape Cod. 25 mile winds. Generator removed and disassembled by Falmouth Marine. Bill arrived aboard *Ebb Tide* with wild stories. We had a ball. Had dinner at Flight Deck." Following this entry my brother sketched a blue marlin in the log, signed his name and added, "Everything shipshape!"

Alfred's decline was precipitous. He began espousing bizarre ideas and quickly lost physical coordination. One day Laurie found her husband talking to himself as he watched a record go round and round on the turntable. Soon she had to put him into a mental hospital. When I.R. visited the institution he found his thirty-six-year-old son crawling on the floor. I.R. pleaded with Laurie, Let me take care of Alfred. I'll build bars on my windows, I want to take him home, I'll watch him every minute. Of course Laurie had to refuse this request. Grandpa demanded of her, Let me have three days alone with my son. She reluctantly agreed. For three days he slept in Alfred's room. I.R. never discussed the visit with Laurie. To the end Grandpa's relationship with his son was private and eclipsed all else. After Grandpa left the hospital, Alfred telephoned to ask his wife to come. Will you bring my shoes? he asked.

A few hours later Alfred died of a heart attack.

I.R. was a blind man without his son. He decided that Alfred's wife was a gold digger and tried to dismiss Laurie with a ten-thousand-dollar check. Don't you ever ask me for another penny, he demanded bitterly of his son's flabbergasted widow. Then he was filled with remorse and fear. What if Laurie kept the grandchildren from him, his connection to Alfred.

Grandpa had pains in his heart for Alfred. He worried, maybe he had given his son too much responsibility. Everything came at once. Business was bad and he had to lay off workers. He had known some of these men thirty years. He told Stella he had to take back the blue Chevy, which was a company car. To save. Stella was angry at him. Why does Thelma keep her Thunderbird?

Because she works for the company. Thelma's gonna take over for Alfred. Someday she'll be president of Globe.

Bullshit, said Mother.

Stella, why do you speak to me this way? I'm an old man. I'm sick. And look how you dress, in torn black stockings? Why do you dress like this?

Grandpa's old law firm, Rubin, Baum and Levin, was a harbor of refuge and stability. Sometimes Grandpa visited his prominent lawyers in their rich, wood-paneled offices. More often the lawyers, including Abe Levin himself, arrived at the 73rd Street apartment fresh from multimillion-dollar negotiations Midtown. They brought thick new drafts of his various wills and trusts along with a stack of new yellow legal pads. They were ready for any and all revisions. They brought hope. The high-priced attorneys wore impeccable pinstriped suits and listened carefully to Grandpa, who sat in his recliner wearing pajamas and slippers. He offered them wisdom about Kennedy and Jacob Javits. He stressed that everything he had ever done was for the family. The attorneys called him I.R. Grandpa felt refreshed and vindicated after these visits.

A few weeks after Alfred's death, my father visited Laurie in her home, which was only a few blocks from our house in Great Neck. He assured her that whatever bad blood existed between him and I.R. had nothing to do with their friendship. He said to Laurie, whenever you need me or want me, pick up the phone and I'll be right over. Count on it. At the time Laurie was beleaguered by her loss and the rejection she felt from I.R. Her meeting with my father was emotional and today my aunt is still moved when she recalls my father's generous words, his ability to brighten a dark time with his irresistible promise of friendship.

But Dad never saw Laurie again. Even while they spoke, the Great Neck house was on the market, and soon after it was sold, Dad moved into a two-room suite at a residential hotel on 44th Street. Although the Concord Hotel was beyond the beginnings of its decline, the move seemed to energize Dad. He woke up to the sound of jackhammers and rivet guns, buildings going up. He entertained customers in the shadow of the Seagram and Socony buildings, his greatest triumphs. With so much action all around it was easy enough to ignore the worn rugs and weary wallpaper in his bedroom. So what? In 1961 the city was pockmarked by massive excavations with derricks lifting, steel girders rising. The need for lighting was all around, and Dad was itching to sell again.

Giving up the house had unburdened me. Manhattan and Riverdale were cheek by jowl. After school Dad and I could meet for Knick games at the Garden. Sometimes I would arrive at the Concord and there would be a message for me at the desk: "Tied up for a half hour. See you at 6:30." He was doing business. I was still intoxicated by his deals. I paced in the lobby craving details. At six-thirty I would be waiting outside his door. Finally it swung open. The customer was shaking Dad's hand, then mine. My father's face was flushed with business, a big deal was in the works. The room smelled of his newly starched shirts, aftershave, sweat, the sweet drift of his bowels, smells I had known my entire life.

After Dad had had a beer or two, we walked outside. The Manhattan night sky was sparkling with fluorescents. Dad wore his trench coat and pointed up to his deals all around. It was so great. The restaurant was my choice and I often picked Sauli Schniderman's place. He was a contractor who had gone broke and then found a backer to open this terrific restaurant with a real French chef who prepared "Chicken Divine" specially for me and Dad. The bar was always crowded with lighting salesmen jostling against beautiful women and there were deals in the air. All the manufacturers and reps came over to our table to say a few words and Sauli would stop by to ask about the chicken. You could tell he admired my father. He knew selling. Then Dad would say to Sauli or one of the salesmen he was going to take his boy to hear some music. Always a big tip to the cigarette girl, who also ran the coatroom, and we were back on the street hailing a cab for Basin Street East or the Embers, which was my favorite because George Shearing often played piano there accompanied by the incomparable Armando Peraza on congas.

For my brother life was anything but shipshape. The sale of the house had thrown him into turmoil and dejection. In his rage at Abe, Bill threw rocks at passing cars on the West Side Highway. He wrote my father off, vowed never again to fish on the *Ebb Tide.* He continued to take the train out to Great Neck. In the darkening afternoon he would stand in front of his house, watch lights come on in the windows and imagine Winnie folding clothes in the little room on the second floor. No one knew where Winnie was. There was no phone number for Bill to call. She had disappeared as though covered over by the earth. The new owner of the house had taken Mother's car out of the rock garden. Bill stood beneath the trees on the front lawn and cried.

My thirteen-year-old brother began to drink bourbon. When he was smashed he would call the new owner of the Great Neck house on the phone to negotiate to buy it back. What will it take? he asked the astonished new home owner. Bill told Mother he was planning to move into an apartment in Great Neck and remain there until he could get the house back. My mother did not know what to do for Bill. She bought him a dog, a German shepherd Bill named Black Jack. But Mother was living in her own reality and found Bill's attachment to Great Neck bizarre. She was free from Abe and beginning to find her own way. Her friends were intensely committed to painting. They lived in cold-water flats and were arrogant about their impoverished lives. Besides Bill, no one she valued had yearnings for the bourgeois life, although when de Kooning came to our Riverdale apartment he commented that he would like to have a lazy Susan like the one we had taken from the Great Neck house. He even took measurements.

From the first days Bill turned the German shepherd against me. By the time Black Jack was a year old, he bared his fangs and growled viciously every time I walked past him. He would attack me on the way to the bathroom. He ripped at my pants and grabbed the sleeves of my shirts. I never had a peaceful day in the apartment with that dog. Some afternoons when Bill was out Black Jack held me hostage in my room. Other times when he had me cornered Bill would make a big show of pulling Black Jack away, chiding him, Now you be good to my brother Fred. He always did this when Mother was around. Then he kissed Black Jack on the lips, on the tongue. Such a sweet dog, he'd say. He knew that this kissing disgusted me. I hated that dog. I couldn't wait to get away from him, to leave for college.

From his balcony on the seventeenth floor Grandpa watched the profusion of rising girders and spires of a veritable new city of glimmering office buildings. But there were no more high-profile jobs for Globe. My father had created Izzy's living hell. Old contractor friends were brusque on the phone and I.R. had no stomach for groveling. There were no more weekend visits from Harry Fischbach for bagels. Only a couple of years earlier, before the divorce was final, Harry had actually asked Grandpa for permission to court Stella. And though such a marriage would have been excellent for Globe, Grandpa had felt proud to turn down the great Harry Fischbach. It was the right thing to do, he decided, because Harry was too old for his daughter.

The unions had always given Izzy an edge, but now they had also turned against him. In the New York area the electrical union mandated a balance manufacturers had to maintain between high-income workers with seniority and inexperienced bottom-of-the-scale laborers. During the Abe years Globe had been given license to employ more low-end workers, but now this policy had been remanded. I.R. was squeezed for high wages when he had no business.

Revenge makes powerful drama, and I must admit that Dad's ingenious work was thrilling to me. I could barely believe it, but the great company was foundering. No one had ever put on such a show of power and finesse in the lighting industry. Of course it was mostly a show for us alone, not something you would take credit for at a Bar Mitzvah or dinner party. Dad would say, "I only want to live long enough to piss on his grave." Then I'd smack him in the shoulder, try to coax a smile.

———

When my grandfather could no longer afford to operate out of New York he assembled a few key guys from the Maspeth plant and moved Globe into a smaller building in Hazleton, Pennsylvania. Hazleton was near Scranton, which was Laurie's hometown. I.R. hoped that Laurie's ties to the community would be helpful, Globe would be welcomed with open arms and maybe the unions would give him a break. He took a small room in a local hotel with an Italian restaurant downstairs and worked late into the night creating designs for his new catalog.

A couple of times when I visited Hazleton, he and I ate in the gloomy restaurant. Once over soggy lasagna Grandpa referred obliquely to "Abe's dark work." His face was turned away from mine and he didn't say any more about it.

Abe Waitzkin's *Ebb Tide* log: "Went fishing from 9AM. Hooked a tuna off the Hens and Chickens. It came in tail wrapped and was eaten at transom by sharks. Changed over to wing fuel tanks at 2 PM. Then the great Les Sagan hooked and landed blue marlin, 123 pounds, a beauty. Back to dock 6 PM. Top boat for the day! Dinner Big Game Club. Great food and of course plenty of booze. Alan will arrive tomorrow." Below this entry another note in a different handwriting: "Today was a day to remember. We're all so lucky to have a friend like Abe. He's an angel." Signed, "Susie."

I never met Susie, although Dad mentioned her to me once or twice. She was a nurse and probably became my father's lover during this first weekend together on Bimini. I imagine a short thirty-year-old with a pleasant face and bobbed hair, white leather shoes, a good-natured girl. I can see her sitting across from my father in the salon of the *Ebb Tide* while Dad ate his lunch of boiled potato and a small piece of meat, chewed slowly and remained attentive to her words, encouraged her to expound upon a difficulty in her life. Perhaps it was a disagreement with her superior at the hospital or the landlord of her building was trying to raise her rent excessively. It might have been anything. I can see my father offering to help out, make a few calls. As he spoke, his eyes were unwavering and seemed to fix her in place. Susie was flattered but also a little flustered by Abe's attention. Although she hardly knew this man she believed that he cared.

More and more Dad was having choking episodes. Phlegm would

catch in his throat and it was hard to breathe. These episodes were alarming to watch. I can see Susie quickly moving to help him and my father gesturing for her to stay put. He knew what to do. With a snapping sound Dad drove air up from his diaphragm to clear himself. He did this again and again. Once more he motioned for her to sit while he gagged and then spat up a ball of brown phlegm into his handkerchief. Then he carefully wiped his mouth. He wasn't at all embarrassed. Soon, Abe was carefully chewing his food, and Susie had the impression that more than eating, he was nurturing himself as if he were a small child.

I can see my father asking Susie for a glass of water, this petite woman bolting from the sofa to get it. There were other simple requests during the hot afternoon of trolling, and always she jumped to do what he asked. Fishing had fallen into the background like the drone of the engines. Susie wanted to help Abe. She found herself stirred by him.

I had frequently watched men and women fall within my father's spell. It was an odd thing. As my father grew older and more frail, his magnetism and power increased. A gesture, a nod or a grimace was enough to spur people to jump, to laugh, to agree. His ability to exercise his will, to sell, achieved a near perfect economy of effort.

. *Tail Wrapped* .

DESPITE PRAYER AND VARIOUS ELABORATE WASHING RITUALS, I would feel illness close upon me like a dark storm. It could happen day or night, lying in bed, walking with a friend or watching a tense basketball game at the Garden. Any manifestation of disease might set me off. A man sitting next to me with a lump in his arm or an article in the newspaper about a dying actor would precipitate a crisis in my life. In an instant my body was covered with the rancid sweat of fear. Death was pointed my way. The constant threat of illness created a new internal logic: Doctors became the agents of bad news. I avoided being around them or even making eye contact when I was forced to be in the same room. I avoided friendships with the children of physicians lest I run into their parents. I steered clear of the news sections of papers like germ-filled rooms. But sometimes even the sports pages described diseased athletes. My eyes would shoot away from dire sentences about stars of the outfield or back court struck down in their prime by leukemia or testicular cancer.

The princess who could feel the pea beneath her mattresses had nothing over me. The faintest ache or twinge had dark meaning and swelling importance. I was forever prodding, testing, discovering my aching ribs or that my jaw hurt to open, the glands under my arms were bigger than usual. My intestines were bloated. The Clinic had missed a few cells of disease. Now it was growing.

One night I was up late finishing a report for school when I went to the bathroom and found a lump in my scrotum. Soon this small nodule between my fingers began to throb. The pain quickly spread until my world itself was this menacing discomfort, my demise.

In the first light of dawn I hailed a cab and raced down the West Side Highway toward my father. I tried to restrain my hysteria as I pounded on his door at the Concord. Why wasn't he coming? Finally Dad opened the door an inch or so but the chain remained latched. He was alarmed by the commotion. I pleaded with him to let me in. But he kept insisting that it was too early, I should come back about nine. I could not believe he would turn me away. I left the door feeling confused and miserable. I sat in a dreary coffee shop on Second Avenue staring out the window.

Shortly before nine I was at his door again. My father was in his robe and had a sheepish expression. Kate, his secretary for a dozen years, was sitting in an armchair in the front room. She was also wearing a robe and her graying hair was badly disheveled. After an awkward silence we took refuge in our old factory banter. I asked about the job they were working on for Ruby and she answered that blueprints were just about finished by the engineering department. Things were moving along. That's terrific. My father's bony leg stuck out from the crack in his bathrobe. None of us was prepared for this. Kate looked out the grimy window at the traffic moving on Third Avenue.

Dad and I walked into the bedroom and I dropped my pants. For a moment my father held my testicle in his fingers, worked his way to the lumpiness and rolled it like tough macaroni. He shrugged and shook his head. "Why don't you see a doctor?"

This hit me like electricity. I paced back and forth. What's the big deal? he said. I don't think he ever realized that for me doctors were shamans. They could kill me with words and innuendo, plant seeds of terror that would take hold months later. I told him finally that I wanted to see Dr. Nelson in Great Neck. He had saved my father on a hundred desperate nights. He was the only one I trusted.

At last my father agreed to the extravagant idea of driving all the way out to Great Neck to see the old doctor. He asked me to stay in the bedroom for a minute while he talked with Kate. The instant he left I turned down the blanket of the double bed and searched the sheets. I quickly found a small round damp spot as though someone had spit and without hesitating I smelled the spot, my nose grazing the cool sheets and the small dampness, surprisingly a neutral smell, next to nothing.

When I came back into the front room, Kate pulled the brush from her hair and avoided my earthy gaze. In her increased wakefulness she was entirely forlorn. But I knew that my balls were fine even before leaving for Great Neck and my last visit with the great healer of my father. I was swelling with well-being.

In this manner my life swung between the blackest illness and manic health. I was thankful for good times and never knew when I would be blindsided. Dad was my lifeline. He always had the answers. Sometimes he brought me to doctors, but often just a few words from him were enough to return me to Riverdale reenergized to hunt the fervent breasts of high school girls, to revel in the melancholia of Keats and Kerouac and to perfect my jump shot at dusk beside the Hudson River. I knew that as long as he lived, I would survive.

Within the course of my last year and a half in high school, all of the families of I.R.'s children had broken apart, the grand houses on Long Island were sold. No more pools, tennis courts and quiet moorings in Great Neck Estates Park; cousins had moved off somewhere, we were all in new schools and rarely heard from one another. Alfred was dead and within a few months Laurie remarried and family members gossiped darkly that this new husband must have been her longtime lover.

If you looked up from the sidewalk at the Globe showroom on 40th Street, the windows were blackened and smudged. The luscious secretaries were no longer directing customers through rooms of infinite fixtures. Globe was out of the huge Maspeth factory. To me this was the most astonishing change. On Friday evenings there was no longer a flood of Globe workers pouring onto Flushing Avenue heading for families and bars and ball games with fists of Grandpa's dollars.

But my dad was at the Concord Hotel landing jobs. He was my

steady compass, proof that we were still on course. Just the sound of his raspy voice on the phone, a little bullying or dismissing, gave me purchase. Dad still knew the right person to call for courtside seats for the Celtic game or airplane tickets to Florida when all the flights were booked. He was so solid. Fixtures remained our glory. Fixtures and big fish. I dreamed of thousand-pound blue marlin cruising off the north end of Bimini in front of George Albert Lyon's majestic home, where he, Ernest Hemingway and Mike Lerner had toasted the sunset with mixed drinks and stories about their ten-hour battles on the blue ocean.

But more and more I began to define myself within arguments I had with my father. While he smirked: Get with it, I'd tell him my ideas about Raymond Radiquet and Keats. I'd talk about Dylan Thomas and the greatness of mutability. Dad, that means the passage of time. He made a bigger smirk and I'd use some word like "pathos" he didn't know. Stupid kid. I could never have moved away from him except that he was there, luring me back.

Dad, I'm thinking of going to Kenyon College in Ohio, I said, bracing for his anger. To study literature. He nodded a couple of times. You know, they have a top English department at Kenyon. Robert Lowell, John Crowe Ransom. I tossed out names I knew nothing about.

So you're a real big shot, he answered. What's wrong with Harvard? It's just around the corner from Celia's house. Is Harvard so goddamned bad?

Dad, I don't have the grades for Harvard. I'd never get in.

That's not your concern, he snapped. You just have to fill out the frig'n application.

I don't know, I said. Dad scowled: Are you nuts? His eyes bulged with incredulity. I knew he could pick up the phone and take care of it. I was tempted. But Kenyon struck a chord, and I figured what's the harm in trying. I could always transfer. Harvard wasn't going anywhere. Dad could always make a phone call.

Some weeks later I visited him again at the Concord and he brought up a conversation with his sister. He had been feeling under the weather, his back was out, and when Celia had called, Dad couldn't stand and had to crawl to pick up the phone. Celia had said to him,

Abe, you don't have to live like this anymore, in a hotel. Come home. I can take care of you. Your family is here in Cambridge. As Dad spoke, I wasn't sure where he was going with this and I thought, What's wrong with her? Doesn't Cele understand the deals he has in the air, what Abe Waitzkin has accomplished in New York?

Celia invited Abe to move back into the house in Cambridge, to have meals at her place on the second floor and share the downstairs with his dad, who was now old and sick. Abe, you can work for Lee, she had said. It's your business.

How ridiculous. Lee Products was hardly more than a garage and had a workforce of only six or seven men. The little shop couldn't manufacture one of his orders in fifteen years. I looked at my father for reassurance. He'd always told me that his sister and her husband were never going to accomplish anything in business, they didn't understand the big picture.

But this was not another occasion to commiserate about his father and brother-in-law's small-mindedness. Dad was making plans to move back to Cambridge to work for Lee Products selling wiring troughs and electrical enclosures as he had done during his first years with Mom. He was looking forward to making a study out of the sunroom of the Fayette Street house, where he'd played with blocks as a little boy, put in a color television.

Dad had already convinced Alan Fischbach to take on Kate as his private secretary. He paused so I could appreciate the loftiness of this legacy. Kate Turner was going to sit at Alan's side at the very top of Fischbach and Moore.

I was speechless. How could he go back to Cambridge? After so many big deals. The UN, the Socony Building. Aqueduct Race Track. What about the lighting business? How could he go back to that droopy house and his sick father who didn't understand selling? Wouldn't he lose all of his connections? What about the Bahamas?

. *Loverman* .

ONE EVENING ON BIMINI I CAME TO THE COMPLEAT ANGLER WITH *Dad, who was still on the mend from major surgery. While he sat outside on the porch I walked through the rooms looking at pictures of Hemingway on the varnished walls—in one of my favorites he was shooting his tommy gun at a giant hammerhead—and read selections from his writing reproduced in large type. There were keenly observed moments of tremendous billfish striking the bait, of anglers strapped into the chair struggling mightily to boat marlin and tuna before the hooked fish were mutilated by sharks. The wanton plenty of the sea pulsed through all of this writing. Boxing matches on the Bimini beach were flavored by the lusty fishing that had preceded them on the blue water north of the island. This writing made me desperate with excitement, and it seemed inconceivable that the author was no longer himself plying the waves pulling baits.*

Abe and Harcourt, Ozzie's father, had sat outside on the porch and I soon joined them. These two clever, wiry men toasted the balmy evening and agreed that they were lucky to have sons who would someday take over their businesses. I had smiled at my father like a puppy. Harcourt was protective of his wounded friend as though they were both part of an elite circle. Even when he was down on his luck, my father arrived in the

Bimini harbor on the bridge of his Ebb Tide *like a maharaja. Although Harcourt was Bimini's most prosperous citizen, owned the power plant and Brown's Hotel and Marina as well as the Compleat Angler Hotel and Bar, it would not have occurred to him that his own business interests far outstripped Abe Waitzkin's.*

Soon after I left Riverdale for Kenyon College, my fourteen-year-old brother ran away from home and settled in central Florida. For months Mother had no idea where he was. She was beside herself. Dad hired detectives, but they couldn't find him. Bill worked on a farm picking cotton and eventually moved to Boca Raton, where he had his hair straightened and dyed jet black like Liz Taylor's. In Boca he met a lady bartender also named Billy, who was twice his age and had two children. Billy believed my brother was eighteen. They fell in love and Bill moved into her place. Late at night while her kids slept, they drank Jack Daniel's. Sometimes they left the kids and walked swiftly to the beach and made love on the cool sand. Holding Billy was beautiful and sad.

After a half a year Bill decided that it was time to move on. When he left Billy she was pregnant and Bill never learned if she had had his baby. The memory of Billy haunted him. Years later he tried to find her in Boca but she had vanished.

Bill moved from Boca Raton to Bimini. By then he had managed to have his German shepherd, Black Jack, shipped south. Bill and Black Jack moved into a room on the top floor of the Bimini Hotel, which was located at the south end of North Bimini overlooking the entrance to the harbor. My brother woke in the morning to the sight of leopard rays and tiger sharks cruising past the white beach on the inside of the reef near the small boat cut.

Bimini assuaged Bill's sense of loss and he decided this was his home. On the island he was free to indulge his love of the sea without the immense weight of his father's fishing hardware and his brother's conventional big game fishing ambitions. Bill quickly discovered Bimini's magic for allowing fantasy to run free.

Living on top of the ocean, he was inspired to write the first draft of his romantic thriller, *Rogue Shark,* in which an eighteen-foot hammerhead wanders through the small boat cut discovering the peaceful island of Bimini. In *Rogue Shark* the islanders are a naïve, idle people with a gross appetite for rum and copulation. Everything changes once the savage creature develops a taste for Biminites.

Many afternoons Bill could be found sitting in a foot of water in the bay near Ansil Saunders's house playing with a baby lemon shark or shovelnose. My brother had the knack of calming these fierce little creatures until they grew docile and allowed petting like cats. Ansil was an accomplished fisherman and fifteen years older than Bill, but still he found himself swept up in my brother's charisma and absurd fishing schemes. Though exhausted from poling his skiff around the flats for bonefish, he and Bill spent nights fishing with handlines from the beach in front of the Bimini Hotel, where big sharks swam in with the tide. The two friends chummed the water with amberjack and bloody tuna and held their thick lines while Bill shared his ideas on the *Carcharodon megalodon* or Egyptian mummies or his plans to climb the ruins of Machu Picchu while taking a break from stalking large black marlin in the Humboldt Current off Cabo Blanco, Peru. Fishing in the blackness with the tide rushing past, the friends were braced for all of life's adventure.

There were scores of nights when they hauled big sharks up onto the beach, the largest a twelve-foot hammerhead that they admired and then pushed back into the ocean. Another night they caught two ten-foot blacktips, and while the beasts heaved on the sand, Ansil found himself convinced by Bill to drag them a hundred yards to the Avis Club's saltwater pool and roll them in. The following morning the two sharks appeared to be asleep on the bottom of the pool. Ansil and Bill were watching from behind a palm tree when a sleepy bather dropped his towel on a chair and took a dive into the deep end. The startled sharks came to the surface in a frenzy, racing around, smacking the walls to break free. The unnerved swimmer burst out of the pool and then stared back at the frantic sharks, shaking his head.

A producer for the popular television show *The American Sportsman* contacted Ansil about doing a piece on the dangerous sharks of Bimini. Soon a television crew was on the island filming the segment starring Bill and Ansil.

In one part of the show, which was Bill's brilliant conception, the two friends stalked two large lemon sharks on the flats east of the island. When the skiff was on top of the two eight-footers, Ansil and

Bill jumped onto their backs. The sharks were powerful and aggressive, and in four or five feet of water they were nearly impossible to control. As Bill and Ansil held their sharks in a bear hug, the creatures twisted and yanked their heads, tried to sink their teeth into thighs and arms. After a few minutes, half-drowned and dizzy, they let the sharks go. Back in the skiff they discovered that their bodies were skinned raw from wrestling against the whipping tails and flanks of the sharks. And to make things worse, their wounds were greased with a foul stinging slime. Bill thought this was hilarious.

Ansil recalls this stunt as one of the dumbest things he ever tried. My brother was so cocksure about handling sharks that Ansil strayed from his sense of caution. But, more, Bill had the ability to elevate outrageous ideas, to make them seem glorious. For another segment of the ABC show, they decided to harpoon a man-eating tiger shark from the fourteen-foot skiff while the cameraman caught the action. After searching for a couple of hours they found a big tiger on a white sand bottom in six feet of water behind South Bimini. The sun was high overhead. The conditions were perfect for filming. Ansil asked the cameraman if he was ready to go and then slowly approached with the skiff. When he was close Bill threw the harpoon, but it only grazed the shark. While my brother retrieved the line attached to the harpoon for another try, the twelve-foot tiger turned sharply and attacked the side of the skiff, throwing everyone off balance. After a few seconds it let go and disappeared from view. While Bill and Ansil tried to locate the shark, it came up astern and charged the skiff again. This time it swam with its head high, planing the water like the white shark years later in the movie *Jaws*. It seized the flimsy transom with a broad mouth of teeth and shook its head, all but ripping the stern from the boat. My brother jabbed the harpoon into its flapping gill to try to get the shark to let go and Ansil shouted to the ABC cameraman to get this on film. But one more attack like the last and the skiff would sink and the three of them would be in the water with the enraged beast. They were lucky. On its third attack the shark grabbed the lower unit of the engine and began to shake its heavy head. Ansil started the engine and gunned the propeller. Teeth and blood splattered into the boat. When the water began to clear, the tiger shark was floating belly up. The scene was more than *The American Sportsman* could have hoped for, but when

Bill and Ansil finally turned their attention to the cameraman, he was cowering facedown on the deck. From the tiger shark's first attack he had been so frightened that he'd never turned on the camera.

To save money Bill shared his room in the hotel with a boy named John, who was several years older and another friend of Ansil's. John had come to the island to do some bonefishing with Ansil before entering Harvard as a freshman. He was petrified of sharks, which Bill found amusing. But John's literary name-dropping and snotty attitude toward *Rogue Shark* wore on my brother's nerves. Whenever Bill was annoyed at someone it quickly showed in Black Jack's demeanor. The German shepherd began snarling and making exploratory lunges at John, putting him on edge. Perhaps Bill saw similarities in this boy to his bookish brother. One night when Bill was entirely fed up with John's pretentiousness, Black Jack came at him with teeth bared and drove John off the Bimini Hotel's little dock, which was a notoriously good place for shark fishing. While John struggled against the current in the blackness, Bill began shrieking at the top of his lungs, "Get out of the water, hammerhead, hammerhead, swim for your life! Hammerhead!"

When Bill called Mother from Florida to say he was coming home, she wasn't sure if she felt joy or anger. She had been desperate about him when he left, but now after a year she thought less about Bill. Stella was living on West 9th Street in the Village, right around the corner from the Cedar Tavern, and had replaced motherhood with extra hours working on her sculpture and teaching. When she hung up the phone with her younger son, her heart was palpitating. She walked to May's Department Store on 14th Street, where two years earlier, when the building was just under construction, she had buried one of her large polyester eggs. May's was one of her favorite stores. She went inside to the appliance department and carefully selected a midsized radio with a wooden cabinet. She put it underneath her coat and walked past a uniformed guard at the door. This was the largest item Mother had ever filched. Stella claimed that shoplifting gave her a rush and distracted her from problems. But I believe she went through this phase of petty stealing mainly to climb in the same boat with Tony.

When Bill arrived in New York he discovered Mom was living with a boyfriend, Tony Fruscella. My brother would have viewed any new man in Mom's life as a rival, but Tony brought qualities that cut to the bone.

Tony Fruscella was a genius jazz musician. He grew up in an orphanage in New Jersey listening to church music until the age of fourteen, when he first heard jazz and began studying trumpet. Following his release from the army he played with the Lester Young band, Gerry Mulligan and Stan Getz and occasionally with Billie Holiday and Charlie Parker. Jazz lovers of the fifties were touched by his emotional trumpet voice, his husky whisper lingering on melody and improvising close to it instead of racing into abstraction, like many of his contemporaries. Tony was often compared to the young Miles Davis. But today listening to his haunting solos I think of Chet Baker.

The recorded oeuvre of Fruscella's music is pitifully meager, although several records from the early and middle fifties attest to his soulful virtuosity and the sadness of his life. By the late fifties Tony was broke and frustrated by lack of recognition. He was doing junk and playing only intermittently. For a time he didn't have a horn and some musicians chipped in and bought him one at a pawnshop. Friends said that he played a great session with Sonny Rollins during the period when Rollins had withdrawn from the public spotlight and was mainly playing by himself on the Brooklyn Bridge. Someone taped it, but the session seems to have been lost.

Mother fell in love with Tony for his music, although by the time she met him, his career was over. At only thirty-eight Fruscella was ruined by drink and drugs, living on rooftops or park benches, and occasionally the couches of friends until he was thrown out.

Wafting through Mother's subterranean 9th Street apartment were the sounds of Tony's solos recorded years earlier with Stan Getz and Phil Woods, lyrical refrains, relaxing and dreamy. Sometimes the music on the hi-fi was Bach and Vivaldi, Tony's favorites, which made Bill impatient because he favored the Supremes and Martha Reeves and the Vandellas. Mixing with the music was the aroma of Mom's chicken soup and gribbenes to heal her wounded men; and the factory smells that came from Mom's kiln, which was cooking in the hall fifteen hours a day. Often it was the odor of hot glass. At the time Mother was melting bottles like caved-in souls. But sometimes it was the acrid smell of melting metal, silver and gold. To maintain his drug habit, Tony was breaking into stores, apartments, going on secret missions was how he put it, grabbing jewelry, small appliances, whatever, bringing loot to Mom's for hiding, melting down precious metals in the kiln before meeting the fence. Mother was mostly oblivious to his capers, or treated them as an aspect of his art.

Tony's immediacy, his wildness and decadence fascinated her. If she took him for a sandwich, Tony would grab the tip when she turned to walk out the door. Mother laughed at his outrages as if they were living in a Warhol movie. Before his introduction to Sadie, Stella's mother, Tony ran around a corner and stole flowers from someone's fenced-in garden.

For Stella, rather than in museums, art was alive in street happenings and improvisational movies and also in abandoned refuse and crippled souls. Tony's fall and beatness were art. One afternoon they were wandering through a flea market on Seventh Avenue. Fruscella picked up an old horn from a table and began to play taps. His sound was so ethereal and captivating people stopped what they were doing and gathered around. Mother was moved by the absurdity and pathos of vegetable vendors and housewives pausing for taps on Seventh Avenue. Afterward Tony said to her, Stella, when I go, I'm gonna leave you my body.

To make a buck Fruscella occasionally worked in a fish market. When he came to 9th Street stinking from the market, with fillets, probably stolen, she told Bill, Tony's into fishing like you. My brother simmered.

One afternoon Bill was walking home from school and noticed the traffic on 9th Street was backed up. Standing in front of the building Tony was brandishing a Japanese sword he'd stolen someplace, dueling cars to a stop like a matador. Despite his rage Bill found this amusing. Tony was not impeded by inhibitions or rules. That's why he's a great artist, said Mother with a glow that irritated my brother.

A couple of months after Bill's return, Tony broke into a boat docked at the 79th Street yacht basin. Escaping over the barbed-wire fence with a big stash, he cut himself up. Tony trailed blood down 9th Street to Mother's basement door. He was a mess and he began bellowing, Stella, Stella, let me in, Stella. Mother wasn't home and Bill was furious and wouldn't open the door. He told Tony to go away, she was in Coney Island, eating at Nathan's. Fruscella hauled his sacks down the block but came back minutes later moaning pitifully, Stella, Stella, please Stella. By now neighbors were looking out windows. When no one answered, Tony piled newspaper and wood against her door and set it on fire.

Bill was in a rage. He called the cops and they arrested Tony with the loot. Fruscella was locked up for three months.

Bill assumed a reasonable tone with his mother, as though he were the sage and forgiving parent. He explained that Tony wasn't a respectable choice. She and Fruscella wouldn't be able to make appearances together at 57th Street gallery openings, not to mention the Museum of Modern Art. With Tony the family would never be accepted back in Great Neck. Mother appeared to agree. She always tried to appease Bill. Then it's all settled, was Bill's manner.

My brother phoned a fishing captain he knew from the Montauk days, Swede Swenson was his name. Swede was rawboned and six foot six. He drove a forty-two-foot Wheeler without the help of a crew. Swede was tough and resourceful and became famous in big game circles for wrestling large game fish aboard without a mate. A few weeks before Tony got out of jail, Bill arranged a date for Mom with Swede Swenson. To please Bill, Stella was pleasant to Swenson when he came by for a cup of coffee. She thought it was comical when this huge man explained how he brought aboard big tunas and broadbills by himself using flying gaffs and meat hooks.

Bill painted his large bedroom dark blue like the Gulf Stream, hung his fish mounts on the wall beside lacquered shark jaws and his prized jars of small sharks in formaldehyde. But he could not re-create Bimini's expansiveness. Bill was hemmed in by big buildings and the banality of school. He'd lost interest in *Rogue Shark* and the daydream of fishing on the beach with Ansil went lifeless. Bill turned on the afternoon soaps or flipped through the channels for Godzilla movies. He drank Jack Daniel's and planned expeditions to South America and the South Pacific. He felt dead without mystery and bold adventure. My brother had his first epileptic seizures during this period. He regarded this illness as humiliating and managed to keep it secret for years.

When Tony got out of jail he was right back to the apartment, needing wine, needing Stella, phoning his ex-wife, jazz vocalist Morgana King (she played the role of Don Corleone's wife opposite

Marlon Brando in *The Godfather*), who always hung up at the sound
of his pleading, plastered voice. Playing against his inebriation, vomiting, manic thievery, bags and boxes of unwanted loot passed on to
Mom with frantic sweaty love, there was "Tony's Blues" or "Night
in Tunisia" or "Lover Man" carrying from the hi-fi down the long,
narrow hall. Mom was painting in the little outdoor garden tapping
her foot or nodding to his sweet music touched with sadness. Musicians said Tony was as good as Chet Baker. For Mother art eclipsed
all sins.

One day Mom said to Tony, I could really love a man who would help
me find old mattress springs. Mother felt limited by the size of her
kiln. She believed if she could develop her melted-bottle sculptures
on a larger scale, she might get a show, begin to make a reputation. In
her view, an old metal mattress frame would make a kind of canvas.
Tony searched abandoned tenements and back alleys for rusting,
burnt-out and battered bedsprings and collected about a dozen. Then
he helped her load them into her station wagon along with boxes of
empty cheap wine and liquor bottles, most of which he had drained
himself in Mother's East 14th Street painting studio, where he slept.
Mother drove off with the junk to Hazleton, Pennsylvania.

The Globe plant in Pennsylvania was only about one-third the
size of the one in Maspeth, but it was brand-new, with concrete
floors unsullied by oil and grease, and many windows, which made
it look bigger than it was. The machinery was top-notch. The automated oven for melting glass lenses and drying lacquer on fixtures
was a hundred feet long, at least the size of the one in Maspeth that
had baked a million of Dad's eight- and ten-footers.

Maybe Mom's beautiful sister Thelma wasn't such a great salesman, but she brought glamour to the new factory and Grandpa liked
that. Once or twice a week she breezed in from New York in her
fancy convertible, unless she was in France or Italy collecting glass
samples for Grandpa's lenses. Thelma turned heads walking through
the plant in a designer dress carrying spiral notebooks filled with up-
beat color combinations for the new line.

But Globe's problems persisted. There wasn't enough business
and labor costs were too high. Grandpa had hoped that the Hazleton
community would greet him with open arms, but the local unions

weren't offering any breaks. Grandpa suspected that his New York enemies were exercising long-distance muscle, Abe was still pulling strings. Probably the truth was that Grandpa had grown too old and weary from loss to pull the company ahead.

When Mom arrived in Hazleton with bedsprings, it was a very slow time and Grandpa was operating with a skeleton crew. More than half the shears, presses and lathes were standing by and the great oven was stone-cold. Mother viewed this as an opportunity. On long tables designed for mounting ballasts and starters into metal housings, she laid out her beat-up mattress supports. Then she began placing liquor bottles on the springs, moving away from these works to gain perspective, while a few sheet metal workers watched and scratched their heads at Thelma's sister with uncombed hair and torn, loose clothing. She arranged bottles with heavy textures leaning against open spaces. Warped and sprung struts were brush-strokes. Stella was allowing figurative images into her work, which added enigma and dark humor. This would rankle Hans Hofmann, the great painting teacher. Was ist das? he would say to her when traces of realism intruded into her abstractions. But Mother always considered impulses and radical departures more important than dogma.

When she was ready she directed Globe workers to place her pieces on the conveyor belt at the mouth of the great oven, which was now hot and ready. Soon the small crew in the factory assembled to watch the emerging red-hot springs smeared with Tony's liquor bottles, which Mother referred to as her "Beds of Pain." Stella found it appealing to make art from junk in her father's temple.

When the sculptures cooled, they were placed in front of windows, and with the white winter sun behind them Mom's bare-boned beds came alive with shimmering light.

From the beginning of her painting life Mother considered white the color of death. "There is finality in white . . . it is pure in the way a bone is pure and clean once freed from the flesh and blood around it," she wrote in a paper for the critic and teacher Meyer Schapiro. During this period, death was a specter in her life. Tony was living right on the edge and he reminded her, like a refrain in his music, Stella, I want you to remember the good times. But in her father's factory, with whiteness pouring through bottles like stillborn souls, one might have taken this work for a new direction in lighting. At least she did. Mother wanted to mass-produce these objects.

Only problem was, the temperature in the Globe oven was too hot or cold or the glass was the wrong type for mattress springs. As she drove back to New York most of the bottles popped off the springs and shattered against the mattress frames. Only a few sculptures from this series survived intact.

Mom tried to keep Tony away from Bill by banishing him to her painting studio on East 14th Street, but Tony missed her and was always coming over to 9th Street. When Bill was home she wouldn't open the door and pretended she no longer cared for Tony. Fruscella would stand on the street calling pitifully, Stella, Stella, let me in. Eventually he would walk back to her studio or head for the Bowery. Some nights Mother would come to 14th Street and other times she would meet him at jazz clubs. One night at the Five Spot, Charlie Mingus invited Tony to sit in with his group. But Tony was boozed up and got on stage with a big cigar, ruined the set with his sorrowful antics. Afterward Mingus came after Tony with a knife while Mother pleaded with the great bass player.

There were nights when Stella didn't come to 14th Street and each time Tony called her apartment Bill picked up the phone and hung up. When he didn't have money for a bottle and was desperate and lonely, Fruscella started fires in the hall outside her door where they kept the trash. He knew that Taylor Mead or another 14th Street neighbor would call Mother to say the building was burning down. She would come out to meet him, whatever the hour, calm Tony down, feed him, make love to him. He didn't understand why he couldn't always be with her. There were a dozen fires, maybe more.

Bill recognized in Tony an adversary he could not defeat. Tony was already beaten to a pulp. And yet for Mother his groveling need and sadness were a pure note, a kind of grace. Tony's battered trumpet was usually in the pawnshop on Third Avenue unless Mom tracked it down and retrieved it for him. Then he'd hold the trumpet in his hand and say in his gruff dockworker voice, Stella, I can't remember how it goes. Help me out. C'mon, Stella. Mother would smile and begin to sing, "'The night is cold and I'm so all alone. I'd give my soul just to call you my own.'" She had a rich emotional voice and Tony loved her so much when she sang "Lover Man." "'I go to bed with the prayer that you'll make love to me. Strange as it seems.'" When Mother finished, Tony would lift the horn and begin to curl around the melody, lingering on low notes until the music ached. He had played it many times for Billie Holiday, but now he no longer had his lip and "Lover Man" had misses and scrapes of pain like Billie's voice during her last year. Always Tony claimed he couldn't remember how the standards went and coaxed Stella to sing before he played the horn.

At Kenyon I was distracted from my mother's degradation by *Beowulf* and *Lycidas.* I was banking information about literature as though it would pay off for me in years like savings bonds; a decade later I would have to forget all the fine tenets of literary criticism to begin to write freely. But I was never a really devoted student. I was diverted by dance halls and townie girls. I played the bongos until dawn in the Kenyon church basement, missed classes fishing in the Kokosing River, while daydreaming about blue marlin rushing at my hula poppers and bloodworms.

On the phone Dad filled me in about the Boston business. He was gradually putting on more men and planning to expand the plant. Almost overnight recessed fluorescents had fallen into the past and Dad had transferred his remarkable selling passion to placing panel boxes and wiring troughs into the dark tangled recesses of factories, garages and sundry buildings. For additional pizzazz he produced specialty items for Alan Fischbach, including stainless steel boxes fashioned to withstand the intense heat of Nike missile launching pads.

Dad promised that someday we'd share the same office and make an unbeatable team selling the Lee Products line throughout New England. Sure I had reservations about the box business, but Dad washed them aside. After his pitch I could feel the splendor of the two of us seated across from one another in our office above the Lee shop, feet on our desks, beating back the competition.

On Martha's Vineyard, the summer before my junior year, I met a girl with long dark hair who loved poetry and didn't get seasick. On our first date Bonnie and I went broadbill swordfishing on the *Ebb Tide.* Easing through the foggy water I couldn't take my eyes off her. I held the wheel and tried to affect the look of a weatherbeaten big game skipper. While I played the hero I ran the bow of the boat into a twelve-foot swordfish that was basking on the surface. We laughed as the fish swam off. Later that night on the tuna tower I kissed Bonnie for the first time and described to her the greatness of trolling big baits for marlin off Bimini. She was from Philadelphia's Main Line and knew nothing about big game fishing, but I went on and on. I stressed how one must be patient dropping a big bonefish back to a blue marlin or else you can pull the bait from his mouth. She nodded earnestly. Such a beautiful girl. I wanted to kiss her forever. Bonnie went to Denison University, which was only fifty miles from Kenyon. It was a miracle.

In Ohio we moved into a little house in a cornfield and I stopped going to classes altogether. We dropped our lines in streams and lakes. We read from Eliot's *The Waste Land* and *The Love Song of J. Alfred Prufrock.* Bonnie understood poems much better than I did but I tried to keep this from her. For some reason she was willing to accept my ideas about a lifetime of trolling. We both knew my plans were hilarious but forged ahead. After discussing all the options we decided after graduating we'd apply to the Peace Corps and ask for an assignment in Chile, where I had heard there was the best swordfishing in the world.

Mother phoned me in Ohio after Tony Fruscella had robbed a church and brought her boxes of religious treasures. Tony was now completely out of control and she was afraid of what Bill would do to him. It is odd she imagined that I would be her ally. I was humiliated by Tony. That such a man would touch my mother. What if Dad found out about it in Boston? He would be appalled, and his rage would have no boundaries. Dad would hire detectives or he might even call the Commissioner.

As a twenty-year-old I never thought of Tony as an artist to be admired or a character Jack Kerouac might have written about in *On the Road.* I hated Tony for loving my mother. He was a bum.

I came home for Thanksgiving with Bonnie, determined to straighten things out. My brother and I spoke to Mom with our arms crossed. She smiled at us and didn't make a fight. I believe she was charmed by our resolve and solid front.

Sometime after dark Tony came to the house carrying a big turkey he had bought with his welfare check. At the door he had a dumb smile and was wearing a new white shirt. Bill and I wouldn't let him into the apartment. Mother stood behind us clutching her hands. Life is tough but we knew what we were doing.

I had learned about crime and punishment from my father. Bill had his own motivations. But did we actually believe we could stop his bleak solos from the street? Or that she would stop listening for him?

. *A Fish from My Brother's Dreams* .

LATER THAT WINTER, BILL AND BONNIE AND I LEFT NEW YORK for Florida. I was surprised and delighted that my brother had actually agreed to go fishing with us. As I drove through the night I explained over and over to Bonnie the art of the dropback. I was afraid that she would strike too soon. For emphasis I gestured to the big marlin rod in Bill's lap in the backseat, a couple of feet of which was sticking out the window. Eventually we settled into conversation about couples we knew from college, their infidelities, emotional breakups and fervent returns, and soon we were ardently exploring the rights and wrongs of our relationship, why we had said this or that last week or a month before. Each nuance of agreement or reservation was so important.

My brother found our intimacy cloying. The ongoing need to probe for honesty was insipid to him. It was my brother's way to be mysterious, to reshape himself behind veils like Mother, to spend the light of day in a darkened bedroom. Bill yawned at my fishing pedantry and glee. I trolled on the surface. In his fishing life my brother was a time traveler, dropped his baits deep for ancient fish. I wanted to understand Bill, to talk. Nothing could interest him less.

Bill's heavy silences didn't matter so much. I was rushing south toward the blue water. I believed that my brother was posturing and would come around in time, become a regular guy. I believed this for years.

We arrived on Islamorada around midnight and pulled into a motel with its sign illuminated by a neon sailfish in full leaping curve. I listened to the ocean teeming with large game fish. Beyond the shadows of palm trees I could hear the flapping of their heavy tails. I could feel Dad behind me, nodding.

I was knotted up with anticipation. This was a rite of passage, game fishing without Dad and his captains or the *Ebb Tide*. I didn't sleep more than an hour or two. In the morning my stomach hurt. What if I screwed up? What if I couldn't find my way back in or we hit a storm or the engine stopped? What if, what if?

Down the road from the motel there was a tiny rundown fishing camp called Estes, built into the mangroves, a little operation with a half-dozen skiffs for rent. Old pelicans were sitting on broken pilings and the office was ramshackle and smelled of old bait. The morning sun was already searing and the flies and mosquitoes were thick and kept getting into our ears and mouths. Look how great this is, I said to Bonnie, pointing to yellowing photographs of big barracudas and tarpon pinned to the walls. On my mouth I could feel Abe Waitzkin's shit-eating grin.

Estes Dock faced the gulf side of Islamorada, offering miles of shallow-water fishing alongside the mangroves and on the flats. There was a chance to catch snappers, ladyfish, bonefish, sea trout, redfish, cobia, possibly tarpon or permit. No marlin, tuna, dolphin or deep-water sharks. They were on the other side of the island in the Gulf Stream. The old-timer who ran the place, I assumed he was Mr. Estes, lectured me that these boats were for the bay only. They weren't fit for the ocean. One of his customers had taken one offshore and it had capsized in a squall, his wife had drowned, he said with distaste. He didn't care about her, only the boat. The man was soured from too many years renting to wannabe fishermen from New Jersey who tortured his old engines and busted propellers on conch beds. I sorely wanted to inform him about the *Ebb Tide*'s tuna tower and the Fin-Nor reels, about all the marlin we'd caught in big seas off the north end of Bimini, hauled them through the teak transom door; but instead I assured him that we would stay in the bay casting to redfish. He pointed to a fourteen-footer that had the classic lines of a large round-bottomed bathtub. Bonnie and I climbed on board and he tossed in two waterlogged life preservers that hit with a thud: Don't go out in the ocean! Who was he talking to?

I headed the outboard north, running in calm muddy water until the view from Estes was blocked by a bend in the island. After another half-mile I saw my brother waving from a little dock behind the Sail-fish Motel. I nosed in and Bill stepped on wearing a white turban and holding Dad's heavy marlin rod and also a lighter one. Then he reached over for some rigged mullets and a bucket he'd bought from a tackle shop. After securing these items he dragged on board the bloody car-cass of a fifty-pound amberjack he'd found on the dock at Bud and Mary's Marina, which was just down the road, on the ocean side of the island. Then we headed north for another few miles until we arrived at the Snake Creek Bridge that spanned Islamorada and Plantation Key. There were a dozen fishermen on the bridge dropping lines and not catching much. I waved at them, trying not to gloat as I headed her into the channel marked by stakes that led into the open ocean.

The sea was running about two feet, nothing to speak of, but the flimsy skiff pounded and skiddered uneasily off each wave. I slowed to a crawl when a forty-footer approached from offshore on her way back in. I smartly decided to take her wake on our quarter, rather than dead ahead, thinking we'd float over and stay dry; but the surge seemed to suck the bottom from the little tub, which went over sickly onto her side and teetered until Bill and I jumped for the high gunwale and the boat caught her balance. A very close call. It would have been humiliating to have capsized in the channel right in front of the snapper fishermen on the bridge.

I shrugged to Bonnie, no big deal. Things happen on big game fishing trips—saltwater dripping down your face, pounding, issues of seamanship come up. It's all part of the game. She didn't know anything about the boats I had sunk in the past. Bonnie, honey, you have to brace your back when we go over waves, I chided gently. And she trusted me, relaxed with her eyes closed, soaking up the sun. Yes, I was jittery. This boat wasn't any more than the one Bill and I had capsized trolling for giant bluefin off Provincetown.

When the green water turned blue I slowed the skiff and we put out two of the smaller mullets on light rods. This settled me down. Even with the morning sun burning my eyes it was a pleasure to watch the baits skip and jiggle across the bubbling wake. Trolling was my favorite fishing. I liked to think about a big marlin or tuna way below slowly angling up in the green water, eyeing baits that were traveling across the immense brightness of the sky.

If we were lucky enough to catch a dolphin, we'd bring it to the chef at the Green Turtle Inn for our dinner that night. Bonnie's hair blew in the wind. She looked at me and smiled.

We weren't trolling twenty minutes when behind one of the mullets I spotted a short bill poking into the air. Then I saw its rapier tail. "Pick up the rod, Bonnie, get ready," I said in a harsh whisper. But the spindly fish was coming much too fast. "What?" she asked, turning my way. The small sailfish was crashing the bait, devouring it.

"Don't look at me, Bonnie. Pick up the rod, fast." She turned toward the rod and looked at it.

"Pick it up," I said more forcefully.

"What's wrong?" she answered, thrown off by my tone of voice. She lifted the rod, which was bowed and heavy with the weight of the pulling sailfish.

"Drop back. Drop back."

She looked at the reel for what to do, and then to me. "What's happening?" she asked, alarmed by the jerky weight on her rod, which suddenly whipped to the right and then swung hard left over the outboard engine as the sailfish tailwalked back across the wake.

"Bonnie, look at the fish. Strike him. Strike him."

With the fish yanking her arms, and a sense that she had forgotten something important, yes, dropping back, she was confused about striking.

"Strike, strike, strike," I called.

Now Bonnie reached for the little lever on the reel, threw the drag into free spool, dropping back.

"No, no, no dropping back. Strike!"

Bonnie remembered to strike then, pulled the rod up in a mountainous strike, a colossal strike, but much too late. There was a cracking sound, like a small-caliber rifle shot. She had dropped back when the fish was already hooked and running and she had forgotten to thumb the reel. The line had bird-nested into a huge tangle at just the instant she reared back to deliver her strike, which had broken the line with a crack.

"I've got him," she said. Now Bonnie was straining to reel, but the handle wouldn't budge because it was stuck in place from the tangled line.

"Bonnie, stop cranking the reel," I said in disgust.

"I've got him."

"You've got nothing." She looked at me with such a wounded expression.

After all of our work she had forgotten to drop back. "Honey, you forgot to drop back. The fish is gone."

"I did drop back," she insisted.

Bill was standing in the bow, laughing and pointing to the sailfish, which was free, jumping a hundred yards off, trying to get rid of the hook, which would lodge in its mouth for a couple of weeks before rusting out. Time after time it jumped, glistening in the late-morning sun.

What a thing it would have been to have landed it from this tiny boat. To have brought it in and shown Estes we were really good fishermen. If only she had struck the fish properly.

But things could have been worse. We were five miles off the island and still floating. A couple of miles ahead there were thirty or more boats fishing, all of them much larger than ours. I knew they were on Alligator Reef.

Now it was Bill's show. We anchored up in about eighty feet of water and my brother began filleting the large amberjack. All around there were boats drift fishing for kingfish or anchored bottom fishing for snappers and groupers. A half-mile off the reef in deeper water the sportfishing fleet trolled ballyhoo and mullet for sailfish.

It was a lovely afternoon, with a few puffy clouds in the sky and a cooling breeze. Bonnie was smiling at nothing in particular, trying to look involved after her big mistake.

After Bill had twenty pounds of white amberjack meat in his chum bucket, he tied the tail of the carcass on a short line and tossed it over the side to scent the water. Then he began mincing the fillets and occasionally throwing a small handful of oily tidbits off the stern. We were rocking gently and birds were yabbering behind the boat. As usual when he chummed I fell into reveries. It might have been ten minutes or an hour. Mother was frying porgies in the galley of our twenty-seven-foot Richardson. I was hungry.

"Throw over the bait," said Bill.

Later my brother would say that a huge shadow had passed beneath the skiff. It was the biggest fish he had ever seen. I tossed over a large rigged mullet that was connected to the marlin rod. Bill stood in the stern with a foot on the transom like a conquistador, the reel in free spool and his thumb on the spool. After a half-minute something picked up the mullet and began moving off. Bill let the line run for a long time, maybe twenty seconds. Then he threw the lever onto strike and hauled the rod into the air. When the line came taut my brother nearly went over the side. He saved himself by backing off on the drag. The marlin rod was much too heavy for stand-up fishing. It must have weighed forty pounds, and with the drag set and a large creature pulling away, it needed to be anchored into the gimbal of a fighting chair. Bill braced himself with a foot on the transom and pushed the drag up. Again he lurched toward the water and had to back off on the drag. Bonnie and I grabbed him by the belt and this time he was able to hold the rod with the drag in place.

With all of us in the stern the bow of the little boat rose in the air and the transom dipped until it was nearly level with the ocean. This was not good. If a wake came our way it would roll into the boat and swamp us. I tried to point this out to Bill but he wasn't listening. I was worried. I could see the three of us in the water waving for help.

My brother was struggling to lift the rod. The fish was swimming very slowly, not really fighting. Maybe the big one hadn't taken the mullet, he wondered aloud. Possibly a kingfish had grabbed the mullet. No, this was no forty-pounder. It wasn't running like a great game fish, but it had tremendous weight, as if we had snagged the bottom. Bill was bent up like a pretzel, trying to pull up against this weight. He had an anguished expression on his face.

When an angler is hooked up to a large fish other boats begin to come around like vultures. They edge closer without thinking they might cut your line in their props. The mystery of what is down there means everything. If they can get a close look, then they can go back to dropping their own lines.

Bill and Bonnie and I began waving for the boats to give us room to fight the fish, but no one backed off. Fishermen could not believe that such a small boat was out here fighting something tremendous. We cursed at them. There were about twenty boats circling us, including two head boats, each with thirty or thirty-five fishermen. From their higher perspective they pointed to the water and drank beer.

After an hour the big fish began to yield. It hadn't really taxed itself yet but seemed disinterested in struggle. Maybe it was sick or old. Bill was cranking the skiff to the fish more than bringing the fish in. Just winding against its great weight was a large effort, and Bill's blue shirt was drenched through. Now the boats were really packed close. One of the head boats was no more than fifty feet off. Islamorada had become Coney Island. Men cursed, threw bottles in the water. We gave them the finger.

If the fish made any kind of run at all it would cut off on one of the boats. But it never ran. Soon we could see the long shadow. And then the shark itself. It was a hammerhead, bigger than we were, much bigger. Perhaps it weighed a thousand pounds. We'd never seen such a fish. Nor had any of the fishermen in the boats.

I had the disquieting thought that this monster shark had caught us. Its ancient head was as broad as the transom of Estes's skiff. Its dorsal was four feet above the surface and the tail was nearly as high. If the hammerhead had taken hold of the lower unit of the engine or rammed us, the boat would have gone over. It could have eaten one of our thrashing arms or legs in a single bite.

But the shark was content basking in the shadow of the skiff. Hanging off its flanks were two thick remora, four feet long. The hammerhead's back was bowed from age, which made it disturbing to look at, menacing and decrepit at the same time. I think the shark would have sat beside the skiff for hours.

Surely it occurred to my brother that he had pulled in the central character of *Rogue Shark*. After admiring the creature for a couple of minutes, Bill cut the line close to the heavy wire leader and connected the swivel clip to our stern rope. He had decided to take the shark back to Estes. I started the outboard and eased it ahead, signaling the boats to let us through.

Of course there was no way we could manage this trip without the cooperation of the hammerhead. If it had decided to swim off, it would have pulled us under unless the cleat ripped from the gunwale. But the sixteen-foot shark followed us like a dog on a leash. It swam behind, slowing undulating its incredible tail.

It was a bizarre sight, all right, Estes's backwater skiff trolling a shark large enough for the movie *Jaws,* with an armada of boats following. We led the shark beneath the Snake Creek Bridge, where we had nearly swamped a few hours before. We waved to the snapper fishermen, who couldn't believe their eyes. Then we idled along the island where the water was only three or four feet deep and the shark stirred up eddies of mud with its tail sweep.

When we rounded the bend and could see Estes, the old man was in his crow's nest above the shack. Every afternoon he went there to look for his precious boats. His little floating dock was crowded with tourists and fishermen from Bud and Mary's Marina who had heard about the giant hammerhead on ship-to-shore.

There must have been fifty people on the tiny dock when I came alongside. They looked like they were ready for a hammerhead barbecue. Someone tossed on board a stout line we could use as a tail rope. People were snapping pictures of the creature that sat on the mud bottom, barely moving except for its gills and an occasional sweep of its tail.

Someone went for a rifle. I guess the idea was to shoot it in the head and hang it by its tail from a nearby tree. People from up and down the Keys would come around to see it and touch its head and rough hide.

The next moment caught me by surprise. Bill went into his back pocket for his fishing pliers and then reached into the water. He cut the wire leader close to the shark's jaw. For a few moments the hammerhead was idle, but then it got the idea, began to paddle its tail slowly. As the shark moved off into the bay, people were yabbering: Why would the kid let it go? That shark was a man-eater. Someone mentioned calling the police. Mr. Estes looked confused, as though time had passed him by. He never said a word to us about taking his skiff into the ocean.

I recently joined Captain Peter Wright to fish off Hatteras, North Carolina. It was a February morning, very cold, and when we reached the Gulf Stream, twenty miles off the coast, steam was rising from the warm ocean as if we had entered an alien place. Almost immediately we begin to see hammerhead sharks. They were swimming north in pods of three or four fish. After an hour or two it became apparent that we had fallen into the midst of a vast population of hammerheads, thousands of them. All around us there were babies as well as ancient creatures with broad heads and humped backs. The sharks were moving very slowly, as if they were all exhausted. We tried to interest them in our bait, but the sharks didn't care about the fresh mossbunkers and mackerels—none of them would eat. During the past decade commercial fishing had decimated the shark population up and down the East Coast—I hadn't seen a hammerhead in years. But for some reason it felt unsettling to come across so many. The entire day hammerheads appeared and disappeared in the mist like an army in retreat. In succeeding days we never saw another one.

. *Stuffed Head Mounts* .

MOTHER CONTINUED TO SPEND TIME WITH TONY, BUT SHE FELT crowded between him and her kids, accommodating, sneaking around. She wasn't painting enough, which put her on edge. Sometimes she had Tony do chores almost like penance.

Stella, you're making me into one of those stuffed fish heads in Bill's room, complained Fruscella one afternoon when Mother had him moving canvases around in the 14th Street studio.

She tore into him: Tony, I'm drowning in your needs. You're the same as Abe.

Such words didn't matter to Tony, who burrowed into drinking and shooting up. Finally, to get him out of the studio, she told him she wouldn't make love to him until he left 14th Street forever.

Deciding that Tony was like Abe gave her resolve. That's how my mother's mind worked. She wouldn't leave him for robbing churches. In the weird and exasperating way Mother made connections, Tony was my father. She rammed this down my throat. Tony was Abe. Though she loathed his memory, Dad remained a locus for my mother, a way to access anger and spur herself out of indecision and torpor.

Mother found Tony a room on the third floor of a dive on 49th Street and Eighth Avenue. Tony brought home a stray cat to keep him company. He called the cat Stella. Mother found this amusing. She bought food for Tony and occasionally spent the night. But she didn't like to stay because the neighborhood was bleak and threatening. In the morning, when it was time to go, men were shooting up in the streets. One night he asked her not to leave and they argued. When she got up to go home Tony threw the cat out the window. Then he ran down the stairs to get her from the street. He came back crying, holding Stella in his arms. The cat was wild-eyed and wounded. Tony fell onto his knees pleading with Mother to stay with him.

Mother saw Tony Fruscella less frequently but left bags of food for him. She kept retrieving his horn from the pawnshop on Third Avenue. As long as he had it, she believed he would survive. One time they arranged to meet in front of the shop so that she could give him back the horn. Right in front of the window there was a trash can and the cat was lying on top of the garbage with a noose around her neck. Mother decided Tony was sending her messages.

She wouldn't see him after this. Mother continued to bring food to the door of Tony's hotel room. When she heard that he was living on the street, she sent him word that she would leave food in a brown bag at the southeast corner of Washington Square Park. Mother did this for months. Sometimes from around corners she would peek until he had picked up the bag of food. Tony set fires a couple of more times outside the front door of the 14th Street studio. He told neighbors and the police that he was Stella's husband.

Sometime after Mom stopped seeing Tony, when he was back on the street and barely surviving, his friend, the great bass player Red Mitchell, composed lyrics to Tony's previously recorded version of "I'll Be Seeing You." Mitchell's words describing Tony's art and painful life were taped over Fruscella's gentle lilting solo. This collaboration over time is a masterpiece that cradles the listener in life's sadness. Fruscella's version had been recorded a decade before the words were added, when he was the toast of a few smoky Village nightclubs, experimenting, blowing, wearing slick clothes, when Fruscella was a giant, a young Miles, they said, doing dreamy junk and playing his breathy solos, singing through the horn, so vulnerable and yet untouchable, as if life could go on and on like this.

In August 1969 Tony died in a friend's apartment. The doctors determined it was a heart attack from too much drugs and drinking, but Mom believed Tony was just worn out and had stopped struggling. At the funeral Stella put Tony's horn into the coffin with him, which angered some of his musician friends who felt it should have been given to a kid, but she insisted.

Mother was the only one to go to the cemetery. In a distant life Tony had been a lieutenant in the army, and now he was honored with a military burial and a bugle playing taps. It is unlikely that the soldier musician knew that he was celebrating a great horn man who had played this lonely tune his whole life. Taps for the vegetable merchants on Seventh Avenue. Taps for Stella and the gravediggers. Afterward they gave my anarchist mother, of all people, the American flag.

. *Betrayal* .

I REMEMBER A NIGHT IN THE CITY WHEN DAD AND I WERE walking on 48th Street, headed toward the Empress Restaurant to meet Leon Conn. They had formed a brief but profitable partnership during Abe's last year in New York before he moved back to Cambridge. My father was angry that Leon owed him commissions from deals, but nothing was in writing. Dad wasn't going to take a screwing from Leon and would set things straight at this dinner. I felt nervous about the meeting. I had always liked Leon and was surprised he was trying to stiff my father.

It was only three blocks from the hotel to the Empress, and it was all my father could do to make it. We walked with my arm around his back and in the cold December air he made blowing sounds like a porpoise. Dad suddenly stopped and I almost knocked him down. He blew sharply, his handkerchief at the hole in his lower throat, and then pulled out his hardware, the stainless steel keepsake of his laryngectomy and permanent tracheotomy, and wiped it dry. A dozen times since the operation he had showed it to me and explained what gauge steel it was, exactly the same stuff he'd used to make special boxes able to withstand tremendous heat on Nike missile launching pads. If you didn't know Dad was talking, you might have thought he was blowing bubbles. As we walked on, I squeezed his elbow and worried about his commissions. How would we ever get it straight? If there were no records his friend could easily lie. Maybe I would have to step in and confront Leon. I worried if I was up to this.

Leon was a few minutes late. We were eating egg rolls when he came to the table with a big smile. During their brief association, he had learned the ropes from Dad and now was closing big jobs on his own. They shook hands warmly and immediately began talking about the lighting business in New York City. Or rather Dad's ex-partner talked and Abe responded with blowing sounds, nods, smirks, occasionally a few salient words written on a little pad. Leon had always looked up to my father, and after reading one of Dad's notes he turned to me, glowing. "No one's got balls like your old man."

According to Leon, New York City was exploding with lighting jobs. The crown jewel was the World Trade Center, which was already in construction and would require the fixtures of twenty good-sized buildings. What a time this was in the industry. My father's chin quivered slightly at the opportunity to land something larger than he had ever imagined. Why not go after it? Which contractor or commissioner was going to say no to him? I was so excited. I said to my father, half under my breath, Maybe you'll decide to come back to New York for a little while. He raised an eyebrow in my direction, maybe, maybe. Dad ate a bite or two and then began to cough and had to clear his stainless tube. I was hoping he wouldn't bring up the commissions and he didn't. With so much opportunity in the air it would have been silly.

After dinner he and I rode in a taxi to the Village, where I was living. On lower Sixth Avenue I helped him out of the cab while the driver waited to take him back to the Concord Hotel. I pointed my father toward the towering cranes and unlit spires of the World Trade Center, a darkened city crawling up into the clouds toward the moon. "Wow," he said silently, taking in its mass and potential, quickly estimating square feet and the miles of fluorescents.

After I graduated from Kenyon, when Dad still had a voice, there had been a period when he and I fought bitterly. Any path I chose was not only wrong, in his view, but devised to cause him pain and embarrassment in front of his business friends, particularly Alan

Fischbach, who supplied parenting advice and political acumen as well as orders for fixtures and wiring troughs. I was incensed by my father's incredulous eyes and tyrannical need to manage my life. If we had dinner and I asked about the boat or his sister, his voice would drip with sarcasm or suspicion, and if I happened to blunder the conversation into my antiwar politics, my choice of wife or struggle to become a writer, we were immediately into a bloodbath of words and silences. With the last scratches of a voice, Dad would correctly point out that I was yelling him down.

After his laryngectomy we no longer argued. This terrible storm had swept past, and he and I were into uncharted but peaceful waters. It wasn't difficult to learn to read Dad's lips and to understand his impassioned guttural sounds. The loudness and cadence of his taps on a glass or tabletop gave dramatic nuance to his appeals and arguments. Assessing the world in our private language, I was accepted as a trusted adviser, nearly an equal. Perhaps this was because I had a knack for anticipating his ideas and even creating some of them. It was a great relief for him to be able to communicate without straining, and Dad had never been more gentle or open with me. I loved my visits to Cambridge. When we were alone late at night in the house, he sipped vodka and shared his big ideas. Sure, Lee Products was small-time, but there was room on the property to double the size of the shop. Dad would take out a yellow pad and sketch the factory with an additional twelve thousand square feet. Maybe we needed five thousand feet more, I suggested boldly, and he tapped his finger on his temple and mouthed the words, You're right, good idea. All of a sudden I was a big cheese like him. Dad showed me where we would place the new shipping department, the automated spray booth and the degreasing tank. He nodded at my suggestions. Soon enough we would sell the shop and move into a factory three times as large. I agreed heartily. Our fantasy swelled by the minute. It wouldn't take long before we'd have a big factory like Globe. Maybe bigger. Then I made myself a corned beef sandwich while Dad waited patiently and sipped from his glass.

The sagging, crumbling Fayette Street house in Cambridge creaked with my father's footsteps. Clues of my childhood hung on the walls or lay carefully organized in his files and drawers. I discovered my third-grade report card signed neatly by Abe Waitzkin, and there was a photograph of him and Mom with a couple of contractors at the Copacabana. Mother was swaying to the strains of the Xavier Cugat Orchestra. Dad was smiling and I could tell that he had the contractors in the palm of his hand.

Our disagreements were ancient history, Dad would say, and now he bragged to his sister or Jerry, the Lee Products shop foreman, that Freddy had written this article or story. He would ask respectfully about Bonnie and was content to leave my radical politics alone. During my frequent trips to Cambridge I was surprised at how easy it was to step away from my New York life and to fall within the sway of Abe's optimism and vision of the future. The truth was, in the absence of his disapproval, my life choices seemed to lack luster and backbone, while Dad's business dreams were brimming with pizzazz and fun. We were drifting into a brief and unusual partnership. Perhaps he had been grooming me all along for this.

Dad quickly decided that returning to New York was a waste of his time, although I don't think he was ever seriously tempted. He was building something special in Boston, he said, with the same mesmerizing confidence I remembered from Great Neck weekends when he had described how he'd wrested the Aqueduct Race Track job away from his juggernaut competitors, Lightolier and Westinghouse. Dad tapped his glass on the kitchen table for emphasis. Lee Products was his company and no one could ever take it away from him. No one. This was more important in the long run than all the New York jobs.

Fuck the World Trade Center. Fuck Leon's commissions. I can imagine him carefully forming the words to his sister Celia when I was back in New York and she visited him late at night with a pint of vanilla ice cream, delicious and soothing for his sore throat. Cele would titter at his ballsy language. Dad always made a nice face as the ice cream went down.

While the Blum family slept upstairs Abe shared his great plans with Cele in the dilapidated kitchen. After ice cream there was coffee at midnight, and Dad regaled her with stories about Alan Fischbach and the Commissioner. She was thrilled by his plots and access to power far beyond the reach of her husband, who did the pricing for small orders at Lee Products. For years there had been the faintly illicit fantasy that she would be a part of Abe's glorious ride to the top. And though she was a caring wife, Cele's love for her brother was so powerful and obvious that it created darkness in Lennie and her eldest son Howie who were coming to abhor Abe's bruising business style.

When Abe was sleepy from his pill she walked him to his room and they talked about business until he was snoring. Dad slept in the green bed from the Great Neck house, right beside Mom's, though the room was sorely cramped with two beds and the lovely matching dresser with wide swinging doors where Winnie had faithfully placed his starched shirts, socks and folded handkerchiefs. The setup suggested that he and Mom could put it back together in a minute. Why not? he once defiantly mouthed to me. And I had no answer.

Cele and Lennie's bedroom was directly above Dad's. Cele always said that living right on top of Abe she would be able to hear him if there was any problem, but one afternoon, a week or ten days after the laryngectomy, Dad was locked out of his apartment and climbed the stairs to her place to get in. Abe had knocked on the door and window but couldn't get his sister's attention at the other end of the house. He walked to the back of the three-story house but he couldn't get into the outside door that led up the stairs to her kitchen. He couldn't call. He had to stand outside in the cold without gloves for an hour. When she found him out there with his nose dripping, Cele nearly burst into tears. Abe didn't have a voice. How could her brother sell the line without a voice?

Even Cele didn't fully understand the power of his fantasy. My father had no interest in pitching the Lee Products line to little distributors in Bangor and Manchester. With or without a voice he intended to close big deals, to get back on top. I would think how hard it was for Dad to carry the little company on his back, living in meager circumstances while trying to build this mite into something he could feel proud about over drinks with his contractor buddies in Vegas or San Juan. While Dad planned bold moves down the line, his father and brother-in-law worried about paying the phone and electric bills and lobbed potshots from the sidelines. They couldn't give a rat's ass about Sammy Davis, Jr., stopping by Abe's table for a drink. Pop and Lennie wanted to run Lee Products like a corner grocery store. No mortgages or loans for adding space or new machines. No risks. Dad's father Joe would complain to his friend, Mr. Glassman from the synagogue, that Abe went to fancy restaurants or Abe didn't get into the shop until eleven A.M. and then he had a glass in his hand. Cele would try to convince her dad that with Abe's contacts he didn't need to get in early to do his selling, but Pop smirked and continued reporting Abe's sins to Mr. Glassman. Dad swallowed his rage. What could he say? It was not right to be furious at his sick eighty-year-old father.

One afternoon my father was sitting in the silent kitchen across from Pop's room on the first floor, wearing shorts and a sleeveless undershirt, pitiably thin—the little he ate ran right through his remaining few feet of intestine. When the doorbell rang, Dad was unwrapping a pound of lean corned beef to make a sandwich. Pop invited Mr. Glassman inside. Mr. Glassman had been walking past on his way home from the synagogue. He was nearly a hundred years old and though he had lost much of his height, his eyes were bright and he could still shuffle along to the synagogue each day. Pop was bitter because he was no longer strong enough to walk to services and had to beg a ride from Cele or one of the kids. Before Mr. Glassman had taken off his coat, Pop began griping about the meat on the table. Abe was always ordering a pound of lean corned beef, sometimes more, when there was already corned beef in the refrigerator, one or two opened packages. Take a look, he said to Mr. Glassman. Pop went into the fridge and pulled out stiff packages of corned beef. Why didn't Abe worry about wasting money? How was he brought up? My father was sitting there in his undershirt smearing mustard on rye bread, not speaking. Now Mr. Glassman and Pop began discussing the synagogue. There were only a few members still alive. An army of dead behind them. Mr. Glassman was concerned about the big bronze sign in the anteroom of the temple with its long list of members past and present. All the deceased members had small illuminated bulbs next to their names. The bulbs were burning out all the time, which made it hard to discern the living from the dead. There was no money in the account for so many bulbs. If money couldn't be raised, Mr. Glassman would have to pay for them himself. It was a disturbing problem.

Abe was into a slow burn. The family was getting in his way. Even without a voice he could close bigger deals than they could imagine. Lennie and Pop were happy to sell three panel boxes at a time. What was wrong with them? Abe still had his connections. In a few weeks he and Alan Fischbach would be taking the *Ebb Tide* to Bimini.

Fischbach was the answer. But Pop and Lennie didn't want Fischbach jobs. Abe smirked, but he didn't try to speak. Now Joe was
complaining to Mr. Glassman about cigarette smoke in the apartment. Who do they think they are anyway? They'd come his way or
Abe would break them. Joe was bitterly sniffing the air while Dad
took a bite of his meat. Abe had given up Luckies, switched to Kent,
with no taste. Wasn't that enough?

When he had his strength back from the laryngectomy, Abe was
again making monthly trips to New York to see Alan Fischbach,
who gave him orders for wiring troughs and panel boxes. Abe also
closed a few side deals with contractors for lighting jobs just to prove
he still could. He walked into familiar offices with a bratty smile and
made his pitch with his finger on the hole in his throat. Dad could
wrap up an order when he was too weak and dizzy to stand.

The Fischbach jobs were not near the megasized orders of the
Globe days, but they were very large by Lee Products standards.
Pop and Lennie were suspicious of these orders, much as I.R. had re-
sisted Dad's fluorescent jobs ten years earlier. Pop and Lennie believed Lee Products should have many customers. They wanted
salesmen on the road servicing distributors throughout New England and to build inventory in the shop so that customers could be
serviced quickly. This was impossible because Abe had the plant's resources and machinery tied up manufacturing Fischbach deals.

Joe Waitzkin, who was now incontinent and increasingly bitter
about his own future, referred to his voiceless son as "the mechanic."
Joe was blind to the glitz and glamour of Fischbach and fumed that
despite Abe's engineering prowess, he would take these big jobs
without considering the technology or resources needed to manufacture them, or even if the job was profitable. His son was driven to
close the deal regardless of the price.

It was not easy for Cele to reconcile her brother's grand schemes
with her father's brutal critiques and Lennie's brooding jealousy. By
now Dad was no longer concealing his scorn for Lennie. My visits to
Cambridge allowed Cele respite from tense family dinners in front
of the counter rotisserie. Dad and I usually dined out in pricey spots
around Boston compliments of Lee Products. We talked business
and planned our fishing trips.

Within months of Abe's laryngectomy Lennie suffered a heart attack, and while he recuperated at home, his eldest son Howie moved up from the factory to the office. Lennie had grown numb to Abe's excesses in the shop, but Howie experienced his uncle's anger with fresh eyes. Abe's lashing style was all the more unnerving for his incomprehensible sounds and brutal silences. Howie was dumbfounded by his uncle's principal attitude that everyone was trying to screw him and he was going to screw them back. Abe fired workers because he suspected they were talking behind his back. He cursed Louie the tool and die maker each time he came into Lee Products with a price, whatever it was, and they fought like cats. Abe pounded the table in frustration and broke pencils writing his damning notes.

Suspicions and vendettas gave Dad resolve to pull on his socks in the morning. He might have sat in a chair looking out the window at the bleak alley between row houses, but fury launched him into fancy offices with his guts in tangles and his vocal cords cut out. My mangled, emaciated father could be a fearsome visage. Fuck 'em, he'd say, spittle bobbing on his lower lip. He'd fire them all, burn the shop down if he didn't get his way. Who was going to stop him? Lennie? Howie? They were mice. Let them carp on about the line. Abe thrived on their resistance and he stuffed Fischbach down their throats. But then he had periods of sweetness, hosting grand corn beef and pastrami lunches in the office, joking with the men; and even while he only took a few bites himself, he loved watching the guys enjoy the food; such camaraderie all but erased the bad taste. Everyone prayed for this Abe to show up at work the next morning.

Unlike his father, Howie would occasionally criticize his uncle and they had terrific blowups. After Howie gave himself a twenty-dollar-a-week raise, my father wouldn't speak with him for a full year. Howie trembled with anger when he walked past my father. Spurred by outrage, my cousin learned the business and became the top inside guy the company needed, figuring out innumerable manufacturing shortcuts; meanwhile the little office crackled with tension and even in the Fayette Street house Howie and Abe no longer spoke or looked at one another.

The atmosphere in Cambridge grew even more incendiary after my father hired Diran Bagdasarian. He was the sales manager of a car dealership, a large, cheerful man with bushy black eyebrows who knew how to lean on a customer and when to back off. Diran was a crackerjack car salesman, but Abe lured him from Pontiacs with the promise of big bucks in the box business, the opportunity to break from tawdriness and mediocrity into the big time.

Abe forced Diran's appointment as sales manager of Lee Products, arguing that the new man would regularly service accounts up and down New England and establish relationships with new distributors. From the start the Blums were suspicious about the arrangement, which obligated the company to pay him commissions on all company sales. Diran was clearly Abe's guy, an Armenian no less, and he would be sharing from a very small pie. Every month Howie or Lennie gave him a list of distributors to visit. Diran neatly filed the paper in his briefcase and drove with Abe to the Pancake House for breakfast.

In fact Abe needed Diran to be his voice, an ally against the Blums, and to drive him around, as Dad was usually wobbly by the afternoon from drinking. Like me Diran had a knack for climbing into Abe's skin. He could read Dad's lips and eventually his mind. Diran learned how to move around his friend's rage, and he was able to soothe my father as no one else except possibly Cele. It was a relief that Dad had such a buddy. They would often call me with the newest gossip about wiring trough jobs. I thought of us as a little team.

Once a month Diran drove Abe to New York to see Fischbach. He did Abe's talking while my father sat patiently, nodding, pointing his forefinger, sipping from his glass. Diran and Abe shared the same hotel room and stayed up late into the night talking business and considering the future. Diran believed that Abe's New York deals were more important than their dollar amounts. He willingly set aside his own needs and family time to chase Abe's vision to the boat, to Fischbach, to one of Dad's steak joints on Second Avenue where lighting salesmen hobnobbed or to hunt down Abe's lost commissions from whoever was pulling a fast one. Diran had decided that this path would eventually lead them both to the exalted place where Dad had once lived before returning to Boston.

I am convinced that Diran's fierce commitment was not about money. He fell in love with my father, as many of us did. Abe's gentleness and empathy were astonishing, the other side of the great storm, mind you, and he could be the truest friend of a lifetime, though it was a little strange that this Abe never held the other one accountable.

Diran wanted to be with Abe all the time. He drove my father through rainstorms and blizzards while Dad sipped his drink. He would help my father inside the creaky house and put him into his bed. With his size Diran could easily lift Abe whenever it was required. My father was so appreciative and his sleepy expression was peaceful and childlike.

Traveling to service the New England accounts seemed trivial to Diran, and Dad was pleased that his friend didn't want to go. They often spent the day doing projects on the *Ebb Tide,* which was berthed at the Boston Harbor Marina. Fuck them, said Abe with his what-are-they-gonna-do-about-it grin.

Into this mixmaster of love and impending war came Bonnie and I with my first boat. Dad had arranged a bargain-basement price for my twenty-foot center-console Sea Craft from the owner of the company, who was a fishing crony from Bimini. Dad recognized that I needed to captain my own ship and never made an argument, which was a great relief. Indeed, his sudden openness to my independence, an unexpected turn of plot, drew me to him, and his caring and reasonable manner seemed to prove the case against my carping and parochial Boston relatives.

Bonnie and I were in Boston the day the Sea Craft arrived on a trailer in front of the Lee Products factory. She had a deep vee bottom and was creamy white with slick racy lines. Soon enough we'd be chasing down marlin off the north end of Bimini in this little fish boat that we also called the *Ebb Tide.* But first she needed setting up. The boat had to be wired bow to stern for running lights, bilge pumps, radios and such. Dad came up with clever design ideas and he pillaged from the shop's workbench for the tools to put into a little brown box tailored for the size of the craft as well as my limited mechanical skills—it would bail me out of ocean jams for many years. He directed Diran to take three men from the shop and they happily ambled outside the dark, noisy factory and went to work on this lovely boat in the sunny parking lot. Dad came by every few hours to check on progress.

Since returning to Boston Abe had made a habit of pulling men from the factory to work on the big *Ebb Tide* whenever he saw the need. In Dad's view his boat brought class and cachet to the business and allowed him to entertain high rollers with cocktails off the Boston lightship or trolling the rip west of Provincetown. But Joe Waitzkin and the Blums were livid whenever Abe took one-third of the Lee Products workforce to clean the *Ebb Tide*'s teak deck or paint her tuna tower or dock boxes. Manufacturing and shipping came to a near halt until the men were back inside the shop degreasing and painting. Then Abe would fly off the handle when they were late delivering boxes to Fischbach.

During our visit Cele tried to pad her way around her brother's audacity. She congratulated us on the new boat and cooked hearty meals for me and Bonnie, which we ate with our cousins, Sereda and Barry. Cele wanted the atmosphere in Fayette Street to be cozy and sharing, full of family and hugs. That was my aunt's character, but she was upset about Abe's style of business and easy manner with her money. She had been thinking her father's way: maybe Abe was a sucker taking his customers to clubs and fancy restaurants, always grabbing the check. And far worse, whenever Abe had to repair the generator on the *Ebb Tide* or fill her four-hundred-gallon gas tanks or pick up pricey odds and ends for Freddy's little *Ebb Tide*, he wrote a Lee Products check without calculating if the remaining balance was sufficient to cover the payroll and the steel delivery; or if she and Lennie minded that he spent their money. When Abe had decided that his boat needed more power he had replaced his gasoline engines with diesels that cost the company more than forty thousand dollars. This had created a cash flow crisis that lasted a year and a half. Cele had suffered the anger and frustration of Lennie and her father and had tried to smooth things over.

But now, while Dad did most of his late-night conniving with Diran or Freddy if he was in town, she felt scorned and shut out. Maybe Abe wasn't worrying about her future anymore. What kind of outrageous promises had her brother made to Diran? Abe had it in for Lennie and Howie, that was for sure. Were Abe and Diran pulling a fast one? Having doubts about Abe were dizzying to my aunt, who had long revered her brother and was devoted to his physical care. But she was seething about Diran taking Lee money while kicking mud in their faces, ordering workers into Abe's boats and walking around the shop like the king of Egypt.

. *The Flying Gaff* .

DAD LOANED US HIS BIG BUICK AND BONNIE AND I TRAILERED THE little *Ebb Tide* south. We almost lost her on I-95 thirty miles north of Lauderdale when the trailer jackknifed. We drove the last miles feeling very shaky. We bought bags and bags of groceries along with hundreds of pounds of horse ballyhoo, split tail mullet and stiff-brined mackerel, which were the best blue marlin baits of all. We were going for marlin that summer, on our own, without a forty-foot sportfishing boat or captain or even my brother. Bill wouldn't come fishing with me anymore, although the meaning and sadness of this had not yet fully registered. It was just the two of us. Bonnie was a very small young woman with little experience on the water. I had my fantasies about being a big-time marlin skipper, but this was the moment of actually stepping into the wild.

As we shopped in the grocery packed with tanned housewives in golf shorts and tennis skirts, I confided in my young wife that what concerned me most about the trip to the Bahamas was the hump. That was what the captains called the middle of the Gulf Stream when the wind was blowing out of the north, against the current, and the seas gathered into steep, menacing waves that could easily swamp a little boat, even a boat like the big *Ebb Tide.* I knew stories about captains riding tuna towers who had lost their boats from under them between Lauderdale and Bimini.

It was her fear of dying on the ocean that first awakened Bonnie to the relevant moral issues. Do you think we should be killing fish for sport or even hurting them with big hooks? she asked as we pulled up to a checkout girl who looked unhappy about our stacked carts. I don't think so, Bonnie mused. A lady behind us looked at me with reproach.

I should never have told Bonnie about the hump. It was a name, lumpen and vulgar, that constellated her fears and brought to her mind mythological boiling seas battering our little boat to smithereens, big ocean sharks feasting on our floating, bloated remains. What's the point of dying on the hump or drowning while trying to kill a few poor fish? she asked me as we struggled with our four carts of groceries into the sweltering parking lot of the Winn-Dixie.

The night before we made the first crossing, her fears had inflamed my own and I couldn't sleep at all worrying about big seas and my own checkered history as a captain. I was sweating in bed and my chest felt tight. Our radio did not have more than a ten-mile range and the crossing was better than sixty. I knew that I must keep my bow into the seas, but our boat was too small for big head seas, and we'd be too low in the water with our heavy load of supplies and bait. Maybe we'd die on this first crossing, and in my last minutes struggling to hold my wife afloat, I'd feel guilty and stupid. I tried to recall Hemingway's inspired writing about marlin and broadbills, but I could only remember his admonitions about going to sea in a small boat.

On the sturdy little craft set up cleverly by my dad, I steered a compass course of 124 degrees for Bimini, more or less the same open ocean faced by Ernest Hemingway three decades earlier on his disastrous first attempt to visit the island. Hemingway and his friends, including John Dos Passos, were still close to the Florida side when a shark hit Hemingway's trolled bait. After he fought the shark to the transom, he gaffed it and then began putting bullets into it from a pistol he carried on board. The twisting shark broke the gaff handle and Hemingway lost his balance and shot himself through both thighs. While the great author bled on the deck and vomited into a bucket, crew members turned back for Florida.

A week later, lured by tales of gigantic marlin off the Bimini Islands, the writer was headed back across the Stream and would soon make pioneering catches of bluefin tuna and marlin, establishing Bimini as the world's greatest fishing ground. Hemingway had also been apprehensive about crossing the hump, which I found reassuring; except that he never made the trip in a boat as small as ours, and whenever he traveled from Florida on his thirty-eight-foot Wheeler he brought along a burly, experienced crew.

When we left the jetties at Port Everglades, the ocean was nearly flat, about what you would expect to find trolling for bass in Manhasset Bay on a calm spring evening, and we looked out nervously for a wall of fierce water ahead. We cruised past water skiers and head boats with anglers dropping silversides and globs of conch for grouper and snapper. I waved to them. They could see Dad's fine rods and reels sitting smartly in my rod holders. These weekend fishermen could tell we were serious marlin hunters. Maybe they were right. When you are young big risks seem negotiable and you get rare chances to become who you want to be. I was reassured by the ocean's kindly movements and the fresh soft smells I had loved since childhood. As the shoreline behind us gradually became indistinct and hazy, I steered a wandering course looking at schools of breaking tunas and promising weed lines or color changes on the water. I was invigorated by working seabirds and the slip of our clean hull through the peaceful ocean. I kept returning to the same heading on the compass without thinking about the southerly breeze and the current that was pushing us north at three and a half knots. I put a couple of baits over for a short time but then decided to return to cruising speed so that we would arrive at the island before dark. It was a beautiful clear afternoon and I felt the wonder of so much open blue water ahead of me, so much adventure ahead. I wanted the trip to go on and on.

Out of sight of land I was no longer monitoring my physical being for twitches, wheezes and aches, all the subtle water signs of breaking down and bowing out. Thankfully this channel in my head had shut down. I took deep breaths of sea air. We were in a tiny boat and there was no land anywhere. The seas had gradually built into rolling mountains of calm ocean and the staunch little boat rode steadily up and down. Perhaps a little seasick, Bonnie nestled alongside me as I steered. This must be the hump. This was where I wanted to be for my life.

After four hours there was still no Bimini ahead, which was perplexing. Maybe with our heavy load of luggage, bait and groceries, we were traveling more slowly than I had imagined. Having crossed to the island many times, I had the impression that Bimini must be dead ahead, as it always had been, like a vast coastline instead of a tiny strip of sand and a few palm trees. But in all of these earlier trips Dad had done the navigating.

Soon it dawned upon us that we were lost at sea. I felt heady more than nervous. I was sure we'd find Bimini and welcomed the challenge, although Bonnie's mood was less sanguine. After a few miles more I spotted two barren rocks dead ahead. There aren't supposed to be rocks in the Atlantic between Fort Lauderdale and Bimini. Bonnie pulled out the chart and began to teach herself navigation. Twenty miles north of the island there were two dots labeled Hens and Chickens. I hadn't known to compensate for the steady breeze and strong northerly Gulf Stream current and steered us to Hens and Chickens instead of Bimini. If we had missed sighting these low rocks, we would have cruised, obliviously, across a short stretch of the Bahamas Bank and then arrived back in the Atlantic until we ran out of gasoline far beyond the effective range of our radio. We might have drifted for days burning in the sun, or capsized in the fierce afternoon squalls that are common in the northern Bahamas. Using Hens and Chickens as a bearing, we were able to plot a successful course to Bimini. We were lucky.

The truth is that Bonnie's grandiose fears about our new deep-sea lives were warranted. My navigational skills were less than primitive and we had no instruments other than a compass. If the Johnson outboard had shut down in the middle of the ocean, we wouldn't have known how to fix it. On the big *Ebb Tide* I had developed angling finesse, but I was no captain, not even a competent mate. The truth is, I didn't even know what there was to learn. Sitting in the fighting chair I had never recognized the unusual challenge of piloting in the

Bahamas. I didn't appreciate the difficulty of "reading" shallow water or the need to approach cays or reef-bound passages with the sun overhead or behind us, thereby lessening the danger of ripping the boat's bottom open on a coral reef obscured by the glare of the sun.

My fishing passion has often warred against prudent boating sense, but particularly in the early days with Bonnie. I always wanted to go farther than the rest of the fleet, to get the baits into untrolled waters. I wanted to stay out later and test the cool night ocean; and I was intrigued by the mystery and gamble of running after dark. On the big *Ebb Tide* I had learned that marlin and wahoo often strike at the edges of a storm, but I didn't think about the power of late-afternoon line squalls or the danger of big wind when you are offshore in a small open boat. I was drawn offshore by Hemingway's and Jack London's sensuous descriptions of wild immense oceans.

The middle thirties, when Hemingway made his Bimini visits, was the golden age of the sport. Marlin were profuse and men were just beginning to understand how to catch them. Each hooked marlin was an adventure fraught with unexpected problems and a bigger-than-life payoff: back then, to go game fishing one had to invent ways to rig and troll baits, to discover how to take up the belly in the line while the fish jumps a quarter-mile away, how to handle these powerful fish close to the boat. It was a revelation that there were fish in the sea powerful enough to snap the heaviest tackle or that three-hundred-pound sharks were lurking nearby to mutilate hooked marlin. Fishing historian George Rieger wrote of this time, "Men fished from dawn to dusk with the enthusiasm of converts to a new religion." That's how I fished with Bonnie, figuring out the sport as we trolled.

During our first trip to Bimini in the little *Ebb Tide,* along with navigational and boating blunders, blue marlin themselves posed an immediate and formidable threat. I should have known this, but I was busy chasing down the quarry of favorite books and childhood dreams.

Blue marlin fishing today bears scant resemblance to Hemingway's depiction of solitary men drift-fishing off Cuba that first captured my imagination as a thirteen-year-old. It is a technically demanding sport that usually employs an experienced angler working with the best tackle and a professional skipper with one or two mates. The boat itself could easily cost a million dollars. It is a beautiful machine, comfortable and fast and loaded with state-of-the-art navigational and fishing gear, including a tender almost the size of our little *Ebb Tide.*

A skillful angler sitting in a sturdy fighting chair with a footrest doesn't use brute strength to win the fight against a big marlin so much as timing and leverage (and, most important, adroit boat handling by the skipper). Nonetheless, since the earliest days of the sport, with notable exceptions, the top anglers have been men who train hard for long fights, building backs and legs by running, lifting weights, pulling sandbags on the beach, using rowing machines and such.

Skippers and mates are usually physically strong men with much knowledge of rigging baits and tackle as well as experience fishing local waters. The best angler in the world will spend idle days if the captain cannot read the water and find fish. Along with refined boat-handling skills, skippers must have a keen sense for the habits and timing of a superfast and powerful game fish on the line. They know, for example, when and *how* to chase a fish with the boat and when the angler must wear the fish out with the raised tip of the rod, the drag of the reel and the strength of his back and legs. Catching the fish requires perfect timing and teamwork between the captain, angler and mate, who will at the end of the fight grab the wire leader. The best mates are coveted around the world by top skippers for their ability to take several wraps of heavy wire or monofilament leader around their gloved hands and to bring the fish the final fifteen feet to the side of the boat. "Wiring" a big tuna or blue marlin is showtime for the professional mate. He has spent years developing a seamless and powerful hand-over-hand pulling motion, along with a sense for when to haul with his full strength and when and *how* to open his hands and allow the coils of wire to slip off if the marlin is about to make a sharp turn or sprint. He mustn't spook the fish with a jerky, indecisive yank and he must be cat quick to get out of the way should a billfish turn and jump at him.

When the marlin is alongside, the mate may tag the fish, then cut the wire leader and let it go, or if a decision has been made to boat the fish, the captain will come down from the bridge and put a big flying gaff into the marlin (the head of a flying gaff, which looks like a meat hook with a twelve-inch diameter, breaks free from its handle when pulled into a fish. The head of the gaff remains secured to the boat by a rope), at which point all hell breaks loose. Now the two of them are trying to gaff the fish a second time while the marlin beats at the boat with his powerful tail and fearful swinging head. They reach into the froth, blood and exhaust smoke, trying to loop a tail rope over the terrified fish without getting hit by the bill or tangled in the line securing the flying gaff to a stern cleat; also they must stay clear of the leader wire, which is still running from the rod tip to the fish's jaw. Even for the best marlin crew in the world, boating a large fish is a tense time and, despite precautions, there are accidents, some of them bizarre and terrible.

One time Bonnie and I were fishing when a friend of ours, Vincente, an experienced mate working on the legendary Tommy Gifford's nearby boat, had his hand pinioned to the transom by the bill of a marlin. Once the marlin had broken itself free, Gifford called us on the radio to come alongside to race the wounded man to shore, as our boat was much faster than his.

Over the years many arms and legs have been broken in cockpits while anglers and crew members attempted to get out of the way of big, struggling fish. Trying to release marlin, mates have impaled themselves on the large hook they are trying to take out of the thrashing fish's jaw. Wiring represents by far the biggest danger and crew members have had their hands crushed by the tightening wire; some have had fingers and hands sheared off when they couldn't let go; and very strong men have become tangled in the leader and been pulled over the side.

Writing for *Motor Boating and Sailing* magazine, Peter Wright, arguably the greatest living marlin skipper, described a tragedy aboard the boat *Trophy Box,* fishing out of Morehead City, North Carolina, in 1994:

> *The strike when it came was fast and without warning—a "crash strike" as big game anglers describe that kind of sudden almost explosive attack on a bait. . . . Angelo Gray Ingram grabbed the rod and got into the fighting chair.*
> *While Ingram fought the fish, mates Chris Bowie and Ronnie*

Fields got everything ready and Ingram's wife Kelly recorded the action on a video camera. In the cockpit, the washdown hose was coiled and hung up. There were no gaff ropes, stray leaders, baits or anything else on the deck to disturb Bowie's footing when he took the leader in his gloved hands to bring the fish alongside the boat after Ingram had wound in the line up to the connecting swivel to which the leader was attached.

According to Wright the crew assembled on the *Trophy Box* was one of the best on the Atlantic Coast. Alan Fields, the captain, had over thirty years of experience. The wire man in the cockpit, Chris Bowie, was an experienced and respected captain himself who had taken over one thousand billfish.

And at 5'9" and 200 pounds, he had kept the powerful, athletic build of his days as a high school wrestler.

When the swivel reached the rod tip, Bowie calmly and carefully took hold of the ... steel piano wire leader. ... Braced against the gunwale, he then began pulling the fish to the boat. ... As the fish [struggled] against Bowie's muscular straining arms, its pectoral fins were iridescent neon-blue that signals an angry or excited state—a color never seen on a tired or beaten marlin. ...

As Bowie pulled the fish closer to the surface, Alan Fields on the bridge called out, "About 175 pounds ..."

[Bowie] pulled the fish toward the surface. His actions as he took his wraps and cleared the wire behind himself were ... calm and deliberate. The marlin darted ahead ... [but] Bowie did not let go of the wire. Bowie probably believed that he could easily hold a fish that size and that it was not really necessary to let go. ...

As Ronnie Fields turned away momentarily ... before cutting the wire to release the fish Bowie held on with his knees and braced below the covering board taking the strain with his back and shoulders. Suddenly he was in the water.

The others on board mainly remember seeing Bowie's shoes as he went overboard. With his footing lost he first fell onto the transom covering board, then was jerked overboard into the water. His sun visor must have been pushed down over his eyes by his head-first entry. The crew saw him at the surface knocking the visor off his head as he started to turn toward the boat, then was pulled back down. He was swimming, not panicked or struggling, just below the surface with his hands outstretched together. They still expected he would be okay.

When Bowie did not immediately come back up to the surface, Alan Fields backed Trophy Box toward him and called to Ingram to "pull him back up." Ingram got a couple of pumps with the rod and was pulling man and fish back toward the surface ... then the wire leader broke.

Wearing shoes, shorts and a T-shirt, Ronnie Fields, a strong swimmer and diver, leaped in to help his friend. He made one dive and came back up for air. He was not able to get down to Bowie who was 30 feet under and was being pulled deeper by the marlin. "I can't get to him," Fields shouted. But he tried again, nonetheless. In a few more seconds, Fields could see neither Bowie nor the marlin in the clear Gulf Stream water.

Marlin fishing in a small open boat is risky enough and I raised the ante greatly with my inexperience and foolishness. It took some time for this to become clear. During the first fishless weeks off Bimini, I didn't know how to rig baits properly or how far they should ride behind the boat or how fast we should troll. I lost hooks because I tied knots improperly, and I wandered into shallow water and had beautiful big baits eaten by barracudas. After I had learned a few basics, we fouled up six or eight chances before we got near a marlin, which was fortunate. Almost always the scenario was the same. After an hour or two blistering in the hot sun, I'd see a brown shape rising behind one of Bonnie's baits, then a dorsal clipping through the white water. I'd begin screaming, "Marlin, marlin, marlin," with the same blast horn fervor usually associated with "Help, murder, murder." Bonnie would look toward me with alarm while I peered astern. Then, flustered and stagestruck, she would pick up the rod and strike with everything she was worth, having forgotten to drop back some slack line to the hungry fish. Time after time our mullets and mackerels came catapulting back at us, ripped out of the marlin's mouth by her premature strikes, and the fish would slowly turn and swim away. Then I would begin berating Bonnie like Mussolini: You struck too soon. You struck too soon. What's wrong with you? Can't you remember to count to ten before striking? Is that so hard? She would look at me bewildered and wounded, deer-eyed. She could barely hold the heavy rod with the weight of the big bait dragging through the water. And then she had to endure my ranting in a pitching piece of fiberglass in the middle of the shark-infested ocean. But marlin possessed me.

We couldn't hook a marlin, but along weed lines several miles off the island I was able to find a few dolphin and sometimes we did well trolling small feathers around schools of blackfin tuna, hard pullers and delicious eating. Then, while the red sun doused itself in the Gulf Stream, I raced the boat inshore and ran along the reef until I came up to the old Avis Club, where Bill and Ansil had put the two black-tip sharks into the pool four or five years earlier; by now the hotel was abandoned and overgrown by trees and vines and its fine rooms were washed out by hurricanes, the fate of a half-dozen undercapitalized hotels on Bimini. I banked the boat sharp to the left through the inside channel I had learned as a kid, keeping her in the deepest water, which meant passing only inches from the sheer wall of coral to my starboard. We bounced a little when the strut of the engine nudged the top of a small sandbar and we were into the harbor. I smiled at Bonnie, who also loved the ride home. We raced the boat along the flats past the Bimini Big Game Fishing Club, noticing which boats carried marlin flags celebrating the day's catch, then we turned west toward the power plant, where the inside channel ran right alongside the shore near Ansil's house and the basketball court, teenaged Wilts, Oscars and Elgins warming up for tonight's big game against the Cat Island All-Stars. Heading north toward Paradise Point we waved at bulky women taking down the wash and young couples hugging one another in the waist-deep warm water of the lagoon. They waved back. We had a few fish in the boat, which made me feel like a hero.

I slowed down when we neared the rickety dock in Porgy Bay, which was right in front of Deacon Davis's aging green shack that Ansil had rented for us for six weeks for a couple hundred dollars.

While Bonnie reached for our bowline, which was coiled and resting on top of a shaky piling set off from the dock, our wake caught up with us and softly lifted the *Ebb Tide,* and then she settled back in the smooth evening water. Here in Porgy Bay I felt like the captain of a forty-footer.

This was our fishing camp. Beneath the sun-bleached planks of the dock the water was busy with fish and fifty yards across the channel there were mangroves with nesting herons and egrets. Sometimes huge leopard rays burst from the calm water. What a beautiful spot. Skinny Dick Davis was sitting on the dock throwing a handline into the channel. A few Porgy Bay kids were resting on their haunches hoping for a fish to take home for dinner. As we learned the waters and brought in bigger catches, more and more kids were waiting for us on the dock. Whenever we walked the roads there were kids in the shadows calling "Freddy and Bonnie."

Bonnie went into the little house to shower and cook dinner. I hosed down the boat while chatting with Dick about the day offshore. He had been a mate during his youth, and I listened closely when he told me where to find big kingfish on the northern edge or the best way to hold a school of dolphin near the boat. He described what it was like fighting on the wire against a big marlin twenty feet below the transom that wouldn't budge. He'd have to wrestle the fish up with his whole strength and he didn't like to let go of the wire, it was a masculine thing. Dick showed me the scars on his hands from where the wire had cut him, and using his handline he demonstrated how he had taken three wraps on the wire. I felt excited and tense when Dick offered advice about wiring, as that would be my job when Bonnie finally hooked a marlin. As it became dark Dick pulled a white bandanna onto his face to keep off the mosquitoes and got serious about his dock fishing.

After dinner I brought out two Heinekens. He barely nodded when I handed one to him. He was a kingly man but dirt poor. His house on the hill was falling down around his bed. No job, no refrigerator to keep the fish and a big family to feed. Sometimes his wife Minnie joined us for night fishing. She had a voice like a lullaby. She was as smart as Dick, had borne eleven children and was still foxy, would lift her skirt to show off her shapely legs, and such a smile.

Minnie remained cheerful against the fall. When Dick's boat had been stolen two years earlier, their lives had changed. He had used the sloop to sail out of the harbor for conch and lobster, to get away from the island for a few hours—the boat had been his freedom. After absorbing this blow, Dick wouldn't lift a hammer or take an odd job. He sat on the porch reading or looking out to sea until it was time to amble across the baseball field to the bay with his handline. Sometimes Dick would say to Minnie, "Dear, I am living in another world." She would answer him, "No, you are not. You are living right here."

Our Porgy Bay dock was a rare fishing spot at night. Dick tossed his line into the current and made memorable catches of big snappers, five- and six-pounders; sometimes a bonefish would grab his bait. He knew just when to lean back and pull on the line with his long arms until the stretch was out of the mono and the hook was set. Occasionally a shark would pull the monofilament line deep into the flesh of Dick's hand. He wouldn't let go, didn't want to give up his line and hook.

When the action grew slack Dick might mention his favorite stories by Poe, Faulkner and Tolstoy. Sometimes he recited Shakespeare in thick, night-crawling Bahamian. I couldn't make out the words and soon grew impatient. I suppose that I was influenced by his blackness and torn shorts and the smell of sweat and conch slop on his skinny arms. I would try to nudge the conversation back to marlin but Dick played to his own drummer. If I didn't care to listen, he recited passages to the evening breeze.

In such a place a colonial mentality settles in peacefully like the sweet east wind off the mangroves or the smell of Bimini bread in the morning when smiling little girls bring the warm loaves. I decided that Dick needed to shape up and be more enterprising. I loaned him a cooler and told him if he filled it with mangrove snappers there would be enough to feed his family and also some left to sell. Dick didn't get the point or he didn't care. He liked fishing, but keeping them was a problem he didn't want to take on. The Davis family had no refrigerator and it wasn't in his character to ask favors of neighbors. Also, late at night Dick had no interest in cleaning fish. After catching a bunch he might gut one or two for the morning, maybe. He just wanted to go to bed and to hell with the fish. Many times he left plump snappers for the dogs. Around Porgy Bay, Dick was dismissed as the fool on the hill.

One evening a couple miles in front of the harbor mouth I came across a school of dolphin taking shade beneath a long floating board. We trolled up fourteen of them. Running back to the island at dusk I couldn't wait to show our catch to Dick, our best yet on Bimini. Bonnie and I would keep one or two and the rest would feed the Davis family for a couple of weeks or Dick could sell some to his neighbors. I was swept up by my own largesse. By the time we got tied up, it was after dark and I felt let down that Dick wasn't fishing on the dock with his handline.

I tossed the dolphin up on the planks and hosed her down. Then I ambled up the hill, slapping mosquitoes. The Davis house was a wreck, its porch buckled, window frames falling apart. I called from outside for Dick to come down to the dock to help with the fish, he could have most of them for Minnie and the kids.

Dick had already taken a bath and was lying on his clean sheets. Even if they didn't have a dollar, Minnie always had clean sheets on the beds. Dick muttered something that I couldn't make out. I was hungry and impatient to give Dick the fish. I knew Minnie could hear that in my voice and she spoke to him sharply and eventually pushed him out the door.

Dick walked behind me, oozing blackness, and by the time we got to the dock, he was muttering but not to me. But it was *about me* and I didn't like the sound of it. I kept turning around to see if he had something in his hand.

The dolphin were laid out on the dock pretty as a picture, the smallest one maybe five pounds, the largest about ten or twelve. Dick ambled up to the fish, muttering and nodding his head righteously. Then with a skinny leg he kicked all fourteen dolphin off the dock. I was too stunned to say a word. Underneath the shallow water the fish glowed iridescent. I thought about getting a gaff, but the tide was running too fast and in a minute they were all gone, tumbling back out toward the harbor mouth.

Except for Dick Davis the several dozen souls in Porgy Bay seemed at peace with their rustic lives, wedged between the blue ocean and the mangroves. A few young men occupied themselves casting from the shore for small bonefish to sell for bait and rustled the bushes at night for land crabs to fatten up in crawls. Crabs and rice was a Porgy Bay specialty. Charlie Rolle manufactured sandy cinder blocks with his strong boys who listened to his every autocratic word; they didn't desire separate lives and would apparently haul blocks into their old age. Reverend Ellis employed local children to collect fiddler crabs, paid them a nickel or a dime depending on the size of the crab, and sent crates of them to Miami for research. Minnie washed our clothes and sang sweet songs while she steamed our groupers.

Porgy Bay was pristine, a world away from Bayley Town and Alicetown down the road where natives longed for the bright lights and bourgeois homes of Miami and the young men coveted gold jewelry and speedboats and mimicked the strut and slang of rich adolescents who visited the island on yachts tied up at Brown's Marina or the Game Club.

Thirty yards north of us on the end of a tiny dock there was a beat-up thirty-two-foot Pacemaker, a top-heavy white whale with weary engines. She was too big for Porgy Bay; there wasn't even room to turn her around in the channel. Craig Tenant lived on the Pacemaker, reading books, sometimes trading books with Dick Davis and taking Judy Hammond fishing when she visited the island every few weeks with her six-year-old daughter. She owned the run-down boat and rented a little cottage only a few yards from ours. On the walls of her living room were photos of her father and mother in the late forties, when they had been members of the exclusive Cat Cay Club. In the photos, her mother, once the winner of a beauty pageant, seemed regal by comparison with Judy. Her parents had owned a fancy fishing boat, and Judy had watched as a kid as they landed marlin and bluefins in the sumptuous company of Vanderbilts and Rockefellers, who were fellow members of the private island resort just down the Turtle Rocks from Bimini. On a shoestring budget, Judy was trying to re-create this romantic earlier time with skinny, snaggletoothed Craig as her captain in Porgy Bay.

Craig was the antimarlin captain. He loved the sea but didn't care how the baits were riding. He rarely looked astern and wouldn't have noticed if his ballyhoos were cleaned off the hooks by barracudas. Craig would have been happy trolling without hooks; the absurdity would have appealed to him much more than catching fish.

In the year and a half that Judy fished with Craig, they never caught one marlin. I don't think they even hooked one. They got drunk on the boat and fucked, and Judy, middle-aged and unhappy in marriage, found some romance in her life with Craig.

When Judy was off the island Craig made a few bucks as an engine mechanic. He worked on the rusted, oil-seeping engines of conch fishermen, engines that were far beyond saving. He got them going again, pirating parts from abandoned engine blocks he found on the beach and with leader wire and hooks. He snickered at the idea of ordering new parts, no challenge. One time my new Johnson was running rough and I asked him to take a look at it. When I came back a few hours later, he had taken the entire engine apart to the last washer and had thrown all of its cylinders, screws and gaskets into a bucket of black oil. I was dismayed and asked him if he could put it back together without a handbook, which I didn't have, and he answered, "I don't know." Craig loved to torment me.

Many nights he would go to the Compleat Angler to drink with his best friend, Ozzie Brown. Before leaving for the bar Craig sat in a corner of our place drinking while Bonnie and I tried to coax him to have dinner. He didn't like to ruin a good drinking night with food.

Craig had come to Bimini from a little town on the Gulf Coast of Florida where he had been running a small marina, but he had grown bored and restless. Life had gone flat for Craig ever since the war. He had flown missions over North Vietnam listening on the radio and cracking enemy codes. He claimed that he was never afraid flying these missions, rather the work had made him feel alive and needed. He had made his way to Porgy Bay, of all places, hoping to find a niche and something that might excite him. He would find it soon enough.

Some nights Bonnie and Craig would agree that my passion for trolling was off the wall. They were uneasy allies—both of them tweaking me, but at the same time, I think, envying my conviction. Bonnie was absorbing this new Fred—night terrors suddenly traded for the all-consuming sea hunt. She wasn't sure how she felt about fishing. She feared the ocean, but every afternoon when we left the dock in Porgy Bay she fell into the pleasant rhythms of the boat. Despite herself she became excited when fish were striking the baits. She would always fish this way, her passion pushing aside reticence.

Toward the end of the summer Bonnie and I were fishing to the north so far out that Bimini was only a small dab on the horizon. There were no other boats. It was overcast and hard to tell where the gray ocean ended and the sky began. In late August the water was nearly always hot and flat and I trolled farther offshore hoping to find fish in a cool current. We were talking about plans for the fall when Bonnie's jaw dropped.

When I looked astern the fish was on top of us, not twenty feet from the transom and right behind the big mackerel on the flat line. It was a huge marlin, shoulders lifted out of the water and coming right at us with a long spear shaking in the air, showing neon blue along its whole surging length, lighting the dead ocean with color. Then an explosion of water when it grabbed the bait and turned. I hadn't noticed that Bonnie had already taken the rod. No need for any dropback. The marlin had hooked itself. Bonnie was attached, her bent legs braced against the drag while the big fish raced for Bimini like a galloping horse. Bonnie tossed me a look: What now?

We had a flimsy fighting chair mounted in the bow on top of the fish box. We struggled up there with my arm around her waist and when she was seated I got back to the controls and spun the twenty-footer around and began chasing the line through the water. The marlin was jumping so far away, maybe a thousand feet off, hard to believe it was the same fish. I urged her to wind the slack. Wind, Bonnie, wind, wind. It is hard to wind a thousand feet of line with a five-hundred-pound fish on the end. Bonnie was sweating and her arm hurt. She reached across herself and cranked with her left arm. She kept winding and I followed the line but with its big belly dragging through the water we were headed in a different direction from where the marlin was jumping; I worried that our fish had broken off.

After twenty-five minutes the fish was about a hundred feet ahead of us, swimming on the surface with its dorsal and tail out. It wasn't pulling hard, just swimming along. I kept running up the line and Bonnie took in the slack. With the long belly out of the water it wasn't so hard to crank. We were closing the distance. The fish was coming easy. Too easy, I thought, recalling how difficult it had been to take a foot of line in the past when I was on the rod. I felt for my cloth gloves on a little shelf below the steering wheel. We were no

more than fifty feet away. The marlin weighed more than five hundred pounds and was maybe twelve feet long. It wasn't struggling. I
hadn't realized before but coming bow first at the fish, instead of
backing down as we did on the big *Ebb Tide,* the white water and vi-
bration of the propeller didn't agitate the marlin and it swam toward
the bow without fight. Bonnie wasn't pulling on the marlin so much
as reeling in slack. The leader wire was no more than ten or twelve
feet away. This was our first fish and I wanted to put it in the boat. I
never stopped to consider how Bonnie and I would ever get such a
heavy fish into the boat. I slipped on my gloves and threw the engine
into neutral. I slid up toward Bonnie and reached for the leader to
wire the fish as Dick Davis had shown me on the dock using his
handline.

Then I began to think a little: I'd never wired a big fish before.
What if it started to sprint off? Dick had told me to wrap the wire
around my hands three times. But maybe Dick wasn't the greatest
authority. Looking at that marlin I felt timid and decided only to
take a single wrap on the wire, even if it meant that the leader would
slip a little through my hands and I couldn't pull with my full
strength.

But with our boat still in the water, it wasn't necessary to pull
hard. The marlin came toward me like a grazing animal. It nestled
along the white fiberglass. Its whole length was lying alongside the
boat like the shark off Islamorada, but this was not a sick or old creature. The marlin was livid with radiant colors, "green," as captains
refer to a fish that hasn't yet played itself out. I was holding a tiger by
the tail.

I told Bonnie to set her rod on the deck and pick up the flying gaff.
While she struggled to pull the heavy gaff off its bracket, I couldn't
decide if the rope from its detachable stainless head should be secured to a stern cleat or if Bonnie should hold the rope in her hand.
One time I had heard of a flying gaff head tearing loose from a fish
and coming back at the deckhands like a lethal boomerang, so I decided against the cleat. Bonnie would have to hold on to the rope.
Then I told her to gaff the marlin.

Dad's gaff must have weighed thirty pounds and it was hard for
her to lift. Bonnie looked fierce straining to hold the gaff above her
head as if she were splitting logs with an ax, but her swipe missed the

marlin completely, though it was only an arm's length away. She wasn't used to the weight and also she wasn't sure how to put it in. We'd never practiced with the flying gaff. Now the fish was beginning to pull on the wire and I told her to try again, quickly, and at that very moment, as she plunged the gaff into the water, I noticed that the big point at the end of the gaff was buried in a large round cork. Dad had put it there so we wouldn't impale ourselves walking around the little boat. That cork may have saved our lives. As I called out for her to take the cork off, Bonnie pulled the sheathed gaff into the underside of the marlin's shoulder.

Then from a near standstill the marlin came out of the water right in front of our faces. I could have touched the whole rising length with my hand and I looked straight at his eye as it passed my own. He fell back, tail slapping the edge of the gunwale, just missing the cockpit by inches. His head came out again a couple of feet away, huge. The marlin fell onto its side, gathered momentum and came out greyhounding toward the island. The single wrapped leader slipped off my hands unnoticed. The eighty-pound-test line snapped like thread.

We sat there looking at one another. We shouldn't have tried to handle the marlin from a still boat. We would soon learn that to control a hot fish on the wire you need forward movement from the boat. If Bonnie had gaffed the marlin, it could have yanked her over or come back at us while we were dead in the water with little freeboard, only a couple of feet between the ocean and the *Ebb Tide*'s gunwale, nowhere to hide.

During our summers fishing out of Porgy Bay, Bonnie was never afraid during tense moments on the boat. Hurricanes and big fish whetted her appetite for adventure. Only in New York, when I began making plans for our next fishing trip, would she express her fears about the ocean. I would remind her how beautiful it had been and how much she had enjoyed our days out on the boat. I would reassure her that I was gradually learning more about being a skipper and that we wouldn't die at sea. She would look at me suspiciously while I kept persuading until eventually I could feel her relax. Gulf Stream trepidations and gentle persuading became our pre-summertime ritual.

. New Journalism .

AFTER DAD HAD ACCEPTED MY CAREER CHOICE, A TACIT ARRANGE-
ment had settled between us that while he prospered on the business
front in Boston, I would smartly move ahead with my writing in New
York. Then when we got together at some swanky restaurant, we
would compare notes over cold shrimps and bottles of beer. But I
worried about holding up my end. In the rush of my young adulthood I felt as though I must be a great writer, but I didn't know how.
I didn't seem to have any plots. I sweated over my pages for a story
line but nothing came besides dark vignettes about my family that
were torture to put on the page and had subjunctives and past par-
ticiples sticking every which way like wobbly elbows. How can you
write stories without plots? Where was the fiction I had always wanted
to write? Mother said to me, Freddy, you just lack imagination, as if
this held the ready answer. She plied me with the offbeat writing of
her friends Jonas Mekas, R. J. Arden and Gregory Corso, but then
suddenly switched gears and suggested, instead of avant-garde stories, I should write with Tolstoy's sweeping vision—thanks, Mom—
and then she insisted that I was blocked because I did not pay proper
attention to the movement of the stars and the key numbers that
guide our lives. She kept me abreast of the days of the month to stay

indoors working and the days when I should venture out into the world. There were other hellish days that were not suited for either writing or going out of the apartment. When I became annoyed with her magical thinking, Mother would sigh, I was no visionary.

While Mother yawned over my stories, my father had become the proud champion of my literary success, bragging to electrical contractors, beefy union guys, favorite cigarette girls, nurses at the Clinic, wholesale bait proprietors who sold us chum, and Diran. I couldn't mention my failures to Dad. I couldn't think of a goddamned plot, but I needed writing to maintain my independence. Even while I continued to admire his wheeling and dealing and brave push for the summit, I worried that if I gave myself to him on more than occasional weekends, our partnership would cease and I would fall into the black bilge of his rage and scorn.

For a time I took a job working for the *New York Post* as a copyboy–editorial assistant. The job made me feel frustrated and thwarted. All I did was sharpen pencils, buy coffee for the rewrite men and deliver copy downstairs to the printer. No one here thought I might have potential. In nearly a year I never had the opportunity to write a sentence for the *Post*. Some days I broke handfuls of pencils and threw them into the garbage. Once on the way to the printer from the rewrite desk, I threw away the copy, just to see what would happen. A few hours later, when the *Post* rolled off the presses, the story wasn't there, another had taken its place. I was excited by this little experiment, which seemed to prove the gratuitous nature of the news.

At the *Post* I became friends with Brian Hamill, another copyboy, a tough good kid, who was the younger brother of my favorite columnist, Pete Hamill. I think the *Post* job was dreary for Brian as well and we talked a lot waiting for the rancorous shout for pencils. One day Brian jolted me with the news that his dad had put in more than twenty years working as an electrical wirer for a lighting company called Globe. Brian, an irreverent kid, spoke with fondness about the company where his dad had been employed; he knew Isadore Rosenblatt as a distant and benevolent figure. It was very odd, because by now I thought of the Globe saga as my own devious and dark invention.

Brian recalled that when Globe had moved from its Brooklyn location near their home to the new plant in Maspeth, his dad, an amputee from the war, had traveled there with some difficulty. Now with the Globe plant in Maspeth closed down, Brian and Pete's dad was out of work.

About the only thing I liked reading in the *Post* besides the sports was Pete Hamill's column and particularly his writing about the war in Vietnam, which heaved with moral outrage and the stench of power and capitalism run amok. I always opened the paper to his column with excitement and jealousy. I never met Pete, although he was sometimes in the office. Maybe I steered clear of him because of the disturbing connection between our fathers and the fear that, journalist that he was, Pete might discover the inside Globe story and write one of his incomparable excoriations. Anyhow, I grew comfortable with the idea that Globe was different things to different people. If Brian and Pete remembered Globe as an undefeated champion put out to pasture, that was fine.

On most days my brother was oblivious to convention, shuffling around New York in a fine bourbon haze, not caring about the day of the week and vaguely pointing toward the next exotic adventure, when his life would kick in. But other times protocol and nostalgia roared with importance for Bill. He suffered terrible grief over his dead pets and commemorated them with formal burials. Bill paid exorbitant fees to ensure perpetual care for the grave sites of his dogs and cats.

Bill had loved Uncle Alfred for his serenity. In my brother's view it had been preposterous for this gentle, sympathetic man to have been in the Globe factory, maneuvering around the tensions and petty deceits of Abe, Thelma and Chet. With an indulgence of self-recrimination Bill admitted that he had been too tied up to visit Alfred's grave before now, but on this morning, for some reason, my brother insisted on going with Grandpa and Mom on one of their regular visits to the cemetery.

Although Bill rarely spoke to his father, he kept a half-dozen of Abe's custom-made Freed and Sons business suits hanging in his closet. Bill treasured these expensive suits, which had been fitted for an emaciated man during the Great Neck days and were now too large for Dad. Bill had shoehorned himself into a dark gray pinstripe, trying for respectability for the cemetery. He had furiously brushed his long bushy hair, but still it gathered in huge side clumps and had ratty tangles and knots.

During the drive back from the grave site Grandpa didn't say a word. His yearning for Alfred sapped the car of hope. While Globe Lighting had continued to shrink and wither, I.R. was tortured by his loss and had nothing left for the business. The legacy of Globe had no meaning to him without Alfred. My brother had his forehead pasted on the window as Long Island gave way to the asphalt and grimy high-rise apartments of Flushing. Coming back from the Island was always an ordeal for Bill. Stella was impatient with the weight of sorrow. Daddy, you have other children, she said, but Grandpa didn't answer.

In Manhattan Grandpa turned south on Second Avenue. In the East Village, across from Ratner's, suddenly the Cadillac swerved and careened ahead onto the curb with the engine racing, throwing people into the air, smacking them off the hood and windshield until the car slammed into a light pole; Grandpa clutched the wheel with the tires spinning in place.

People were lying on the sidewalk. After the police arrived, Grandpa climbed out of the big car looking righteous and wounded, as though someone had accused him of this mayhem. This was what my brother remembered for years, the bewilderment of his grandfather trying to explain that the engine had raced and the brakes wouldn't work. He had done the right thing. The car didn't work properly.

I was at the *Post* sitting around with Brian and some other copy-boys when the call came from one of my aunts, or maybe it was Mother, describing Grandpa's terrible accident. One elderly man had died and four others had been badly injured. Grandpa had decided to give up his license, I was told, as if this would give the event immediate closure. But there was one other thing. Someone in the family had come up with the brainstorm that as I worked for the *Post* I would be able to kill the story. I went across the room to a more private place to speak. I tried to explain I wasn't a big shot like Pete Hamill, but my excuses were tossed aside. Otherwise Grandpa's picture and this sorrowful story would be plastered on page one and sold at every newsstand in the state.

I knew that in the next couple of hours someone would bark "Copy" and one of us would hustle the story of Grandpa's accident downstairs to the pressroom. If along the way the smudged pages fell into the garbage, the accident would miss the early edition of the *Post* and then something more important might happen in the world to push my grandfather off page one—this was my plan. News is only news if it goes into the paper.

Somehow the shameful pages got past me; but as it turned out, there hadn't been much to worry about. To the surprise of the family, the article about Grandpa's accident was only a few paragraphs on page forty-seven. It was hardly there at all, like Globe itself.

After this terrible event my brother wandered further from the main highway. In New York he had been writing occasional magazine profiles about afternoon soap opera stars and now he stopped doing this. He decided that he had already experienced the mundane side of life and no longer considered making a living viable.

My tight allegiance with Dad was unbearable to Bill, senseless and ugly. My kid brother had no interest in competing for Dad's affections. He gave us the Gulf Stream, all the islands and sharks and marlins. He yawned at my Bimini tales and referred obliquely to a stratum of experience beyond the horizon of my conventional attitudes and married life. In distant places there were delectable possibilities enhanced in ways he wouldn't explain, variations I could not imagine with multiple partners, the smell of curry and tiny dark-skinned girls. He became coy or dismissive when I asked him particulars. Then Bill would change the subject to my precarious health just to hear my voice go quivery at the mention of disease. With his face in a mask of solicitous sorrow, Bill appraised his big brother mired in fear, his father and the box business. My weakness made him soar, convinced him that he was right about Elizabeth Taylor and the timeless beauty of Great Neck.

For my father Bill had become occasional postcards from distant places: Hi Dad. I'm here exploring the ruins of Machu Picchu. I'm trying to find time to get out fishing in the Humboldt Current for black marlin. Wouldn't it be great if I landed a two-thousand-pounder? Sometimes he drew the outline of a hefty marlin at the bottom of his postcards. It was very similar to the fish he began drawing at eleven on his school assignments.

What could my salesman father make of Bill's grand airs and great escapes, his need for drama and shadowy worlds? My brother was putting it to both of us.

My friends saw Bill as Dean Moriarty, racing off on oddball quests, gathering his rosebuds in the androgynous wild country of San Francisco and Tangier, sipping deeply of the night. Bill fed me tidbits. He wanted to buy a proper home in the Mediterranean and was planning a wild caper to raise the money. He showed me a gun, and in his *toujours gai* style hinted he was going to rob a bank or smuggle drugs to get the money. My baby brother left me sputtering or preaching pitifully.

I can imagine Aunt Celia pretending that there was no crisis in her family. A break with Abe was unthinkable, and whenever she came to the brink of war with her brother she backed off. She tried to assuage Joe Waitzkin's rage against his profligate son who went to fancy restaurants and sent back his food uneaten. Abe is a sick man, she said to Pop, who was now dying himself, bleeding in the toilet and not telling anyone so he wouldn't have to go back into the hospital.

She would tell herself, Abe loves the boat. So what if it costs us a few bucks to fix it? No one is starving at 15 Fayette Street. In no time Abe would be leaving for Florida. Her frail brother could no longer take the cold of Boston and had spent the last few winters in a friend's Fort Lauderdale home on a canal off the intracoastal waterway. Cele had visited her brother there, and she knew the routine. Abe liked to have drinks on the patio with his friend Bob and Bob's elderly mother, Frances, while admiring the *Ebb Tide,* which was docked behind the house. When late afternoon storms blew over from the Everglades, they grabbed their drinks and scurried into the Marlin Room, decorated with fish mounts and Abe's Tycoon rods and Fin-Nor reels, which hung from the ceiling on a tricky little bracket Abe had invented and manufactured. In the Marlin Room they nibbled hors d'oeuvres and had a picture window view of the boat riding out the lashing wind and rain. On lovely evenings they would take the *Ebb Tide* to one of the trendy marinas on the intracoastal for drinks and dinner.

Cele could easily fall into the old habit of enjoying her brother's hoity-toity lifestyle even if she was burdened by the cost. He deserves it, she would sometimes say to Lennie, all the pain he has suffered. And Lennie would nod sullenly. After Abe left they would rarely hear from him except for monthly canceled checks and a few postcards extolling sunsets on the intracoastal or marlin hookups off Bimini.

In the meantime Cele made steak and salad dinners, hoping that the family would knit together. She would feed Howie before it was time for Abe slowly to climb the squeaking back stairs that led from his kitchen door to hers. Howie rushed through his meal, which made Cele unhappy. Then, before Abe arrived, Howie quickly left to visit his friend who owned a Baskin-Robbins ice cream store in Central Square.

At the brightly lit kitchen table Abe would carefully chew his meat, trying not to choke. He'd meticulously form the words, it's good, to his sister; and after she'd served him sherbet for his throat, thank you. He wiped his face neatly. During these dinners Lennie would occasionally make a stale joke and Abe would smile, though he'd heard it two dozen times before. She took this as a good sign.

She knew that once the cold weather had driven Abe south, Howie would again linger over dinner with the family and her oldest son would have his way in the shop. Soon enough Howie would become the president of Lee Products. With Abe in Fort Lauderdale Lennie would be able to relax and she wouldn't worry so much about his heart. Just cool it until Abe left for Florida.

Except one morning over breakfast Dad told Celia that it was time to put the business back into his name. Abe was looking very collected in a white business shirt, smelling of starch and morning coffee, glancing at the sports section of the paper. It was a new day and he hadn't had a drink. Give the lawyer a call, he wrote on his pad. It was very reasonable. There was nothing more to discuss and Dad turned back to the newspaper after spelling it out for her.

A dozen years before, Abe had transferred his fifty percent ownership in the business and its real estate to his sister to protect the shop from I.R.'s schemes against him during the divorce proceedings with Stella. In those black days when Abe was still weak from surgery and I.R. had put him into the mental hospital and then forced Abe out of Globe, his sister had been the only one he could trust. Without her he couldn't have survived the conniving and deception, the humiliation.

Celia was dismayed, though she responded in her singsong voice with hands on her hips, puffing out her ample chest, What's the big rush, Abe? Why all of a sudden call the lawyers? Do it today! She didn't like it when her brother gave her orders as if she were a secretary. Dad smiled at her show. He was such a master of timing. Maybe this was not the right time to push Cele? But why should he have to push? He wanted the goddamned shares back in his name.

Abe backed off but Cele worried now that something very bad was happening behind her back, in her own home. Why did Abe want this change? They gave him everything he wanted. Cele had worried about Diran ever since he had left the car dealership for Lee Products. Why come into their tiny company to earn less than he had made selling Pontiacs? What promises had Abe made to Diran? She knew better than anyone the power of her brother's ambition and avarice. Abe played by his own rules and he never looked back. She decided Abe and Diran were planning to push Howie and Lennie out of the company and her brother was pressuring her to give him the leverage.

Celia went to her sick father for advice and Joe reminded her that Abe's kids had a rich grandfather. From the Great Neck days Joe remembered Globe as a vast city of men and machines supplying lighting for communities across America. Pop had always admired Izzy Rosenblatt, an immigrant like himself, who had come to this country with nothing and had become a legend in the industry. Cele needed to protect her own children, insisted Pop, who urged her not to return Abe's shares in the family business.

Cele continued to be indirect with her brother. What's the problem, Abe? There's no rush, she would say when he asked about fixing the paperwork. We'll see about it during the winter. Her tight, angry smile told another story.

Diran called me on the phone with the news. In the big man's voice there was a tension I had never heard before, a lack of clarity and direction. Diran had always had all of Abe's answers, but now Dad was concerned and uncertain. He had assumed that his sister would stand by him. For all the married years it was Cele who had grasped Abe's vision, had ennobled his razzle-dazzle and dark maneuverings while Stella was out to lunch. Diran was only a diversion and now his bluster was making Abe impatient. Diran was window dressing. It was Cele who had energized Dad and made him glow. She had bathed his seeping wounds when Dad was too weak to stand, had propped him back up—now an enemy from deep within the camp. Abe was incredulous and daunted. She knew all his weaknesses and fears, the pills and props of his weird, irresistible strength. She knew where he spent the money, how he closed the deals.

Maybe Cele was pulling a fast one. We'll see, said Diran reaching for the old cockiness.

By now Pop was back in the hospital, dying. Dad was in the bleak house by himself. He couldn't speak on the phone. He was drinking at breakfast, missing days of work, and he no longer went upstairs for his dinner. No more late-night visits from his sister but sometimes Cele dropped by a plate of food. Dad was too damning and tense to eat it, his longing for her turning to bile. No one would ever take this business away from him. Never. He couldn't look at his sister. He wanted to break them. But then he felt weak and sick, dizzy. Loneliness and wretched aversion were all over him. He was losing weight from his bones and skin. He had stomach cramps like the Great Neck days and he fought them back. But he was hurting bad, as if old surgeries were coming apart. He would dial my number in New York.

Dad, how ya doin'?

He would tap faintly like demise.

Things are going badly with Cele and Lennie? They won't give back your shares?

Frantic flutter of taps with his fingernail.

They're trying to screw you, Pop?

They're trying to screw me. My dumb son-of-a-bitch brother-in-law. I want to get him. I want to get the prick bastard.

Can't Diran help you?

No, a slow sullen beat.

You mean he can't handle it? Diran doesn't know what to do? Bing, bing, on his glass with a spoon. That's right.

Is he spending more time with his family? You don't want to go over and visit Diran in his house?

That's right.

You feel out of place there now with the problems on your mind? That's right.

Listen, Pop, don't worry. I'll come up next weekend and we'll figure it out, come up with a plan. Stop worrying. It's gonna work out. Now listen to me. Just one thing. I want you to back off on the bottle a little. Only one or two drinks, no more. Promise me that. Promise me.

Dad promised with a tap.

———

I visited Cambridge and we had long talks. My father's destitution empowered me and I gushed with bright ideas. I calmed him down. We went out and Dad watched me eat linguine with shrimps and clams. He took pleasure from my appetite. We spent evenings on the musty sofa watching the Celtics run the fast break and drank beer together and talked. We were having a rough time, I agreed, but it would turn out okay. I believed that. He smiled sweetly. I was his boy. There was still a bright light at the end of the tunnel.

I remembered the name of a lawyer friend, a hard drinker who fished in the spring in the Bahamas for bluefin. I was surprised Dad hadn't thought of calling him. He was a partner in one of Boston's biggest and best law firms. The lawyer was delighted to hear from me and was appalled by Dad's difficulties with his sister. Abe is such a great guy, he said, and recalled good times with Dad in the islands. We retained the firm to fight for Dad's shares. Dad felt relieved having such a good plan.

Cele and Lennie were afraid of being crushed by this giant and they retained a firm equally costly and prestigious. Two monster firms. Either of them might have defended a major suit against a massive public corporation or represented a Kennedy. Teams of sage partners and whiz-smart interns rolled up their sleeves and began the lengthy litigation over Lee Products.

It was a game. That's how I thought of my business life with Dad, all the big plans, the action and drama—a testing ground with a lifetime of second chances. For a moment the game had gotten away from us. It was very close. Anyone might have made a reasonable phone call. Cele was wretched in her isolation from her brother, guilt-ridden about not giving him back the shares that were indisputably his. But there was so much anger and passion for the fight. Dad had once closed the biggest deals in the city and now Lee Products was his domain. Cele was defending bravely against a massive hostile takeover. None of us ever thought we were battling over a few ruined machines and a crumbling building.

I knew we'd win. I encouraged Dad to leave for Florida, where he would be living with his friends. I would watch over the lawsuit against Cele and my cousins. I'd handle it. We planned to visit in Florida and take the *Ebb Tide* to the Bahamas.

. The Last Marlin .

FROM OFFSHORE, BIMINI FIRST APPEARS LIKE A MISTAKE—A FEW *fuzzy treetops planted in the expanse of choppy ocean. When I blink, this trace of land is gone and I wonder if I've imagined it, which is sometimes the case. Eventually I can make out a dash of sand and the roofs of a few homes.*

In fact, the island is only a hundred sandy yards across, a tenuous place. A small tidal wave could easily obliterate the entire tiny civilization of fifteen hundred poor souls with their hopes and sadnesses, state-of-the-art satellite dishes nailed onto woeful shaky shacks, glistening new washing machines standing on rotting porches; everywhere there are legacies of the drug trade, a minifleet of Camrys and pickups smoothly gathering speed for the three-mile trip to the north or south, an island of teenage boys without dreams selling crack to smaller boys, of beached fishermen dreaming of fleets of motor scooters and golf carts, a single wave could wash it all onto the flats with the barracudas, bonefish and hammerheads.

But this is the perspective of an outsider and after only a few days I am drawn into this place. The water is clear and warm, the same striation of colors that moved me so as a teenager, the same night air and sandy streets, the inside channel peaceful and evocative, as if all of this has been waiting for me. The bonefishermen search the flats for muds and tails.

The girls are still young and flirtatious. I become lost in time. Bimini
cured my father again and again, kept him alive and selling. It keeps me
alive. Bimini memories are still sensuous and deepened by evening
breezes and the deep sea.

Somehow it makes perfect sense that Eric Sawyer on the hill has long
conversations with his grandfather, who has been dead now for thirty
years. They argue over small details. At night Hemingway's old skipper
dreams of a huge marlin rising behind his boat as it trolls down the
Queens Highway. While Eric prepares for the strike his outriggers tangle
in palm trees and the huge fish lunges past motor scooters and golf carts
trying to get at the skipping bait. Eric loses his fish again and again.
"Waitzkin, there are a thousand ways to lose a marlin," he explains to me
philosophically.

I am thinking of my father and Craig. I am hungry for them.

While I tended to my father's legal affairs, my brother arrived at
the weighty decision to construct a life-sized model of the jaw of an
eighty-foot *Carcharodon megalodon.* It incensed him that the *Car-*
charodon megalodon jaw at the Museum of Natural History was
constructed inaccurately, using teeth of the same size instead of
larger, hand-sized ones in front, with progressively smaller teeth
toward the back of the jaw. Bill had discussed this terrible blunder
with an ichthyologist at the museum and mentioned an expedition he
was planning to South Carolina to search for giant shark teeth to
make a perfect jaw. I could imagine my brother's bourbon-slurred
words as he expressed his outrage about the museum's shoddy work.

Bill traveled to South Carolina and moved in with a hippie couple
who lived near the marshlands. There was much marijuana and night
partying but on most days my brother pulled on his hip boots and
trudged into the bog searching for giant fossilized shark teeth, exhausting work, particularly with Bill's arthritis, which made bending
painful. He spent weeks there and returned to the city with hundreds
of teeth, although only a half-dozen were exactly right for the mammoth jaw. There would need to be several more trips. Bill sorted the
teeth by size, stored them in jars and showed them to his friends.
They were his treasure.

I tried to explain to Bill what was going on between Dad and his sister and that our father was sick and depressed. Only now had it become clear to me that Dad had little money and his only valuable asset was the boat. If he lost the case, how would he survive? It was not possible for him to continue living in the viperous Cambridge atmosphere where he began drinking before breakfast. Dad was now our responsibility, I said to my brother collegially, trying to enlist his support but feeling his attention drift. With Dad in trouble conversations with Bill were even more exasperating. My brother's life played out in front of him like a Broadway musical. When he finished constructing the jaw, and it was in place in the museum, he intended to move to Morocco and settle down overlooking the Mediterranean attended by loyal servants. Occasionally he would return to the States for Mother's gallery openings. And perhaps someday he might come back to live in Great Neck. Dad was not in Bill's plans. He wanted me to understand this.

On an inspiration I called my aunt on the phone and urged her to return my father's shares of Lee Products, just give back what you know is his, Cele. Then we could forget the lawyers and all the anger would soon disappear. My aunt's voice was cheerful but unyielding. I could not believe that she would say no. Then I had this terrific idea and I just spoke it to my aunt. If you persist in this, someone is going to die, Cele. I let this hang dramatically. She knew what I meant, my father or her husband Lennie. It was such a preposterous thing to say, but in my youthful miasma I believed my aunt would shudder and buckle. Instead she closed like a fist around my visionary prattle. Her fury made me righteous. I got off the phone with her and called the lawyers, talked strategy, felt like a big shot. Like Abe.

Several weeks after Dad left for Florida I heard from his friend Bob, who owned the house in Fort Lauderdale where my father stayed and tied up his boat. My father had been sick with cramps for a week. Food wouldn't pass through him. Abe had told Bob that he needed a shot but they couldn't find a doctor to come over to the house and give him one. Abe drank more and more but the cramps wouldn't ease up. He vomited green foam. Finally Bob had taken Abe to the Holy Cross Hospital and a few hours later Dad was operated on for an intestinal blockage.

I had flown to Florida many times and always with the expectation of fishing or sitting on a veranda by the water with my father sipping a drink and talking about his deals. In Florida we usually food-shopped for the boat, bought bait, Japanese feathers, line and such, got ready to leave for Bimini. There was terrific excitement. Flying with Bonnie to Fort Lauderdale I found it hard to escape this mind-set. My life with him moved ahead like a wave.

Sitting up in the hospital bed with his hair neatly brushed, Dad looked great, as if he were expecting a customer. He gave me a wave and grinned at his intravenous tubes. No big deal, he'd had much worse than this. I read his lips and the meticulous movements of his hands, like a conductor's, lingering on a point or raising its emphasis. We were soon into our own world of business deals and great plans. He was jaunty and ready to go. I loved it that none of the doctors and nurses who busied themselves about his bedside had any idea what we were talking about. I told him that my writing was going terrifically, although I was hardly writing at all. Dad expected to get out of the hospital soon and go back to Bob's house. Fischbach was coming down. He needed to have work done on the diesels before he could leave for the islands.

When the phone rang it was Cele. She had learned about Dad's surgery from his friend Bob. I pointed to the receiver and Dad shook his head, mouthed the words, No way, and then, I want the god-damned shares back. Then we'll talk. This was vintage Abe Waitzkin, tightening the screws, using sickbed leverage.

Bonnie and I went out to dinner at the Raindancer Steak House on Commercial Boulevard, Dad's favorite restaurant. We stayed in the forward bunks of the *Ebb Tide*. We made love and she assured me that my pains weren't cancer or colitis, just a tight stomach.

The next day in the hospital Dad was living in another place and time. He was staring up at the ceiling with a perturbed expression. He reached up with his hand and turned something. Than he put his finger on his temple and thought deeply.

What's he doing? asked the nurse.

He was trying to install the electric garage door in the Great Neck house. It wouldn't go up or down. I recalled this cold winter afternoon very well. I had been there holding his tools while he figured out the answer. Dad tightened something with a screwdriver. The wiring diagram was all wrong and he was disgusted. Then he began testing wires with his ohmmeter. A few days later Dad had gone into the hospital for his colostomy.

When I called him back Dad looked at me suspiciously, his face dark as though someone had crossed him. All morning he had been vomiting green bile. The doctor said that it was only a question of time before his digestion kicked back in, not to worry.

Later that evening Dad was standing in a corner of his hospital room. No one was around and it was almost dusk. Soon they would roll in his dinner. He had to move quickly or he would be discovered. He was late for his flight but he couldn't find his pants or his watch with his name printed above the leaping sailfish painted on the dial. And then he had to go to the toilet, he had to go terrible. But he couldn't find the bathroom. The nurse found him standing with his intravenous wires pulled out of his arm, an emaciated man with a hand covering his wound, his excrement looking like corn flakes coming out from between his fingers. It was a sweet smell, not unpleasant.

What are you doing, standing there, she asked him. You've pulled out your wires.

I have to take a crap, he mouthed the words. I have to go terrible.

Are you hungry, sweetheart? she asked without looking at what he was saying. We'll take care of that. Tonight we have pot roast and mashed potatoes. You just climb back into bed.

I have to take a goddamned crap. I have to go bad.

Don't you pull out your wires again. You hear me. Or I'll have to tie you down.

He was shaking his head, no, no, no. I gotta go real bad. I gotta go something terrible. She wasn't listening to him and he was disgusted.

The young doctor explained that Dad was shaking like a leaf from alcohol withdrawal and his blood chemistry was off. As soon as corrections were made, he would be back to his old self. The doctor was cheerful and I felt assured. Except now I wanted to ask him about the pains in my stomach. But I was too embarrassed to mention it. I was terrified by the traffic of medical apparatus and doctors. As if I had pressing business I rushed from Dad's room whenever a nurse came to change his dressing. I was impelled by the superstition that I wouldn't survive if I saw my father's wounds and blood.

After ten days Bonnie went back to her job in New York. My brother Bill arrived flushed with the drama and solemnity of Dad's grave illness and imminent passing. Bill felt empowered by formal occasions. I would look at my brother's face for a sign of affection for his father, something he'd been hiding or saving for the right moment, but this wasn't it. After a week Bill grew restless waiting and returned to New York.

Cele kept calling the hospital almost every day. I would explain that Dad was too tired to come to the phone, but she knew that Abe wouldn't speak to her. And I knew the pain it caused her. This was my father's plan for winning. I never told her about the times he was living in another world. I kept hoping that she would send the papers down to Florida and Dad would get better.

There were days when Dad was so far away I feared he would never make it back. His eyes raced around the room and he reported fires burning outside the window. He smiled and then fell into despair, witnessed terrible things. A world of pain and success whirled by him. He persuaded his customers. Eventually he grew calm and sleepy, childlike. Some afternoons he worked on the garage door or his diesels. I waited for him to come back.

I waited for two months. There was hardly anything left of Dad. Food poured through him like an open pipe. I stayed on the *Ebb Tide* and ate steak in the Raindancer, believing it would help. Occasionally, late at night, he would surprise me with a phone call, tap with his fingernail on the receiver. Things were going good or he was feeling sleepy. These taps revived my optimism. Somehow he lived.

And there were days when my father's clarity was startling. He'd smile at me and ask about the legal case against Cele and Lennie. He made sharp suggestions. Again he was calling the shots, and I believed that he would get us out of this mess. Dad was concerned about the dwindling balance in his checkbook and suggested that maybe we would have to let the boat go. This was reasonable, as boat expenses were bleeding away his little money, but I couldn't deal with the idea.

Sometimes Dad looked at my face and he knew that I was afraid. He took my hand and said I was okay, not to worry about my health.

I admitted that I was concerned about my blood pressure. Every couple of hours they checked his while I believed that mine was sky-high. My head was bursting from pressure. Once or twice when he was sleeping, I fumbled with the apparatus myself, wound it around my arm like when I was a kid and had tried to teach myself how to tie the phylacteries around my wrists and forehead, so that Dad and I would live and not get diseases. Dad asked a young nurse to check my blood pressure and she seemed happy to do it. After this, whenever it was her shift, she took my pressure and said that I was doing fine. I would feel better for a few hours.

One morning Dad's lawyer from Boston called to tell us that my aunt was returning Abe's ownership in the business. Celia couldn't bear this break from her sick brother. She was guilt-ridden and had made the decision without consulting her husband and son, who would later become very angry with her.

The terrible fight was over. It was a miracle. In a couple of days Dad's lawyer would fly to Florida with the papers for Abe to sign. He would have money again and there would be no more talk of selling the boat.

I tried to tell Dad the great news, but he wasn't listening and his face was dark. I needed him to hear that he had won the case. I tried to trick him. I said it would be fun to go down to the parking lot in a wheelchair and look at his Buick. He didn't want to go but I wanted to jolt him, bring him back. I was sure that the smell of the new car would be a tonic for him. By the time we reached the car he was beating on the arms of the chair. I don't give a fuck, he said. What are you trying to get away with! He was appalled that I had brought him out into the sunny parking lot.

When we got back to the hospital room, Bob's mother, Frances, was waiting for him. She was a robust, matronly lady, about seventy years old, with white hair. Many evenings she and Abe had sat on the patio of Bob's house looking at the *Ebb Tide* while sipping a drink.

Oh how are you, Abe, Frances said, engulfing my father in her huge chest. Good, he said, gathering himself for a lady caller. He told me to leave, he wanted to be alone with Frances.

I left them for half an hour, and when I returned, Dad had fallen asleep.

Look at this, poor boy, said Frances shaking her head. "Don't tell anyone," my father had scrawled on a napkin. "They're keeping me here against my will. I'm going to run away with my boys. I'll call when I can."

When the lawyer from Boston arrived at the hospital my father was out of touch: Hi, Abe, I've brought you something. Do you want to take a look and sign these papers, Abe? Abe! Dad gave him a wilting stare and added the words, Are you fuck'n kidding me? No way.

There was no forcing him, and I suggested to the attorney that we should sit quietly and let time pass. I knew this must seem odd to a man who billed at a high rate for his hours and was scheduled to fly back to Boston in the early afternoon. Dad wasn't anywhere close and I was afraid that after twenty minutes the lawyer would stand up and take his leave of this surreal meeting. But instead he took off his jacket and sat by the bed. Hours passed and he missed the flight back to Boston. We waited for Dad to come back. Dad had told me that this man was a great tuna fisherman and that on Bimini he had a reputation for partying through the night, a wild man, was how Dad put it. But now the attorney had fallen into quiet waiting, a kind of reverie with me and Dad, who had eventually grown still.

It was around dusk and Dad had a sweet, peaceful expression. The attorney quietly asked him to sign the papers and my father looked at me and asked mildly, Freddy, do you think I should?

Dad, I think you should sign. I think it's fine, Dad.

He signed the papers with his favorite Parker pen but I don't think Dad knew what he was signing or that he'd won.

A few days later I was sleeping late on the boat when the phone rang. My father was tapping rapidly, all business. I'll be right over, Dad.

When I arrived in his hospital room he was sitting up with a concerned expression. Look at this, he said, pulling aside his sheet. Dad's stomach and legs were covered with blood. He hadn't shown anyone but he wanted me to know. I raced for the nurse, who started making phone calls while my father bled. Everyone had gone to lunch. I ran down the hall looking for a doctor, any doctor. I asked a janitor who was mopping the floor to help me. My father was bleeding to death.

It took forever before a surgeon was in the room and they were pushing Dad back into the operating room. His eyes were back in his head.

I had to get out of the hospital. I knew he was dying and I couldn't bear waiting for the nurse or doctor to come back to his room to tell me my father was gone. I drove to the boat and phoned Bonnie and my mother. I couldn't stop crying and they said soothing things— now he's gone to a better place, his pain is over.

But Abe didn't die. I came the next morning and was stunned to find him sitting up in bed with a weary but cheerful expression. They had stitched him up and given him blood and now Dad was feeling better, as he put it. He was hungry. And he had made the decision to go back to Boston. He wanted to go to the Clinic to be with his doctors—they would know how to fix him up.

I was confused and exhausted. I had spent the night considering how I would make it without him. Now I didn't want to read his lips. I had fallen off the wave. I didn't want to make arrangements and talk plans, but he still needed me.

With a nurse we flew north on Eastern, his favorite airline. Dad seemed energized and collected being in the plane. He'd flown to so many cities to meet with his customers to close deals.

In the Clinic all of his doctor friends came to visit as they had so many times before when he came in for operations and follow-ups. They came up with an ambitious plan to build his strength. It involved feeding him with a tube that entered an artery in his chest. Dad looked pleased with the idea, although every night he fought with the nurses and pulled out the feeding tube. In the morning I would find his arms tied to the bed and he would tell me that in the night the nurses had done bad things to him. When I asked if they beat him, he nodded that they had.

Celia came to visit him every day. I don't think that my father had any memory of the legal case or the terrible rift with his sister. Even in the evening, when he grew distracted and suspicious, he allowed Celia to hold his hand.

One night when I came to his room, Dad was hopping like a puppet on a string, smiling, crying, explaining how to wire a fixture or maybe it was the garage door in the old house. Then he began persuading, gesturing with his hands. You had to believe him. That's how I saw him the last time.

Alan Fischbach didn't come to my father's funeral, which surprised me greatly and seemed to compromise the affair. So many of his orders had been at the center of my father's happiness. Some other key customers also weren't able to make it because of the cold, raw weather. But the Commissioner came up from New York with several big men I didn't recognize. The Commissioner's friends wore dark suits and sunglasses and flanked him on both sides. My mother sat next to Celia. Their tenderness toward one another surprised me.

I wrote a few pages about my father and Diran read them. I had wanted to describe Dad's incomparable selling—that he pulled out all the stops to close the deal. But it seemed as though no one, even the salesmen attending, would understand why I idolized his selling, which was unremitting and sometimes involved extravagant and unattractive tactics; it might sound as though I were belittling him, and so I wrote something tame and considered. At funerals there is the pull to put everyone into the ground with the same kind words.

At the end of the service the Commissioner came over to where I was sitting, and when he leaned to whisper in my ear, my heart began jumping: if you ever need a favor, anything, anything at all, you call me. He handed me a card with a phone number and then his hand lingered on my shoulder in a manner both majestic and sinister. The Commissioner could bestow giant favors or he could exact awful revenge. To the best of my knowledge he had never once failed my father and I shuddered with the power of his offering.

At the funerals of family members and beloved pets, my brother stepped forward, made sharp decisions and showed an attention to detail not generally apparent in his daily life. I think at such times the past came alive for Bill and he felt a calling and responsibility. He had long been fascinated by the pharaohs and had studied the *Book of the Dead*. He believed in a connection between the meticulous preparation of the grave site and some form of eternal life. While I was spooked and tentative around my father's death, it was my brother who selected Abe's coffin. He knew what color and style were best for Dad, what shaped pillow and what little objects—pliers, pen, writing pad, cigarette lighter—to place in the pockets of his business suit, and which suit, which little shoes would travel with Dad through all of time.

And now weeks after Abe's death, Celia, Bill and I were seated in a cramped office with two dusty desks piled high with notebooks, directories and old stencils. On the plate-glass window was a sign that read, "Sam Canter & Sons, Artistic Granite Monuments."

My aunt's face was puffy and red. It's not fair, she said, wiping her eyes.

Sam Canter, a portly man, nodded to her in a caring manner. Sam understood the slow and intractable rhythms of grief. He had walked with a thousand customers down this path.

My brother was wearing the pants from one of Dad's old suits, his stomach bulging over the top, and his beard was full, his bushy hair brushed back for the occasion and held in place with a rubber band.

You know, you look like a rabbi, my aunt said, trying to smile. She used to say that to calm my father down when he was incensed about Bill's appearance and incomprehensible life choices.

Sam was very smooth and we hardly noticed when he brought out the big and shiny book of possibilities. There were gray and red gravestones, one big black one, an imposing stone. That one is rarely used, he said in such a way as to imply an impropriety. My aunt shook her head decisively, never, never that one. But size really wasn't an issue. The stone would be the same height and gray color as those to the left and right, his father and cousin. We wouldn't want to make it look like he was a king, right? she asked Sam Canter, who nodded and paused a beat.

The big thing, he explained, is whether to choose the polished or the natural surface and whether you want the top of the stone straight horizontal cut or one of several sloping curves and the kind of border you want, which depends completely on whether you choose polished or natural and, of course, the wording of the stone itself. But the big decision would be between the natural or polished stone: that's what determines the lettering technique and the border, Sam repeated.

It was a confusing and painful choice made more difficult by the plastic page coverings that protected Sam's photographs from rough handling but made it difficult to tell the difference between natural and polished.

After some time we decided that the polished was best for Abe.

Then Sam pulled out his drawing pad in order to sketch out a few stones. Should we keep it simple? he asked drawing with dexterity. Usually it's the Hebrew name over the American, although we can do it the other way. What is the Hebrew name? he inquired looking up from his sketch. Avram, my aunt said tentatively.

Sam nodded and took a solemn breath. Avram above Abraham, he continued. Then comes the dates below the names; or you can have it the other way around, put Abraham over Avram. Sam was sketching it both ways, so we could make a considered decision, when my brother spoke up.

I'd like to put a fish at the top of the stone.

A fish?

Well no, not just a fish. A blue marlin. That's a very special game fish.

Celia stretched her skirt lower on her legs. She had been hoping this idea would go away.

It might be wrong, she said emotionally.

Is this fish on a line?

No, it's free. In the evening when the sun is setting, marlin sometimes jump like this. No one knows why they do it. I want the marlin leaping off the top of the stone. I'll draw the fish. And you make a stencil from my drawing. Just like these stencils of flowers here on your desk. Except this will be a leaping marlin. That's it.

Was your father in the fishing business? Sam asked, absorbing a new wrinkle in an old business.

No, my father was in the electrical business.

Sam shrugged.

Are you sure there's nothing wrong with it? my aunt asked. Nothing in the Jewish Law which says we shouldn't?

Sam seemed to be searching through the Jewish Law for the answer.

I don't know anything in the Jewish Law which says we can't put a marlin on the stone.

Are you sure, Sam? she pressed him.

There is one thing. You people decided on the polished stone. But with this fish we'll have to cut it on the natural.

———

Later that night Bill drew the blue marlin. It was a simple outline of a stout jumping fish that looked remarkably similar to marlin he began drawing as a kid in Great Neck on his school assignments. My brother had dragged the marlin of his childhood across the years and put it more or less unchanged onto the margins of his favorite books like *Madame Bovary* and *Gone with the Wind* and on the pages of rough drafts of his magazine profiles of afternoon soap stars. He also put them at the bottom of postcards from distant places to me and Dad, like a signature. To the best of my knowledge my brother stopped sketching this frisky, guileless marlin after the one he gave to Sam Canter for Dad's stone.

PART III
PUSHING SOUTH

. Stella's Books .

I WENT THROUGH DAD'S APARTMENT IN CAMBRIDGE, CAREFULLY
packing away manila folders of business letters and canceled checks
as if these trappings might contain crucial clues or someday would
bring me great pleasure. I went through his clothing and was surprised to find that his white business shirts were threadbare at the
collar and the terry-cloth bathrobe given to him by Alan Fischbach
on his birthday was worn through at the elbows. I became upset
about the bathrobe, deciding that Alan's gift had been less than top
quality.

Diran tried to persuade me that I could write and sell wiring
troughs at the same time, together we could make calls on Fischbach
and build Lee Products into a powerhouse company. I felt bad letting him down, but without Dad the family business had no allure
for me. In fact it seemed alien. I sold Dad's interest to my aunt and
uncle for a modest sum. Diran felt betrayed, I suppose. He wouldn't
talk to me after this.

Even when I was a teenager pledging to Mother that I would spend
my life selling fluorescent lighting, I felt like an oddball around Dad's
electrical contractors and union guys. I had no gift for small talk with
Alan Fischbach and Charlie Zweifel. But now, leaden and dull-witted

without my father, and despite giving up the business, I believed that Abe's connections gave me an edge.

I wanted it both ways. I coveted my father's power to pick up the phone and take care of matters, and also I wanted the license to explore subterranean worlds like writers I admired or even my brother. Settling Dad's affairs had left a void, as my so-called career at this point was mainly the desire and ambition to write—not much was coming out of me. Dad's connections were a part of my fantasy life along with the New York Knicks and fishing. I could always call the commissioner and ask him to help me out with the magazines that were sending back my stories and proposals. I sometimes imagined meeting Alan Fischbach for dinner at one of the steak joints frequented by lighting guys, soaking in the glow of being Abe's son. Abe's doctors at the Clinic, the contractors and the Commissioner were power and cachet in reserve.

Three or four months after Dad's funeral I was thrilled to receive a letter from Alan Fischbach. I expected an apology and explanation for missing the service and then some extravagant offer or invitation, which I would probably refuse, at least for the present. We'd both leave the door wide open.

In Alan's one-page typed letter he came right to the point. He said that I was a bad son who had caused my father a lot of pain. I had embarrassed my father by demonstrating against the war in Vietnam. I had fought with him up and down the line, and after his death I had let my father down by selling his business instead of going into it as Abe had desired. Alan made it crystal clear that this letter would be our final communication. He would never again speak to me in person or on the phone.

As I read these lines my face was burning. Maybe Alan was afraid that I would ask a big favor or maybe it had struck a deep chord, years before, when Dad had complained about my antiwar activities. I read Fischbach's letter again and this time noticed on the bottom left of the page the initials "KT," which stood for Kate Turner, Dad's longtime secretary whom he had passed on to Alan when Dad moved back to Boston. Kate had typed the letter, maybe she had even composed it for Fischbach. Many times Dad would give Kate a general idea of what he wanted to say and she would compose the letter herself, putting her initials on the lower left of the page. Dad was proud of her ability to write his letters and always called her a terrific secretary. I felt such shame that Kate had been a part of this. I ripped the letter up and threw it in the trash. Kate and I had spent a hundred afternoons together figuring deals and looking at blueprints.

Surely Alan had told everyone in the trade that Abe's son was a bum, an ingrate. He would have told the Commissioner. Forget any favors. I was out. Dad's friends could give you every deal in the city or they could shut you out.

There was no way to pay the upkeep, and I had to sell the big *Ebb Tide*. The fishing boat of our dreams was worth hardly anything, explained the yacht broker in Fort Lauderdale, old, slow and made of wood, while the newest generation of sportfishing boats was speedy and constructed of fiberglass, requiring much less maintenance. It was difficult to sell the boat at any price at all, like an old horse, but finally a charter skipper from North Carolina took the *Ebb Tide,* and we never saw it again. My brother made some kind remarks before leaving for his new life in Morocco, but in truth I felt hardly anything for the boat.

I wrote a few articles and taught literature classes to senior citizens. These seventy- and eighty-year-olds had much more energy than I had and the classes exhausted me. I walked the city streets like a sick man. I rarely laughed and had no interest in seeing friends.

Stella was impatient about Abe. No fond memories. He treated me like a postage stamp, she said acerbically. He stuck me on the boat or with his business cronies, wherever he wanted. Mother rushed ahead unfettered by nostalgia.

She moved into the Chelsea Hotel soon after my brother left for Tangier. For more than a century the hotel had catered to the quirky needs of artists, including Dylan Thomas, Brendan Behan, Arthur Miller, Arthur Clarke, Janis Joplin, Willem de Kooning, just to mention a few. My father wouldn't have cared about this august history. He would have felt contempt for the ungroomed, oddly dressed patrons rushing through the lobby studying manuscripts or carrying instruments or canvases up the grimy elevators to their small rooms and crucial, lonely work. Abe would have regarded the Chelsea Hotel as a freak show, and I didn't know what to think. I couldn't tell which attitudes were mine and which were his. I was out of it on my best days and even more dampened by the surfeit of art and commitment at the Chelsea.

The hotel was run by Stanley Bard, harried, materialistic and saddled with an enormous hostelry of demanding eccentrics. Racing from his office to a disaster on the fifth floor, Stanley couldn't believe what he had to put up with to earn a buck: dissipated lives, alcoholism, drugs, unusual sexual behavior, early despair and suicide. He continually surprised himself with the sympathy he felt for artists and the favors he had bestowed over the years—as if his largesse went against all reason. Stanley had been known to give painters a break on the rent or to allow them to pay a month late, and sometimes he even bartered rent for canvases and sculptures. Artists would constantly press him for better deals.

They're not like us, he would complain to me when I visited the hotel and he had me cornered in the lobby. Maybe it was my blue button-down shirts, or something on my face that told Stanley that at the core I was a businessman and wheeler-dealer like him—as if we could calm one another down or offer solace. To the best of my knowledge Stanley knew nothing of my father and my persistent yearnings to hear the talk of lighting fixture salesmen, as if this would brighten my life. He usually approached me to seek consolation about my mother.

Your mother is crazy, Stanley complained to me, as if Stella were someone else's mother.

Why do you say that, Stanley?

She never wants to pay the rent. She expects me to carry her. A couple of months ago, when I asked for money, your mother got all red in the face and I ran away from her because I was afraid she'd have a heart attack.

Every night, it seemed, police officers were in the lobby trying to deal with a soul who had gone mad or to investigate an assault or suicide. Stella was charming and conspiratorial at the edge of chaos and dissipation. She made chicken soup for me and whispered about the police in the hall on the day the critic Barry Schwartz leaped out of his fifth-floor window directly above her apartment, splattering onto 23rd Street. His huge despair was a function of his genius,

Mother explained to me as I ate her matzoh balls. Mom was friends with George Kleinsinger, the composer of "Tubby the Tuba," who lived on the top floor within a forest of tropical plants, monkeys, rare birds and large snakes. George liked to show his place off and we often visited. Around the time of Barry Schwartz's suicide, Kleinsinger's young black girlfriend was murdered, and for a week their friends drank sangría in the Quixote Bar and speculated about whether George had killed her. This didn't turn out to be the case, but the rumor was thrilling and seemed to spin writers, filmmakers and composers into months of composition. At the Chelsea life's biggest downers and disasters were first and foremost grist for the art mill.

Mom still melted glass in her kiln, no more gold, and her hi-fi poured out Coltrane, Monk, Garner, Fruscella and her musician friend Dollar Brand, who was living down the hall. For several years she had been making polyester resin sculptures of books. Books were perfect for Mom as she was foremost a storyteller and illusionist. She was allowing faces and forms to come into her work like the lyrical refrains that surfaced in the jazz of Coltrane and Monk.

She called her floor-to-ceiling living room of books "Details of a Lost Library," and on many nights writers, painters and musicians came by and perused Stella's myths, dictionaries, novels and religious texts, all of them without words; they sampled her chicken soup and chopped liver and listened to her advice about the future based upon numerology and her interpretation of the stars. Her apartment was a stimulating place to visit, even for me, although I was navigating through the night and taking bearings from Dad. I smirked like him when she read the stars for writers I respected like Claude Brown, Gregory Corso and Allen Ginsberg.

By now I admired my mother's art but I still believed that she should live a more proper and tidy life. I was able to find the energy to battle with her over issues of propriety; maybe I persisted just to feel myself alive. It bothered me that one-third of the Persian rug from Great Neck was rock-hard from resin overflow when she poured the toxic material into molds for her books. She didn't notice that she had destroyed the rug and that her apartment reeked of resin and that when she worked, the fumes drifted down the hall and drove her neighbors crazy—they beat on her door, which she found amusing, and they complained to Stanley Bard, who complained to me. I gave her a gas mask for her birthday and urged her to pour on newspapers.

When I criticized her eccentricities and sloppy habits, Mother laughed in my face. Stella insisted that great art had to be raw, immediate, gestural, ragged, emotional, uncompromising; it wasn't neat or carefully controlled or pretty. Mother also believed that art demanded pain and poverty—worldly success was the kiss of death for a serious artist. She dressed like a bag lady and never told a soul that she had spent a dozen years in Great Neck with Abe or that her father, now very old and sick, had once brightened cities and towns with his lighting fixtures. I think Mom actually convinced herself that she was dirt-poor and couldn't afford the rent. Her roots were mortifying to Stella. She felt great anger toward Abe and her father for their years of chicanery and lies, and she cultivated this rage for power and energy in her art. She was often angry with me and repeatedly called me a bullshit artist like Abe.

One evening I was sitting with Allen Ginsberg smoking grass on the ruined Persian rug. He was entranced by her books. "Words are lies, Allen," Mother said, which jolted me—he was the great musician of words. *Howl* gave me goose bumps whenever I read the first lines. Ginsberg smiled sweetly and looked around. Mother had learned how to paint within the resin and in some works, faces and stories emerged from a livid atmosphere of color, fissures and crusts. Blackened self-portraits stared up from bleeding bindings. In one book Moby Dick was decomposing, wrapped in kelp and despair; in a few volumes stillborn angels writhed under glass; there were bound pages of Bartleby's ledgers, mostly indiscernible and evoking futility. There were many tragedies and religious stories with pranks mixed in: strange fruit dripping from shelves, birds nesting in bindings, a deformed broadbill eating fat squids the color of lemons. On another wall there were rows of more or less opaque volumes where hidden details gave way to long sweeps of color like the furious paintings of the Great Neck days, and the sculptures also shared the same crusty textures and dark hues of earlier work. Also on the shelves were a few photographs of her father as a young man when he was still a laborer before Globe, a seascape my brother painted as a kid, and a couple of recent photographs of Bill with long hair and a withering stare. This environment was constantly changing as Stella tinkered and replaced volumes according to her mood. Some days the whole sweep of volumes was alive and beguiling, while other times the massive work seemed claustrophobic and dead as bones.

Allen Ginsberg had brought along a lady friend. She wasn't feeling well. She coughed throughout the long evening and didn't speak much. At one point Ginsberg drew a manuscript of new poems out of his leather briefcase and read us a half-dozen. He was delighted by Mother's bookish world and soon began playing his harmonica and singing. Then when it was time to leave, this girl started to vomit. Ginsberg paused for maybe a beat, and then he opened his briefcase with his manuscript of new poems and she vomited all over the pages while he held her head. I drove them back to the East Village and found myself wondering if Ginsberg would have sacrificed his poems if not for Mother's remarks about words. Probably.

My brother's absence paced Mother's art life. She told her friends that Bill was away writing novels and plays. Mother worked her way into this fantasy—they were both making books. She poured at night on her tiny balcony, and despite the toxic fumes she brought wet sculptures into her bedroom so she could see them with a fresh eye in the morning. She believed that things would go bad and she wouldn't be able to work when Bill came back from Morocco. Stanley Bard finally convinced her to stop pouring resin in her apartment by allowing her to use a small room in the basement of the hotel. Neither of them anticipated that the noxious fumes would rise through the air shafts and sicken half the Chelsea residents. Then Mother took refuge in the art colonies, Yaddo and MacDowell, where she could work with her toxic materials in a proper studio or outdoors. She was the first artist to have a solo show treating the book as a sculptural object. She later had many exhibitions and tributes for her work, including the Pollock-Krasner Lifetime Achievement Award. But Stella was dismissive about the trappings of success and often construed good notices or even compliments from friends as lies or slaps in the face—maybe she was afraid of losing her working anger. What truly mattered to Stella was working every day and, of course, Bill.

In Mom's bedroom in the Chelsea there was a prized photograph of Bill with a bearded friend, each of them holding five large bricks of dark-chocolate-colored hashish. They had smuggled the drugs in from Mexico and Bill would soon use his money for a new life. His friend looked goofy holding the drugs, but my brother appeared calm and resolute on the eve of great adventure. Always in Bill's adult life there was a need for danger and new beginnings pulling against an unctuous dissolute yearning for home that stuck to him like a shameful habit.

Bill was mysterious about his Tangier life and tried to manage the fragments and rumors that came to us from the Casbah. He was writing a play and taking trips into the Sahara like a character in a Paul Bowles novel. On the narrow streets of the city he wore his djellaba and passed for Moroccan or Lebanese. In this outfit I could imagine my brother feeling like royalty in disguise, a Great Neck aristocrat slumming at the Café of the Dancing Boy, smoking his bejeweled hashish pipe, watching the men play checkers while the little boy danced in regal clothes. John Clemans, my college roommate, visited Tangier and reflected afterward that in his days with my brother not much transpired but there was always the anticipation that something unusual would soon take place, something erotic or on the edge.

Bill discovered a stunning house built into a cliff two hundred feet above the Mediterranean. "From the air the house looks like a ship about to be launched," he wrote in a letter to Mother. He intended to live his life in this house above the sea.

. The Ghosts of Big Tuna .

ON BIMINI THE BLUE WATER'S DINING ROOM ON THE HILL WAS ABE'S *favorite breakfast spot, offering a luscious view of the Gulf Stream, comfortable captain's chairs, hearty meals. In the morning the room was filled with the crews and owners of sportfishing boats wolfing down big breakfasts, sharing plans for the day, checking the wind. The wind told a lot about the fishing day, particularly in the spring. Dad smoked a cigarette and looked content, which made me happy.*

My father drew conviction from the bustle and purpose of the crews, the strength of hefty anglers who pulled sandbags down the Bimini beach to train for giant bluefin tuna. When he was sitting around with the guys at breakfast his face would flush with excitement and I might punch him lightly on the shoulder; Dad would draw back his fist as if he were going to unload one on me.

One morning he and I were eating breakfast here when the room emptied of fishermen in a half-minute. One of the guys had seen a school of six-hundred-pound bluefin pushing through the light blue water right in front of the hotel. The fishing crews went racing down the hill to their boats, trying to be the first to bait the school. Dad stiffened a little as if we were missing out on the action; maybe we should go after them, crank up the Ebb Tide *and try to put a big tuna in the boat. But we weren't rigged*

*for bluefin. A little later we left the harbor and trolled for marlin a mile
or two offshore of the tuna boats. In the spring we had the whole Gulf
Stream of marlin to ourselves—the other boats were all after giant tuna.*

*In those years, when the wind blew briskly from the southwest, tremen-
dous schools of bluefin came to the surface and swam along the edge of the
Gulf Stream where you could see their massive shadows against the sand
bottom. Between May and the beginning of July hundreds of thousands of
these gigantic, graceful fish passed the Bimini Islands heading north from
Cuba and the southern cays. In the morning the finest sportfishing boats in
the world raced one another out of the Bimini harbor, creating a bedlam
of roaring engines and big churning wakes, any small boat in their way be
damned. These custom-built superfast fishing machines sprinted south
along the edge of the Stream, which was called "the alley." The captains
rode in towers thirty or forty feet above the water peering into the waves.
When a captain spotted a school he wheeled the boat around and chased
the fish full-throttle, and when he was close, a mate in the cockpit threw
over a single bait. The captain tried to pass it right in front of the fish. Usually the first boat to bait a school was the one that got a strike and the trail-
ing boats encountered wary or disinterested tuna. The competition was so
fierce to be the first to a school that captains wouldn't risk coming off the
lurching towers for a minute; they would eat lunch in big seas while holding on for life, piss in plastic bags while staring into the water for giant
shadows and fins riding down waves. Often when boats chased down
schools they cut one another off like racing cars, occasionally they collided
and there were terrible accidents with boats going down.*

*During the golden tuna days of the fifties, sixties and seventies, the mi-
grating schools seemed limitless and boats often came into the marinas
with three or four giant bluefin shoehorned into the cockpit. Occasionally
the fish swam right into the Bimini harbor and the boats hooked up six-
and seven-hundred-pounders beside the flats in shallow water and all the
local people stood on shore and watched tuna make their incomparable
runs while the anglers hauled back on rods so stout they barely bent despite the tremendous strain on backs and knees. What a show! Captains
whiplashed transmissions from forward hard into reverse chasing down
fish and frequently transmissions and engines came apart. The owners
flew in mechanics and costly new diesels from the States and the massive
engines were replaced at the dock. No expense was too great for bluefin.*

For years owners and crews of the boats debated whether or not the big fish should be boated or brought alongside and then released. "Releasing a tuna is like having a great piece of ass and not coming" was a refrain often heard from macho man anglers on the docks of Bimini and Cat Cay.

"Now the tuna don't hardly come through anymore," says James Rolle, who was the greatest of all Bimini's tuna mates, a powerful and adroit wire man who these days runs a tiny corner grocery store on the hill a little ways up from the Blue Waters dining room. "We don't need to debate anymore about releasing tuna because they're almost all gone."

Gulf Stream crossings were usually a buffer, a transition between worlds. Coming over from Florida I looked for fish and tried to let go of concerns of the city, which wasn't always easy. On some trips the fifty-mile expanse of ocean was just sloppy and cold, the water stinging our eyes all the way across. On the first trip to Bimini after Dad, the Stream was flat and hot, full of glare and fouled from days of stillness. There were no fish in this ocean. We felt drugged out there, hopeless.

The twenty-footer was weighed down by a thousand pounds of food, bait, Dad's heavy rods and reels that I had taken off the big *Ebb Tide*, luggage, supplies for Bimini friends, an air conditioner, a small freezer for the little shack we had rented in Porgy Bay and also by malaise and hospital memories. We had no freeboard and any big breaking sea would have washed over the bow and filled the boat. I steered through thick ridges of seaweed and had to shut her down a half-dozen times to unwind warm slimy weed from the prop. It was dangerous to cross with such a heavy load, but there was no sea to speak of. The water was rotten and listless and there was no hump.

A customs official noticed us cruising through the harbor mouth at dusk. He hauled us into the station and accused us of smuggling supplies onto the island at night to avoid paying duty. He was right. I paid the fine.

The first days back the ocean seemed lonely and I couldn't imagine which way to head, north or south, who cares. Pulling baits across the calm water I felt as if I had fled New York and all the reasonable choices and ambitions of adulthood. My shaky writing career atomized in the insufferable midday heat. Bonnie moped and complained about the sun burning her skin and that we were spending all of our money to catch fish. But we couldn't catch a fish. Barracudas wouldn't strike my baits. We argued and I hardly cared if the baits were dragging clumps of seaweed. The heat wave and becalmed ocean worked against us.

My friend Craig came out with us and agreed with Bonnie that fishing was pointless. I tried to will myself back into the ocean. While I watched the baits Craig chain-smoked and mulled over his future. He was no longer running the boat for Judy Hammond. Day after day he wore the same chinos and work shirt. Craig was basically homeless, sleeping here or there, sometimes on our sofa.

Maybe it was the third or fourth day on the island, we were trolling in front of the harbor mouth at about five in the evening. The ocean was slick calm and blinding with glare, the worst conditions for billfishing, where you want some white water for skipping baits. I looked toward the shore and saw a mast, I thought it was a mast, about four or five hundred yards off. But it was curved like a dorsal fin. Much too tall for a fin, but I eased the boat in that direction. It was three times the height of any marlin fin I had ever seen before and splintered at the top from battle or perhaps age. I trolled a bait in front of this mythic fish, it must have been fifteen or sixteen feet long, but the marlin never stopped moving to the north. It had no interest in our bait and, of course, we could never have landed such a creature. Eventually the fish started to go down but very slowly. After a few minutes I could still see the tip of the dorsal, and even after it slipped under, the marlin made a rippling wake on the surface. On Bimini we described this two-thousand-pounder to a couple of the captains of the big fishing boats, but they considered Bonnie and me rank amateurs telling fish stories.

A few days later the weather turned and we headed offshore into a stiff breeze and a four-foot head sea. We were wet from spray and invigorated by the new weather. Schools of baby flying fish broke off the tops of waves like shattering glass. A few flying fish landed on the gunwale and Bonnie tossed them over. It was hard to stay in the boat in the breaking sea but it was fun. On Bimini the wind can change everything. In the afternoon we hooked a couple of dolphin on feathers.

Ocean fishing in the twenty-footer was gritty and basic, especially when the wind was blowing. We went to the bathroom over the gunwale, got our asses wet from the white water. We trolled big bonefish and mackerel through valleys of ocean, turned into big breakers to avoid broaching or steered away from head seas when we could get away with it. To keep from being tossed over, we held on or braced against the gunwale while we rigged a live bonito. It was a whole day of isometric exercises. We were sore from banging against the steering wheel, the side of the console or the reels. If the fishing was good we were covered with slime and wet all day, literally a step away from the waves. It was a different life than on the bridge of a big sportfishing boat, where you could put your feet up like a tourist.

Maybe ten days into the trip Bonnie hooked a small marlin and fought it standing up wearing a belly harness. She had the hundred-pounder alongside in a half hour. I wired it without difficulty and then Bonnie leaned over the side and snatched the bill of the fish in her two hands. She reached with one hand to pull the hook out and continued to tow the fish alongside to force water through its gills until the marlin got back its strength and then she let it go. Bonnie didn't worry about getting yanked over or speared. She'd left all of her fears in New York. We'd caught our first marlin by ourselves in the twenty-footer. The following day we caught a sailfish and had another chance at a marlin.

Sometimes the ocean just opens up, reveals itself. All of a sudden there's no more resistance or dead water, the clues are sharp and urgent. Color changes, wind and weed lines, edges of storms and tidal rips are fresh trails. You move ahead like a scout, body tingling and sweating, no more small talk with wives and friends, just listening to the seabirds, watching each dip and flutter—the birds will show where to put the baits. In such moments I can smell fish, and even the first time this sensation felt familiar. When a captain is in a zone he can fill his boat while other fishermen are hardly getting a strike. I've seen it many times.

That summer we learned to catch permit, a tough-fighting, platter-shaped fish, by casting crabs on the deep flats and channels around Sandy Cay, twenty miles south of Bimini. To the north of the island we used a downrigger and trolled for kingfish. We brought in two over eighty pounds. We caught a fifty-pound African pompano.

After we ate it and threw away the carcass, someone told me that it was almost surely a world record. That fish gave us both ciguatera poisoning, aching joints and a little nausea, but we kept fishing.

I discovered that I had this knack for finding fish; more and more I could anticipate the strikes before they happened. But I wasn't good at the mechanical side of the sport. Craig kept our engine running, and Bonnie charmed captains and mates on the dock to teach her the best knot to use for double lines or the newest way to rig bonito for live baiting.

All the kids in Porgy Bay urged us to register for the annual Native Fishing Tournament, the biggest event of the summer. Winners were the toast of Bimini. But frankly I had no interest in fishing tournaments and dreaded the appearance of hundreds of Florida boats on the island. Fishing as a competition seemed off the mark.

I enjoyed our solitary fishing day, getting up late in the morning, rigging for the afternoon and leaving the dock around two. By four o'clock the local charter boats were headed back in and we were usually the only boat pulling baits off the north end of the island. Even in my twenties I didn't mind lulls in the action, and fantasies were a big part of my fishing. As the summer wore on, the success of an individual day hardly registered as the weeks blended and New York malaise disappeared. But don't get me wrong, we caught fish. One day Bonnie hooked ten marlin and brought five to the side of the boat. You couldn't help catching fish off Bimini.

By now we were feeding the Porgy Bay community with our kingfish, dolphin, grouper, tuna and cero mackerel. I was learning all the best drops around the island and the cays to the south. Even when we were trolling for marlin I came in on the edge for an hour in the afternoon to catch fish for the Porgy Bay kids to take home to their families.

In the evening skinny Dick Davis climbed on board chortling while he took a look in our fish box. He was talking to himself that summer but would interrupt an argument or admonition to say something about our fishing—some little advice from another world. While I was washing down the boat Minnie would sit on the dock, her legs dangling toward the water, her skirt pulled up on her thighs. We all know what a Dick can do, she'd recall with a twinkle while her lost love sat at the end of the dock wearing ragged shorts, mumbling or laughing. Then she'd slowly nod at the inexorable passing of all things—her kids growing up and moving out; her poor walls and roof blowing down around their beds while Dick spent days on the porch poring through volumes of Melville and Shakespeare, sometimes crying.

At dusk ten or twelve kids set off for home carrying fish in the air—the smaller ones dragging a dolphin or kingfish along the dirt road across the baseball field to their houses on the hill.

Craig would occasionally come by the dock holding a beer but he was spending more and more time with Jeff and Wendy, who rented a little house fifty yards north of ours. Jeff was a terrific diver. Usually he worked the Turtle Rocks just south of Bimini, free diving for big groupers and snappers in seventy feet of water while she ran the boat in her ribbon bikini. They adored one another. A couple of times Jeff invited us over and barbecued a big snapper stuffed with crawfish. Someone mentioned that they were making their money racing marijuana across the Stream at night to a house in Fort Lauderdale. I was doing the best fishing of my life and didn't pay much attention.

Every year there were a half-dozen tournaments on the island offering trophies, substantial cash prizes, but most important, bragging rights: which was the top boat, the best captain, the most skillful angler. These events were cutthroat competitions featuring all the elite crews and million-dollar fish boats from up and down the East Coast. The biggest of all the events was the Bimini Native Fishing Tournament, which was held each August. As many as three hundred boats glutted the Bimini harbor for the tournament—you couldn't find an empty slip or hotel room on the island. There was a bonefish class, a big boat division, and a division for boats under twenty-five feet. We were badgered into registering for the small boat division by the Porgy Bay kids, who boasted on Brown's dock that we would win. It was embarrassing.

Everyone on the island knew the favorites—the same boats took top places year after year. Some of the owners and captains bet big bucks against one another in side competitions called calcuttas. Among them were skippers I had known a decade earlier at the Montauk Yacht Club, where I had gained notoriety for sinking a borrowed skiff with my brother. Dad had revered these peripatetic skippers, almost like the surgeons at the Clinic, and was always trying to hire one cheap to guide his *Ebb Tide* to mako and marlin.

In the bonefish division my old friend Ansil Saunders was the favored captain. Bonefish Cordell sought to wrest away the title, but year after year Ansil Saunders came away with the first-place trophy.

At seven A.M. of the first day hundreds of boats of all sizes left the dock and jockeyed for position to go through the harbor mouth. I worried about getting trammeled by a fifty-footer before we even got into the open ocean. By eight o'clock this flotilla crowded the best water to the north of the island like Sheepshead Bay on a Saturday in summer. We knew that we had no chance competing against the top fish hawks from Florida. Bonnie and I trolled far to the north, trying to stay away from the fleet. It was our plan to fish short hours and enjoy the parties in the evening.

The first day the ocean was lumpy, weather was headed our way. We didn't catch a thing until about two in the afternoon when I noticed some working birds. I trolled beneath them and Bonnie caught a few blackfin tuna. Usually after a couple of passes a school of tuna will go down and the birds will rise high in the air searching until the fish come up again or disappear for good. This school stayed right on top feeding on small bait. There were no other boats within a half-mile and we had them to ourselves. I trolled around and around the breaking tuna and Bonnie hooked them on feathers. After two hours, when it was time to pull in the lines, we had about twenty fish in the boat.

All the boats weighed in their catch at Brown's Marina. A big crowd of locals were waiting on the dock dancing to junkanoo music coming from the patio. It was exciting to see all the fish and to speculate who had the early lead and figured to win thousands in the calcutta. The mates in the cockpits of the forty-footers stuck out their chests after tossing a nice sailfish or wahoo on the dock. Natives romanced their favorite captains for beers and fish to take home and put in their freezers. Fish were the harvest of the island and everyone went home happy. But first each fish was weighed and points were awarded depending on the species, with marlin, bonefish, tuna and wahoo getting premium points and barracuda and groupers getting smaller numbers of points per pound.

At the end of the first day the top boat in the small boat division was the *Ebb Tide*. None of the Florida guys knew anything about this twenty-footer, a two-person operation with a small lady angler who doubled as mate. No woman had ever won the small boat division of the Native Fishing Tournament.

I knew that our early lead was luck. I'd stumbled across a school of tuna that had committed suicide. But first place confers a responsibility. That night I couldn't fall asleep trying to figure out how we could keep pace with the top boats.

On the second day the wind was blowing twenty-five out of the southeast. It was rough, and most of the boats fished in front of the island, which offered a lee, or up to the north, which was best for marlin. I decided to run to Sandy Cay, twenty miles to the south. I knew that no other boats in our division would want to take a beating going so far. It took us more than two hours to get there pounding into six-foot head seas. It was a gamble. Running so far meant much less time for fishing.

There were no other boats within sight and we put out our baits above ledges seventy feet down that looked like lush green hills in the clear water on calmer mornings. In those days fishermen rarely traveled to the reefs and atolls stringing to the south of Sandy Cay. The waters were alive with hungry fish unused to seeing rigged baits or lures. Almost immediately a big kingfish leaped high into the air and pounced on a ballyhoo. After a dogged fight Bonnie landed the forty-pounder.

All morning the fishing was red-hot and Bonnie often had hookups on all three lines. Schools of mackerel and jacks flashed at the baits. Wahoo and kings were hitting before we could get ballyhoo twenty feet behind the boat and the surface feeding incited an army below. Sometimes she couldn't get a big grouper into the boat before it was ripped off the hook by barracudas and sharks. Once she was pulling a mackerel over the side when a cuda leaped after it and landed in the cockpit. Then it jumped back into the water. My job was mainly to find the fish and pull them aboard with the gaff. Bonnie cranked the reels and took fish off the hook, rigged leaders, tried to keep slime off the deck so we wouldn't go over the side. After a couple of hours we had no more bait, but it didn't matter: cero mackerel and wahoo hit feathers and even bare hooks. We filled the box with mackerels, hefty groupers, barracuda, kings and wahoo. By the end of the second day we were exhausted and still held a lead over a hundred thirty boats.

During the last two days of the tournament, competitors from Florida shadowed us to the southern cays. There were several boats fishing nearby and they followed us from one atoll or reef to the next. The boats were bigger, more commodious and far more efficient than we were. In each of them an angler sat all day in a canopied fighting chair cranking fish while the captain steered and a hired mate rigged baits and leaders, unhooked fish and carefully laid them in coolers, handed out sodas. We were helter-skelter and had fish flopping on the deck.

Going into the last day we had fallen behind one of the Florida boats. Again, it was a rough sea and the fish were hitting. The lead boat appeared to be doing better than we were, but I couldn't really be certain while trying to help Bonnie and then jumping back to the wheel to get turned around before we took a wave in the cockpit. I would never have guessed the way this tournament had possessed me. Bonnie and I fished without a break until the late afternoon, when our lines became tangled and we were completely out of rigs. I was furious at the men in the other boats who pulled their lines over my secret drops. We drifted around for three-quarters of an hour watching our competition boat fish while we tried to put things in order.

Later that night at the awards ceremony Ansil Saunders took first place in the bonefish division. Each year Ansil won the tournament as though it were preordained and would always be this way. We were talking to Ansil when Bonnie was called to the podium.

My young wife won best-angler prize ahead of all the men, just barely edging out the top-scoring Florida boat. Now and again I look at the color photograph taken that night of Bonnie holding her huge trophy and cup. I am standing beside her with a shit-eating smile clutching a much smaller trophy awarded to the top captain.

. *Square Grouper* .

IN NEW YORK, IN THE LATE SEVENTIES, I WAS MAKING A BELATED *run at adulthood and career, but the ruins of our family were inescapable and even beguiling. My grandfather was spending dying afternoons with his venerable lawyers. The great factory was gone, turned into thick trusts and wills and massive legal bills. But the senior law partners called him I.R. with the old snap as if he might still mount the great Cadillac and put things in order.*

One afternoon when I visited my grandfather on 73rd Street, he was in a deep lethargy in front of the TV, a few white hairs blown by a breeze off the river. Suddenly he roused himself and remarked, "Mister, your father did terrible things. Terrible." I pressed him to tell me. I was hungry for any scrap about my dad, but he shook his head. "He was your father. I don't want to poison your mind against him." This was not possible, but Grandpa wouldn't say another word about Abe.

My mother was sculpting her ancient texts from resin, her anger toward me hardening as Bill defiantly plunged into illness and drugged oblivion. She blamed me for Bill's decline. I never understood this. She would say to me, "You're smart, like Abe. You can figure out what to do." But I didn't have the answers.

A couple of times a week I visited my brother, who was now living in a Manhattan apartment amid the broken furniture, old fish mounts and sundry objects of Great Neck years, when he had contemplated dinosaurs and ninety-foot sharks. Bill now walked with a list and spoke with slurred words. Each time I came to visit he asked me which button switched on his new VCR, he couldn't keep it straight. I kept thinking that my brother could turn his life around; it was a simple question of will. I urged him to stop eating pills from the street and watching old Godzilla movies over and over, poring through photo albums of Liz Taylor and afternoon soap stars of the fifties. My brother's rooms were suffocating with dust and recycled memories. I couldn't wait to get out of his apartment. Through the thickness he smiled at me—there is nothing you can do about my choices, kid. The next day or three days later I'd get a phone call from the bank across from his building, my brother was on the floor mumbling to himself. I took him home from the bank, put him back on the black leather sofa from the Great Neck house. I was angry at him. Bill smiled at me sweetly, his slurred words, "The ship is sinking, kid. The bow is going under."

In the days following the Bimini Native Fishing Tournament we were the heroes of Porgy Bay. The kids held running races in our honor and talked incessantly about next year's tournament, when we would surely win again and bring more glory to Porgy Bay. Every year we would be champions, they believed, like the great Ansil Saunders. And so it was a big surprise when we came back to the island the following July and discovered that the children of Porgy Bay had lost interest in our fishing exploits. Once again we rented Charlie Rolle's little house and trolled long afternoons through the month of July. But only a few of the children stopped by in the evening to take fish home to their families. Since our last visit the culinary taste of Porgy Bay had undergone a change. Locals claimed to be bored with fish and were shopping at King Brown's grocery store for chickens. Even Minnie Davis bought chicken from King Brown, who each week imported crates of frozen meat and poultry from Florida.

Bimini had entered a building boom, with scores of cinder-block houses and several hotels in various states of construction. One man was putting up a three-story mansion on the bay and was dredging a small harbor for his new fleet of boats. In the bay there were a dozen new and costly twin-screw ocean speedboats moored or tied up at small docks. In the evening the young men of the island roared their new boats up and down the inside channel, disturbing old-timers handlining for snappers in skiffs and throwing big wakes up on conch piles and sandy backyards. There were a half-dozen shiny new cars on the island, big four-door sedans suitable for a limo service in Manhattan. Fishermen cruised the cars up and down the three-mile stretch of road with windows closed, air conditioners whirring and stereos pumping out Barry White or Marvin Gaye. There was a wildness in the air, new chances, Bimini men strutting and making deals at the edge of the bay.

When I trolled offshore with Bonnie I occasionally turned on the radio to hear what the other captains were catching. There was the normal palaver about the water looking dead or some boat breaking off a nice marlin but also Bimini skippers would ask one another if they had seen any "square grouper." On the bay in the evening conch and lobster fishermen reported snaring square grouper on the banks to the east of the island; and the young men who owned the sleek new speedboats were hunting exclusively for this new breed off the southern cays where Bonnie and I had prospered the previous summer winning the Native Tournament. "Square grouper" was the name locals used for sixty-pound bales of marijuana. Square grouper had become the fish of choice on this small Bahamian island.

Almost everyone on Bimini was making money off the refuse of a new delivery route used by the Colombian drug trade. Many nights planes from Central America and the southern Bahamas flew close to Bimini and dumped bales of marijuana into the ocean. Standing by below were fast, expensive speedboats with Colombians brandishing automatic weapons on the lookout for DEA helicopters and U.S. Coast Guard cutters. When the plastic-covered bundles dropped from the sky, the men quickly loaded them on the boats and raced across the Gulf Stream headed for safe houses in southeast Florida. Invariably during these nervous night transfers, bales of marijuana were lost and floated north toward Great Isaac lighthouse or east onto the Bahamas bank, depending on the wind and tide. There were nights when Colombian planes running low on fuel weren't able to locate the waiting boats and jettisoned their entire cargo into Bimini waters, hundreds of bales.

Every morning the Bimini fleet of small boats that had formerly supplied local restaurants with conch, lobster and grouper now hunted exclusively for floating bales of marijuana. There was such an abundance that you didn't even need a boat. Like the giant bluefin tuna during Abe's years, there were days when scores of bales came right into the Bimini harbor with the tide; the wealth of Solomon bobbed in front of the Big Game Club, the Blue Water Marina or the power company; sometimes bales became tangled in the mangroves or they tumbled up onto the beach in the surf. It was common to see men, women, children, dockhands, pastors, laundry ladies wading into the lagoon pulling out waterlogged bales.

During the first year or two of the drug prosperity, everything was out in the open. Men who owned trucks rented them for top prices to lucky fishermen who came to the town dock with a big catch, and I once saw three or four of the Porgy Bay kids struggling to push a heavy bale across the baseball field to their shack on the hill. Bimini ladies dried soggy grass on their back porches or on the sun-bleached roofs of their little homes and sold it to a few hippie smugglers in Porgy Bay or to my friend Craig. The ladies felt graced by marijuana. At last they could buy all of the dreamy appliances of modern life. One summer Sunday services came to an abrupt halt at churches on the hill when parishioners noticed thousands of pounds of marijuana floating in the beautiful light blue water twenty yards off the beach. Everyone raced out of the pews to collect bales and one seventy-year-old lady called after her grandchildren to bring her home a share. "If God made it, it must be good," she reflected. Indeed, ministers on Bimini had stashes of marijuana. The new churches were the sturdiest structures on the island and during hurricane season their basements were rented out as safe houses for grass.

"Smuggling is ninety percent boredom, punctuated by moments of sheer terror," said Craig, quoting Henri de Monfreid. Craig had set up his ragged operation at the old Bimini Hotel on the southern end of the island, where my brother and his German shepherd had once lived on the top floor writing his romantic thriller, *Rogue Shark*. But the rooms in the hotel were no longer suitable for guests and the breezy top floors with a wonderful view of the changing sea were now open to the weather.

Most evenings Craig sat alone at a derelict bar on the downstairs floor manning the phone and looking out the harbor mouth at the sunset or glancing at his thirty-foot Chris Craft, which was tied casually with a single line to a broken piling. It amused him to watch the boat come around 180 degrees with the tide without touching the seawall, or if it banged a few times, so what. Craig was no yachtsman. The boat's windshield was cracked from hairy night crossings in twelve-foot seas, and there were empty Heineken bottles rolling on the deck. The thirty-footer looked like it belonged in a junkyard, but it was powered by 350-horsepower Crusaders and could run at thirty-five knots under a full load. It was named the *M.S.T.*—moments of sheer terror—and beneath the fiberglass deck were secret compartments Craig had built for storing up to a thousand pounds of marijuana.

Craig was slight of build with long sun-bleached hair and a face gaunt from little food and long drinking days. He had allowed a bushy mustache to fall over his mouth, partly obscuring bad teeth. When I was around Craig I often thought of my father. Maybe it was Craig's alcoholism and emaciated body, his mechanical excellence. He kept my boat running. I felt safe when he was around.

In his new incarnation Craig enjoyed having a wad of big bills in his pocket, pretending to be a player drinking at the Compleat Angler. But mostly Craig believed that his smuggling life was hilarious, and his biggest and best deals were crafted for garish audacity more than maximum profit. Craig was a gentle man and could never have survived as a drug kingpin in New York or Miami, but on Bimini he was intrigued by the absurdity of turtle fishermen harvesting marijuana on the bank, of pastors and little kids searching the mangroves for bales.

Funny, Abe had always suspected that natives were smoking grass, or tea, as he called it, twenty years before they had ever heard of marijuana. Craig made good bargains because in the early months of the trade, locals hadn't learned what the foul-smelling stuff was worth. Sometimes he allowed bales to accumulate on the patio while he drank beer, unconcerned that a drunk might run off with one.

Eventually he loaded the bales on a dolly and pushed them down the road to a broken shed next to Chalk's Flying Service, a stone's throw from a little house on the water's edge where Hemingway had once composed chapters of *Islands in the Stream.* Usually Craig's marijuana was damp from floating in saltwater and it smelled like cow manure. If there was a breeze from the south, the stench from the shed carried up the road toward the marinas. Craig paid the local police to ignore the smell. Even the most proper citizens handed money to the officers, encouraging them to spend the day napping on the second-story porch of the police station, which had a splendid view of the bonefish flats and mangroves.

Whenever Craig had collected a thousand pounds or was in the right mood, he loaded the compartments of the *M.S.T.,* fitted back the fiberglass deck and headed out the harbor mouth into the night ocean for Lauderdale. The *M.S.T.* was a wet boat when loaded down with marijuana. For hours crossing the black Gulf Stream he was drenched and looking out for the lights of Coast Guard cutters patrolling the fifty-mile stretch to Florida. A few times when they spotted him, Craig gambled and raced the patrol boats to the coast, lost them in the winding intracoastals north of Fort Lauderdale. Other times he gambled, allowing seamen holding guns to come alongside and search the *M.S.T.*

"If you were with me when the Coast Guard came on board, I'd be nervous," he said to me. "They could see the fear in your eyes. You're no smuggler. . . . When I'm by myself I invite the young men on board and offer them a beer, urge them to look anywhere they want. If you play it cool or if you really don't care what happens, they won't look very hard or they won't look at all. The truth is that some days I really don't care if they catch me. If I'm thrown into jail, I'll read some good books for a year."

Craig pushed the envelope. He had a deep boredom and needed the fix of outrageous dares. One day he was approached by the head of Bimini immigration who said that he had a cousin living on Ragged Island, three hundred miles to the south, who had a ton of Colombian gold perfectly dry—it had never even been in the water. Craig wasn't set up for transporting a ton of marijuana from Ragged

Island, but it tickled him to work in partnership with the head of immigration—a few months earlier this tedious stern-faced official had wanted to ship Craig off Bimini.

Craig might have rented the mail boat or any one of a half-dozen cruisers on Bimini that could easily carry enough fuel for such a trip and would blend into the seascape of the quiet southern Bahamas, but instead he approached a veteran pilot who flew the big Chalk's seaplane into Bimini each afternoon. In the Bahamas Chalk's was a virtual icon of safe, reliable transportation. Craig offered the pilot five thousand dollars to fly the drugs, and when the man agreed, Craig traveled to the Chalk's terminal on MacArthur Causeway in Miami to charter the plane and pilot for a day of sightseeing in the Bahamas. Craig was entranced with the idea of this lumbering big craft that everyone recognized landing next to a rickety dock on Flamenco Cay in the Ragged Island chain and loading up with bales.

It was Craig's plan for the pilot to pick up the bales on Ragged Island and then Craig would meet the Chalk's seaplane in the *M.S.T.* on the flats south of the lavish resort island of Cat Cay. That's what happened, except there were a few complications. When the seaplane arrived from Ragged Island, the evening sea was choppy and it was exhausting work lifting bales onto the Chris Craft, which was tied up to the seaplane's pontoon. There was much too much marijuana to store in Craig's secret compartments, so the bales were all over the deck and piled floor to ceiling in the small salon. Craig had forgotten to bring a broom. The pilot tried to clean the plane with his fingers, but it was hopeless and he went back to Miami dirty with seeds and sticks.

Craig was too tired to run across and he spent the night anchored near a half-dozen trawler yachts in the lee of Cat Cay, where Vanderbilts and Rockefellers owned homes and Richard Nixon often visited his pal Bebe Rebozo. Craig slept in the cockpit on top of the bales. In the morning he plowed across the Gulf Stream, too heavy to make any speed with the marijuana in full view. If a Coast Guard helicopter or plane had passed over he would have gone directly to jail. Craig pulled up to a house he had rented for the day in Key Biscayne. There was supposed to be an adjacent boathouse where he could transfer the marijuana into a waiting van, but there was no boathouse.

Craig and another man hustled the bales across the lawn and piled them into the van with a few neighbors watching. Then he raced the *M.S.T.* back to Bimini.

So much money floating in the ocean had changed the essence of Bimini life. Fishermen no longer worried about the declining bluefin run or whether wahoo would arrive in the fall. The enormous diesel generators in the power plant were idle much of that summer because mechanics were searching for grass in skiffs, and Donnie Marie, the plant manager, was flying around the out islands in a small plane trying to buy a ton of grass cheap to make a killing like Craig. Biminites purchased brand-new appliances, although there was no electrical power. They imported Honda generators, which powered VCRs, big-screen TVs and powerful stereos. Up and down the island little generators screeched through the night like buzz saws.

Bonnie and I kept fishing. I had never had so much energy for fishing, as if this shearing away of tradition had raised the stakes for me. I needed to be out there pulling baits and looking for color changes and birds, feeling the movement of the boat. Three or four times a week, after trolling much of the day, I'd come back to Porgy Bay, take a shower and suggest to Bonnie that we should spend the night catching mutton snapper or chumming for yellowtail off South Cat Cay. When there was no sea running, she loved spending nights on the water away from the screech of generators. Sometimes we headed way offshore and dropped baits deep for broadbill swordfish. While we drifted north in soft swells Bimini to the east looked like a few blinking stars.

In our second Native Tournament there were fewer entries by a third as some Florida fishermen were scared away by articles in the *Miami Herald* about drug smuggling on Bimini. The tournament was still quite large, about two hundred boats, but there was far less energy and conviction for fishing. Crowds were no longer waiting on Brown's dock to admire the catch and to bring fish home for the freezer. Biminites had more important things to do. Sadly, many fish were wasted, kicked back into the water for the sharks.

During party nights on shore, booze and money talk incited Florida skippers, even men who ran million-dollar Rybovich and Merritt fish boats, who grunged up to Bimini lowlifes trying to buy cheap bales to bring home. A couple of bales hidden in the bilge could pay for a Mercedes or a year's college tuition for a kid. In the morning, while the Florida guys trolled baits, they asked one another on the radio about sighting any unusual grouper. A few got lucky.

Bonnie and I pushed resolutely to the south. Once again the wind was blowing up big seas, but we traveled even farther from Bimini exploring reefs and deep drops south of a remote atoll called South Riding Rock. This year it was much harder fishing for all the boats. The marlin were scarce and during the intervening months a fleet of Cuban fishing boats had wiped out the thirty-mile string of reefs south of Cat Cay. The surviving fish had grown wiser, it seemed, but we coaxed some strikes using the downrigger and a few northern lures I'd brought to try in the Bahamas.

Bonnie had become a great angler. She was now better than I was, more reliable on the strikes and strong, too. I loved the Riding Rock days without any boats in sight, trying out new ideas, but at Brown's dock we both felt guilty weighing in wahoo, kings and grouper without our rooting section of Porgy Bay kids waiting to carry home the catch. None of our friends were focused on the tournament. Dick Davis was keeping to himself and Craig was in Jamaica doing business. Bonnie won the top angler prize for the second year in a row— I was best captain—a rare encore performance that played to a half-empty house.

One day in the middle of August scores of bales were floating near the pristine bathing beach just down from the cemetery on the hill near Minnie's house in Porgy Bay. All the boys who used to wait for us on Charlie Rolle's dock jumped into the sea and collected fortunes; wriggly three-year-olds without underwear splashed into the ocean to help their big brothers pull at the black garbage bags. Minnie's beautiful thirteen-year-old daughter stood on the beach. Ava couldn't swim a stroke. All of this money floating in front of her and Ava didn't have pretty clothes or a radio to listen to music. She ran into the ocean and threw herself onto a bale as if it were a life preserver. One of the bigger boys wrestled her off and she almost drowned in the placid water. On the beach she screamed at the boy, "I can't swim, can't fuck'n swim. I risked my life. Give it back." He was ashamed and gave it back to her. The Davis family dried the bale on their back porch. A policeman came around and was going to take it away but Minnie thought to hand him an envelope. Ava got eight thousand dollars for her bale.

Dick Davis didn't have the energy to look for marijuana. He sat on the porch in his T-shirt, reading and sometimes crying. He believed that he was placed on earth for bigger things than doing yard work or maybe a little house painting, but he didn't know what; and the children collecting fortunes on the beach deepened his sense of futility. A few nights Dick flew into a rage and beat Minnie and she ran to a neighbor's. When she came back to the little shack the following morning, he asked her like a child, "Dear, what did you buy for me to eat?"

In his patient voice Dick explained to Minnie he would look for drugs on the bank if he still had his skiff, a beautiful sloop with an outboard on the transom. Three years before the boat had been stolen. "I lost everything," he said to Minnie. He had looked everywhere for it, even traveled to Miami and walked the docks along the Miami River, no luck. After that Dick became impotent.

"What are you laughing about, dear?" he called to her from the porch.

"Would you rather see me laugh or cry?" Minnie would respond.

While Dick sat on the porch watching or reading one of his great books, Porgy Bay was booming. Nearly all the homes were replaced or improved by drug money, but the Davis family only sold the one bale and all the kids and grandkids needed something. Several of the Porgy Bay teenagers with fast boats made many thousands and built lavish homes with imported shrubbery and private docks where they tied up their boats. They built concrete walls and guarded their pocket estates with vicious dogs.

Dick began suffering excruciating headaches. He'd reach for *Don Quixote* or *Lord Jim* and press the volume down on his skull. Ava came home from school to find Daddy grimacing under a book. When she switched on the television inside, he screamed, "Turn it off, I don't want to hear that." Then a few minutes later in a sweet voice, "Minnie, dear, you must come and read this." Minnie was inside sweeping and tending her pot of crabs and rice. From the porch he tried to interest her in a passage from *Don Quixote,* but she didn't have time for that.

"Dear, are you jealous of me?" he called to her through the broken pane of glass. "I'm not talking to you. I'm living in another world." A few minutes later, "Dear, let me kiss you. I just want to kiss you." Minnie didn't answer but she giggled at his foolishness.

In the evening Minnie carried water from Charlie Rolle's well and heated it for Dick's bath. She put clean sheets on his bed, rubbed lotion on his skinny legs. She did what she could until they were both frustrated.

In the middle of the night he was back on the porch, feeling the offshore breeze and calling to her through the broken glass. "Dear, I just want to kiss you. I love you, dear." Minnie pretended to be asleep.

"Dear, I could put you in my lap and cut your throat and you couldn't do a thing."

At the end of August, a week before Bonnie and I ran the little boat back across the Gulf Stream and trailed it north with Dad's Buick, Dick Davis died of a stroke. That was our last summer in Porgy Bay. The following year Charlie Rolle found a permanent tenant for his cottage, and Bonnie and I weren't able to rent a house on North Bimini. Maybe it was time to find new waters. We took a small plane and visited Chub Cay and the out islands, San Salvador, Cat Island, Long Island. We discovered rustic marinas where men were openly discussing marijuana, making deals, moving bales north to Bimini or directly to Florida in planes and boats. No one was talking fishing.

. *The Colombians* .

ON OUR LAST FISHING TRIP WITH ABE, BONNIE AND I JOINED HIM *in Fort Lauderdale and we took a small plane to the tiny island of Chub Cay, about a hundred miles east of Bimini. The* Ebb Tide *was waiting for us at the private marina along with a young man who was running her for Dad, Don Lash. I had long wanted to take the big* Ebb Tide *and fish one of the more remote southern islands. Off Chub, boats used live lobster for bait and caught hundred-pound cubera snapper—wild.*

But we found the Ebb Tide *broken down at the dock. Don couldn't get the port engine to fire. He was covered with grease and he looked beaten. Abe took off his white business shirt and climbed onto the engine, pulling off wires and testing with his meter. He had been ill, his face gaunt and very stern. After a half hour he signaled with his hand for me to go onto the bridge and hit the starter. She turned over. Dad made a disgusted expression—why do I have to do everything? He sent Bonnie for cigarettes, sat in the salon with smirks and sent us scurrying: find my lighter, my slippers, buy J&B, pick up the galley.*

The following morning we fished near the island. It was rough and overcast. I ran the boat all day and we never had a strike, no birds. As we approached the dock, Dad came out from the salon where he had been resting, tapped against the ladder with his cigarette lighter, to say, let

Don bring her in. I said, that's okay, I'll do it. Dad widened his eyes, and I turned away from him, looked at the dock. I had never brought her into a slip by myself. The wind was blowing about twenty and sweat began running down my sides. Maybe I'd bang her up. Fuck it.

I spun the Ebb Tide *around and backed her in, pulled the transmissions in and out of gear, compensating for the wind, put her right between the pilings. It wasn't hard. I'd been practicing in my head for ten years. I tried not to look at his face.*

The following morning the port engine wouldn't start and Dad was back in the bilge with his tools. The big diesels were still hot from the previous day's running. His chest was sweaty. I don't know where he found the strength to pull the wrenches. I should have been able to do this for him, but I didn't know how. He worked on the engine for hours but he couldn't figure the problem. He was choking and dizzy when he climbed out. His anger spread all over the boat.

Don and I decided to leave for Fort Lauderdale on one engine. Abe was below, smoldering. We tried to pretend he wasn't there. In the late afternoon we moved slowly across the shallow Bahama bank, a seventy-mile stretch where the translucent water is rarely deeper than ten feet— on calm days from the bridge it's like peering into the world's largest fish tank. I stayed on the bridge with Don trying to admire skiddering sharks and cudas, enjoy the breeze, trying to forget him, but I couldn't. He had this pull, could make your world come apart.

About ten o'clock at night we could see the light from Gun Cay, twelve miles off, it was blowing twenty-five and building. We kept coming ahead. By the time we apprached Gun, it was blowing a gale out of the east. The wind was behind us and on the starboard quarter, throwing the boat ahead into bucking seas. It felt reckless running into blackness and tumult. Don steered and I held a flashlight on the compass and watched the Fathometer. I went down below and took a glance. Abe was slowly chewing a boiled potato. He didn't say a word. I told Bonnie to come onto the bridge.

We decided to go through the cut between Cat Cay and Gun, hoping that on the north side of the Bimini Islands we would find some protection from the wind. But with only one engine we were getting nudged toward the reef that runs north a couple of hundred yards between Cat Cay and the deep passage alongside Gun. Too dangerous. We should turn around and beat back into the gale. It was too late. Without a port engine we couldn't get around in time against the wind and seas—we'd wash broadside onto the reef. Don steered for the cut, but there was only thirty yards of good water. I thought of Abe down below, stewing, no idea what was ahead. We were showered with water, shallow seas breaking every which way, Don pulling the wheel hard to starboard. I turned the flashlight on his face and Don looked crazed or ecstatic, as if he were going over a waterfall. Bonnie kept her courage—she always did.

Now we were entering the passage but I could tell from the dark shape of the shore to my right that we were too far south of the bluff— we weren't going to make it. With the flashlight I could see the Fathometer marking no water beneath the hull. We were on top of the coral. If she caught a rudder in the reef, we'd go over, water flooding the cockpit and the salon. We'd be thrown over the side into the breakers and coral, Dad trapped below. I considered racing down the ladder, getting him onto the bridge somehow or putting him in a life preserver. But there was no time. I felt the rudder catch the bottom, hit twice, bump. I tried to think what we should do. Then a breaker caught us and the Ebb Tide spun around, broaching; another wave hit us broadside, filling the cockpit and lifting us like a stick; the forty-footer heeled way over, the three of us holding on to the bridge. But when we came down into the trough there was no more bumping and scraping. We had been tossed over the reef, still bucking in big seas, water in the cockpit, but now there was some ocean under us. I ran down the ladder and opened the fish door in the transom so the cockpit would drain out.

Don slowly turned back into the wind and we made our way north, using the ribbon of islands as protection from the storm. It took us almost two hours to idle up to Bimini, where we recognized the lights and familiar shapes of the shore, dropped the hook right in front of the Blue Water's dining room, where Dad and I liked to go for breakfast.

Down below, Abe was calm now, a sleepy expression on his face. Go figure. I helped him make his way into his bunk up forward. I kissed his cheek and pulled the blanket up under his chin. What a relief. When Dad was past his anger, the whole world opened up.

It wasn't time to leave Bimini, not for another fifteen years, as it turned out. Ansil Saunders told me about a house on South Bimini that had been on the market for some time. It was a breezy, comfortable place, he said, only a couple of minutes from the Gulf Stream. Under the living room floor there was a huge fifteen-thousand-gallon cistern—we would never run out of water, he promised. And we could buy the house dirt cheap.

I recall the first South Bimini night very well. After crossing the Gulf Stream with two-year-old Josh, we pulled up to our own private dock shaded by Australian pines and coconut palms. Herons and egrets nested across the canal in the mangroves, and Bonnie noticed lobsters in the shallow water beneath the warped planks of the dock. What a beautiful spot! We unloaded groceries, bait and clothes and put sheets on the bed, set up Josh's portable playpen. We had caught a nice dolphin coming across and Bonnie seasoned the fillets for frying. At about seven in the evening, the oil was sizzling when the power went out. While we waited for someone to turn it back on, we talked about dinner and the great fishing we would do in the morning. We were happy to be in our own house at the edge of the Gulf Stream. As time passed in the dark we listened to the crawling crackling feeding sounds of the canal. The house grew hotter. The baby cried and Bonnie rocked him and made a breeze on his sweaty face with a magazine. We searched for candles and potato chips. There were no phone lines or we would have learned that weary island generators were always shut down at night and frequently they were broken for weeks at a time. There was no way to run the water pump to flush the toilet or to refrigerate the groceries or to paddle the moist hot air with our brand-new Hunter fan above the bed. We discovered that our cinder-block walls, built to withstand hurricane-force winds, also retained and radiated the sweltering midday heat like a brick oven. Worst of all, we were scratching and swatting bugs.

The biggest impediment to gracious suburban living on the north end of South Bimini was the magnificent mangrove that spread east toward the Bahamas bank and the Tongue of the Ocean. The mangrove was a breeding ground for untold billions of mosquitoes, and in the late afternoon dark clouds of them fell upon our shady secluded dock, settled on the roof and windowsills, covered our stretched and torn screens like fur and worked themselves inside. By nightfall we were defending against a whining blizzard of mosquitoes, rolling windows shut, shoving towels under the doors, and still we were swatting and slapping. After dark one could not walk onto our dock and survive. We spent nocturnal hours fortressed in, sweltering, sticking close to our coils, scratching welts and swellings, calming the baby. Porgy Bay was just across the lagoon but South Bimini was a different universe. Our Bimini friends were reluctant to visit the house because of the pestilence of bugs.

We had put all our savings into the South Bimini house and I was resolved to make it work. By candlelight we slathered on repellents before bed, and I assuaged Bonnie with the promise of great fishing offshore. The morning breeze would be cool and the sky dark with birds working above schools of feeding fish. We'd have great action. In point of fact, the action was spotty. By the time we moved into the house there were fewer sailfish and marlin offshore. Days would pass without a billfish strike and I rarely found birds marking schools of tuna. But I was a patient fisherman and I enjoyed trolling north of the island where the deep ledges and weed lines were familiar as the vacant lots and little wooded areas I had played in as a kid. For me, the chance to raise a big one, dreaming about him and searching, was more arresting than the actual hours hooked up and pulling on the heavy rod and chasing down a marlin with the boat. Every day I was excited to leave the dock. The Bimini ocean was deep and compelling, the blue ocean of my childhood.

Bonnie was hearty and forgiving, and put up with slow game fishing, relentless sun and never-ending insects living on the hellish canal. We learned how to manage. We brought over our own little generator, which was noisy but turned the fans and powered a small air conditioner in the bedroom. I poured Clorox into the fifteen-thousand-gallon cistern, fouled from years of floating bugs and drowned rats, so we could take showers. With the proper cocktail of sprays and repellents, we could race onto the dock and throw off the lines in the evening to go to town for dinner.

If the offshore fishing was slow, the South Bimini house provided adventure. We taught Josh the game of squashing scorpions with his shoe. We soon discovered that our enormous cistern created the perfect environment for nesting scorpions. One night I woke in bed with two of them crawling in my hair. We developed a healthy let's-get-them-before-they-get-us philosophy and crushed scores of them. Josh loved South Bimini. In the early afternoon he stood on the dock and tried to spot bonefish and tarpon swimming in the canal. Big sharks and even a sawfish came in with the tide. When he was two and a half I taught him to fish and he spent hours hooking baby snapper beneath my bait table, putting them into his bucket, and when he was in the mood pouring them back into the canal. After a rain at dusk he and Bonnie would go crabbing in the bush with Brownie, an island dog we had adopted. Once in the dark of the moon Josh was chased out of the bush by a wild boar. Bonnie caged the ugly crabs with blue biters the size of a man's fist on the porch and fed them bread until they were "clean" and ready to stew in their own fat with rice.

During my father's days on Bimini, the best sportfishing boats in the world jockeyed into their slips at the Game Club and the crews set big bait freezers on the dock for a month or longer while the boats trolled north of the island. By the late seventies the dearth of marlin along with drug operations had given the island a black eye. The million-dollar Rybovich and Merritt boats with their fine cabinetry and varnish work did their blue marlin fishing farther to the south, out of San Salvador and Rum Cay in the southern Bahamas, Providenciales in the Turks and Caicos or Saint Thomas in the Virgin Islands or farther south in the waters of Belize or Venezuela. They rarely stopped at the Game Club except for maybe a night to refuel en route with tackle and arsenals of weapons stashed below and freezers lashed on the teak decks. These migrating crews stayed off the streets and ate on board. Nearly every day Florida newspapers carried stories about drug trafficking around Bimini, including incidents of Colombians having commandeered boats at sea, throwing American families overboard.

From the days on the big *Ebb Tide* with Abe, I knew many of the captains who docked overnight at the Game Club on their way south. They would tell me about phenomenal catches off distant islands. They wondered why we were still hanging out in Bimini, where there were no more fish. "Abe was one of a kind," or "What a guy your dad was," they'd say, hustling down the dock to pay the bill or pulling aboard the lines and easing out of the slip. I'd watch them head out the harbor mouth and imagine what they knew of my father.

One summer we didn't raise a single billfish in six weeks of trolling. A couple of local captains who continued fishing in front of the island were sure the marlin would come back. They believed the poor fishing had to do with vagaries of migration in the Gulf Stream rather than worldwide depletion of pelagic fish. Nonetheless, pulling baits offshore began to feel pointless, even for a stoic troller such as myself. We did more permit fishing off Sandy Cay and began making the thirty-five-mile run to the South Riding Rock, where I could usually find cero mackerel, kings and grouper. Some days as Bonnie and I trolled around the reefs we kept an eye on fat phallic forty-footers with big engines rumbling near an atoll a half-mile away. The speedy boats were waiting for planes coming up from South America and the remoteness of South Riding Rock made it a location of choice for Colombian drug transfers. We shared this terrain uneasily with a keen feel for personal space; for if we trolled within a hundred yards of one of the drug boats, men appeared from below holding automatic weapons and the boat began to ease in our direction. If I stayed a quarter-mile off, they tolerated our presence. We carried a shotgun, although I knew we wouldn't have a chance if it came down to a fight. Whenever the Colombians were within sight I eyeballed the shortest sprint to the bank, where we could probably get away in shallow water.

Over time the Colombians grew bolder. They pulled up to the Big Game Club in their powerful machines and walked up to Porgy Bay buying back their own marijuana and selling different drugs to the young men. They gradually settled on Bimini and paid off the police and other officials. The Colombians didn't tolerate competition. The hippie smugglers knew they were out of their league and soon left Bimini to study meditation in California. The Colombians set up their operation at the extreme south end of our canal, around the bend but only about three hundred yards from our house. They took over an abandoned marina, which they used as a storage depot for drugs. Almost every night planes landed on the South Bimini airstrip. Bimini men were paid well to haul marijuana to the marina. Sometimes there were mixups in timing between pilots and the men waiting on South Bimini for shipments. By the time the planes made it to Bimini, they were out of fuel, and when there were no lights on the runway, the planes ditched on the bonefish flats or the reefs east of South Bimini, where the wrecks made good hiding places for spiny crawfish. By 1980 there were scores of planes littering the waters around the island and also many wrecks on the outskirts of the airport where pilots had missed the runway in the black of night.

After dark the big speedboats rumbled up to the derelict marina at the south end of the canal, loaded up with drugs and left for Florida. Usually they idled past our house, but still the throb of their big engines pulsed through our walls. Other nights the boats came past at thirty knots and their wakes threw the *Ebb Tide* hard against the pilings and eroded the canal banks, exposing the pine tree roots to the sun and undermining our dock, which eventually fell into the water. We rebuilt it.

At the extreme north end of our canal was another small marina that had been abandoned for about ten years. A local guy, Cornelius Hannah, Jr., recognized a chance to make a buck. In the fifties Cornelius had owned the Bimini Bakery right behind the Game Club. He had also worked as a waiter at the club and played guitar for hotel guests, including Abe and Stella. When I was a kid I had once spent an afternoon sailing with him in his little boat, which he used to get to South Bimini where he grew vegetables on a plot owned by his parents. Cornelius was a jack-of-all-trades, like many Bimini men of his generation.

In the dilapidated marina a hundred fifty yards north of our house, Cornelius had set up an operation for smuggling Haitians into the States. Often when we came in from trolling Cornelius would wave me over to ask if I had any fish to sell him for his clients, and one afternoon we agreed on a price for a hundred-forty-pound wahoo, a tremendous fish.

Usually there were six or eight impoverished Haitians squatting on the docks or lying on the sand, slapping at mosquitoes, waiting, worrying if they'd make it alive to Florida or get shipped back to Haiti. A sorrowful scene.

Craig sometimes visited our house in the *M.S.T.* He came through the door ostentatiously slapping himself, amused that our house was blanketed by mosquitoes and sandwiched between Haitian refugees and bloodcurdling Colombians. We laughed over the absurdity of our lives: he was smuggling drugs on the *M.S.T.* and I was making my stand on the canal. Out of the blue I would find myself describing dark moments to Craig—he had that effect upon me. He knew that in New York I was often besotted by fears, but on this island, or bobbing offshore, I felt charmed and safe. After my father's death I had come to believe that my happiness and resourcefulness as an adult—raising a family, writing, enduring failure and boredom, warding off illness—depended upon periods of time trolling or hanging out with the bonefishermen on the wall by the Game Club dock. In the city I lived off the interest of Bimini time.

I felt the loss of Craig even while he was around. I worried about his drinking and sloppy seamanship. Like me, Craig felt unfit for the mainland, shaky. He was in his element at the bar of the abandoned hotel on the south end of North Bimini, where he sat by himself drinking beer, smoking, watching the tide, occasionally taking a trip in his derelict boat, although business was way off. But he never cared about money. Craig didn't worry about the Colombians visiting him at night. What could they do to him, was his attitude.

Of course there were major differences between us. I had a few dollars and another life in New York, diverse ambitions, a family. I came in the summer and went home. Sometimes it annoyed Craig that I measured my risks; I asked him about his capers, fed off the energy of the smuggling life, but I stayed clean. I wasn't going to jail.

A couple of times Craig arrived in the *M.S.T.,* her secret compartments loaded with a thousand pounds of grass for the trip to Florida. It was a test—how much do you love me? He knew I didn't want marijuana near my house. Craig watched me worry about the police swooping in on us and seemed to count minutes until I was jumping out of my skin and told him to leave and not come back here with dope. He took a pull on his beer and smirked, said he was going across to visit his friend Ozzie Brown at the Compleat Angler. I wouldn't see him again for a week.

Other times he came over half-drunk and sat on the sofa, a Heineken bottle in his hand. When he was nearly incoherent, Craig warned me that he wouldn't be alive much longer, to expect his friend Jeff, another marijuana smuggler, to call me in the city one day with word of what had happened to him. Through his drunkenness he gauged my discomfort. How much do you love me? Will you miss me, remember me?

———

It is amazing that we went back each summer. My mother was furious at me. "You'll die at sea," she railed. "You're the same as Abe. You're wasting your life." Art was everything to Stella, fishing was absurd. She never understood or cared that on the little boat I felt whole.

We trolled, caught a few. Josh grew up. Katya was born. Minnie took care of her summers in the South Bimini house, calmed the crying baby girl with her cool hand. The Gulf Stream remained intoxicating. On any day we might raise a big one. Josh became a great fisherman and diver. And a chess champion.

The changes on the island occurred slowly, which made them tolerable, almost remedial, blending with so much of the past, even when the phone call to New York came one winter afternoon from Jeff, as Craig had warned. Craig's decomposed body had been found floating under a dock in a canal in Fort Lauderdale. The coroner hypothesized that death was accidental—maybe he had fallen into the canal after a Super Bowl party—but Craig's mother didn't believe it, nor did I. Her boy was too strong a swimmer to drown in a canal.

The blue ocean absorbed bad news, made big promises. It was impossible to stay away, even though fishing seemed preposterous—hardly any fish while we trolled at the edge of a war.

It was a pitiful little war. The Colombians resented local competition and killed some young Bimini men; other natives crashed in small planes trying to escape DEA pursuit. By night Bahamian Defense Force boats harassed us, searched our little boat for bales while we chummed for snapper off Picket Rock. In the afternoon, while we trolled offshore looking for birds, Bonnie and I observed Defense Force cutters rendezvous with Colombian speedboats waiting for drug drops in the lee of the islands. The Defense Force guys made their side deals. Everyone on Bimini was on the take, except the young men rotting in Florida jails.

In 1993 we bought an old forty-two-foot Hatteras with my buddy Tom Chernoff, a Fort Lauderdale–based salesman with a great appetite for adventure and a sweet pitch—everyone believed in Tom and especially me. The sportfishing boat was beamy and comfortable, very much like Abe's. Eventually—inevitably—we renamed her the *Ebb Tide*. We trolled farther to the south, where there were more fish, but we always came back to Bimini to visit friends and to

pull Japanese feathers for wahoo on the deep edge north of the island. By now the marlin business was mostly dead, there was less
marijuana around, and Bimini's best blue water skippers spent their
days on shore renting out golf carts and motor scooters. Young Bimini men sat sullenly on the wall just south of the Game Club, hoping for marijuana to float in with the tide. It was rumored that a
Japanese consortium would put up a big casino on the north end of
the island, great turrets would face the Gulf Stream brandishing
replicas of larger-than-life leaping blue marlin. Bimini would be
saved.

. *I'll Be Seeing You* .

MY BROTHER BILL DIED AT THIRTY-SIX. SOON AFTER THAT, STELLA left New York and moved into a small house on Martha's Vineyard. She rarely saw people. On cold winter days my mother would bring a small folding chair to South Beach, where she had spread Bill's ashes. She mourned for ten years. I didn't think that she would survive.

Today she lives alone in her house on Music Street in West Tisbury. She spends her days painting and sculpting, and much of the time she won't tolerate visitors. But when I'm on the island and she is in the mood for company, we have wonderful evenings—both of us greedy for conversation and good jazz. She even lets me kiss her cheek and give her a big hug when I'm leaving—she finds these moments amusing. Occasionally we still argue about Abe, and Mother says to me, "But you know, you turned out more like me than him."

Sometimes when I ask her about events that have gone hazy involving my father or Bill, Stella can't remember. She draws a blank. This alarms me. Who is left to remember? The greatest are forgotten in a minute, it seems, salesmen and artists alike. My whole life I've had trouble with this.

There are a few guys who play jazz on the island, and Stella keeps

track of where they are appearing and on what nights. These fellows
are always touched when we show up to hear them play Horace Silver, Coltrane and Thelonious Monk selections. More than once
Mom and I have been the only diners in the restaurant.

One winter evening there were a half-dozen of us in Louis's Italian restaurant, across from the supermarket in Vineyard Haven, eating spaghetti and tapping to the music of pianist John Alaimo, and
bass player Jimmy B. They got big hands for "Mysterioso" and
"Song for My Father," and then John had us standing and cheering
for his rollicking version of Herbie Hancock's "Watermelon Man."
What a great night of music—an evening that flies in the face of mutability.

Jimmy B., a big burly guy, a mover by day, came over to our table
and we started talking about jazz and somehow got on to comparing
favorite trumpet players. I mentioned Chet Baker and that both of my
children are crazy about Miles Davis, and Jimmy, very opinionated
about his music, shook his head as if to say, Nice, but surely not the
greatest. After a pause he said, "The best I've ever heard on the trumpet was Tony Fruscella." Mother and I flashed our biggest I've-seen-
a-ghost expressions. To us, Tony was an icon of loss, a trumpet player
long covered over by time. "Come on. I'll show you," said Jimmy B.

We walked outside. It was snowing and icing, frigid, absolutely
the worst weather. I was afraid my mother would fall and break her
hip. Jimmy B. hustled his bass into the back of his tiny station
wagon. It didn't fit all the way in, so he traveled to gigs around the island with the rear window open, even in blizzard conditions. It felt
like a deep freeze in the car. Mother's old coat had no buttons and I
tried to hold it closed for her. Jimmy fiddled in his glove compart-
ment for the tape he wanted. "Here it is. I want you to hear this cut,"
he said. The little speakers crackled and then played clearly for Tony
Fruscella's version of "I'll Be Seeing You" with Red Mitchell's vocal
laid on top describing Tony's rough life. We were shaking in the cold
and listening to Tony's sad trumpet refrain. It was the first time that
Mother and I had ever heard the recording—we didn't know it even
existed or that anyone listened anymore to Tony Fruscella's music.
Mother, almost eighty, was nodding like a hipster. "No one plays the
horn better than that," said Jimmy B. "That's as good as it gets."

. *Pushing South* .

DURING THE NINETIES THERE HAS BEEN MUCH ATTENTION GIVEN to the devastation of worldwide populations of both pelagic and bottom-feeding fish. Marine scientists have predicted a fishless ocean unless commercial harvesting is severely limited. And yet during this crisis time sportsmen have witnessed miracles of abundance that are almost without precedent. For example, in 1993, it was discovered that numerous marlin over a thousand pounds were in residence in front of the small island of Madeira in the eastern Atlantic. Boats and crews flocked to the island at considerable expense, and hooking "granders," thousand-pound marlin, became commonplace. World records were shattered. No one had ever heard of so many huge marlin gathering in just a few acres of ocean, and fishermen wanted to believe that this surfeit was evidence of a great revival of the world's marlin population. However, two years later the big marlin vanished from Madeira.

Similarly, in the winter of 1993 off Hatteras, North Carolina, there was an astonishing and inexplicable profusion of medium-sized bluefin tuna—three- to-five-hundred-pounders—as if the earth had been tilted and most of the endangered tuna stock had poured into this small stretch of ocean. Fishermen traveled to Hatteras with the expectation of battling thirty or even forty giant bluefins in a single day—such feats had never taken place in all of game fishing history. This sudden wealth of hefty tuna incited contentious political debate between commercial fishermen and sportsmen about the quantities of tuna each group should be allowed to keep each season, as though passion and legislation conferred permanence; but soon enough most of the tuna were gone from Hatteras.

These ephemeral pockets of abundance have had a powerful effect upon sport fishermen. The wealthiest have built larger and more expensive boats than ever before—virtual ships—that can sustain fishing expeditions on distant oceans. When there is word that big fish have been discovered off the Canary Islands, Costa Rica or in the Coral Sea, boats with cruising range to make the trip cast off. Trolling in this twilight is uniquely compelling; there is still time.

In August 1998, we are pulling lures twenty miles east of Eleuthera Island, headed south. There is no land in sight but a mile or two ahead of the Hatteras there are a few birds on the horizon or at least I think so. I squint my eyes trying to bring the birds into focus. I'm nervous and excited. We haven't caught a good fish all summer, but I like this oily calm stretch of gray water between Eleuthera and Little San Salvador. There is current running and I have that feeling, my skin tingling, a kind of whole body intuition—I'm feeling big fish, tuna or marlin. But as I stare ahead I begin to feel less confident. More and more I've been predicting big strikes and then nothing comes up behind the baits. I'm not sure about the birds, dammit.

For the last few years I have been seeing birds in my head whenever I stare at the horizon, as if a mural of working seabirds has become imprinted in my brain. It is something more perverse than deteriorating eyesight; I never see working birds in front of office buildings or even when I'm walking along the Hudson River in the evening. And it's even worse. When the birds are real I don't notice them. My twenty-one-year-old son, Josh, bounds up the ladder in two athletic steps, and says impatiently, "Dad, you see the birds over there to the port, a couple of hundred yards off? Look, will you!" And I nod to him, got 'em, and turn the wheel squinting to see the birds. "Not there, Dad," Josh says, grabbing the wheel and turning sharply until the bow comes around another thirty degrees and he asks again, "Can you see the birds?" I nod yes. But I still can't see the damn birds. "Okay, keep steering this way. You'll see them. There's a lot of birds in front of you."

I am looking at these birds, or whatever, way ahead of the *Ebb Tide,* as we troll toward Little San Salvador. At this speed it will take the old Hatteras three more hours to reach the uninhabited island, one of my favorite places. Little San Salvador is tiny, with a white, perfectly made half-moon beach, no litter, no buildings, no people, good holding for the anchor, lovely reefs for snorkeling, and the island affords a natural lee for the prevailing southeast wind this time of year. Usually when we pull into the lagoon there are no other boats anchored. It is way off the beaten track. Sleeping in this anchorage is exquisitely restful. I dream about this place.

The birds are still fluttering in the distance, no change to speak of, and by now I'm pretty sure they are my own wispy flock. Oddly enough, this takes the pressure off. The fishing has been slow all summer, but trolling is its own reward, peaceful and prescient. As long as we are covering ground with the lures, we could raise anything. Hooking up can be anticlimatic, even boring. But I should add that this eastern trolling spirit makes my son impatient and he sometimes accuses me of steering away from fish.

Josh is seated below on the bait freezer watching the lures in the wake, as I did, religiously, on my dad's boat. Josh is our deckhand, fast and savvy. He has great eyes and is the only one on the *Ebb Tide* strong enough to wire a big fish and wrestle it aboard. He could make a career of being a mate except that he is a professional chess player, needs to study a lot and often travels abroad to play. Josh loves to fish but worries that the time he gives us on the boat in the summer is costing him.

Katya, my thirteen-year-old daughter, is in the salon painting her nails black, tapping her foot, listening to Fiona Apple through her earphones and sometimes singing along, her voice husky with decadence. She is in another world. I often wonder what Katya is thinking about. She won't tell me. She scribbles in her journal and snaps it closed when I walk past. Josh used to tell me everything, but with Katya it's a guessing game. She has wandered into adolescence with the most lovely musing smile, and I already miss her terribly.

Even with reservations about killing fish, Katya has become a good angler. In fact, on our crack fishing team, Katya *is* the angler. Josh is the deckhand. Bonnie navigates. I steer the boat and use my wisdom and guile to guide us to fish—the big game captain fantasy persists against the logic of the time.

There has been a change. The flock has thickened and turned black, swung in our direction, so many goddamn birds a quarter-mile ahead that I am suddenly sapped of confidence. I keep squinting and trying to clear my head.

"Bonnie, would you please take a look ahead and tell me if you see what I see?"

"Not now." Bonnie is seated beside me on the bridge, her head in a thick novel. I nudge her, but she won't look up. At fifty-four Bonnie will only come on the boat if I'm willing to accept her terms. She is semiretired from fishing and refuses to stare at the baits behind the boat—considers it a waste of her time and rarely picks up a rod. She doesn't reminisce about the long frenetic days in the cockpit when she won the Bimini Native Tournament an unheard-of three times in four years. And I know she could still fish with the old zest if she wanted to. This tension exists between us—that she doesn't want to anymore. But Bonnie has trained me to take what I can get.

"Honey, are those birds? You just wouldn't believe how many birds I see."

"Ah huh." She won't look up from the book.

"Hey Dad, way to go!" Josh calls from below with a tremendous grin. He is standing on the gunwale and pointing ahead of the boat where the sky is congested with diving, hovering, yapping birds.

I smirk back at Josh and nod as if I knew it all along. I spotted the birds miles away and have been stalking for twenty minutes like the great Ansil Saunders. It actually feels cold when we enter this dark aviary. I see a big tuna come out of the water, then more and more tuna, hundred-pounders bounding along, hundreds of hundred-pounders. Such beautiful big fish with black backs traced with golden yellow. We haven't been able to find one all summer. They are all here off the southern tip of Eleuthera, in gray water, the sky stormy with birds.

Now the tuna are ripping through schools of bait fish and the birds are diving into the mix, racing off with tidbits. Brown boobies with broad wings are wheeling only inches from the surface. I suspect that there are marlin here as well, feeding below the tuna, and certainly big sharks and probably wahoo. Bonnie is standing now, looking over this great opulence, shaking her head. You could walk across the broad backs of tuna, acres of tuna.

"Katya, Katya," Josh is bellowing like a foghorn for his sister. "Kaatyaaaa." He smacks the bulkhead with his fist.

Katya comes bolting through the door, earphones dangling from her neck, trying to keep her wet black nails off the varnish.

"Look at the birds!" he shrieks.

Katya rolls her eyes, you called me outside for birds. Give me a break. I'm busy, don't you know. She tosses her head and goes back below, her teenaged musings much larger than some birds or the unassailable purpose of our trip to this remote patch of ocean with no land in sight, no friends, no social life. Birds! Please.

I see the fish come up behind the flatline bait. It looks like an ox, big, dark and broad, big black tuna, as my friend James Rolle says, it's coming hard at the lure, grabs the plastic and heads for New York.

"Katya, Kaaatyaaaaa!!!" Josh is screaming so loud the air is shaking and again she charges through the door, blowing on her nails, the fifty-pound-test rod in the holder bent nearly in half, line pouring off.

"Get in the goddamned chair. What's wrong with you? I told you to get out here. First time we've seen fish—"

"What's your problem, Josh," she says, facing off with her brother while line empties from the reel.

"Katya, I fuckin' told you—"

"You told me to look at the birds, Josh."

"Katya, look at what you're doing," he says, laughing in disbelief. We're losing this fish and Katya's asserting herself. It's now a quarter mile behind the boat and steaming. The rod between Katya's legs is bucking with big fish power.

"Don't talk to me in that voice, Mr. Big Shot."

"Jesus Christ, reel, Katya."

"How can I reel?"

She's right. Line is still running off. What a fish. Katya is holding the rod with both of her hands while Josh puts the kidney harness around her back. There is too much line off the reel to turn the boat around. We'd probably lose the rest of the line from the spool if I tried this maneuver. I start to back down on the tuna. One engine in reverse, and then the other, to keep the line right behind the transom—I hope the transmission stays together. The fish is no longer running and Katya is pushing hard against the footrest, leaning back against the fish and then swinging down and taking up slack line, rocking and reeling, while I back the boat and water splashes over the transom onto my daughter's shapely brown legs.

There's a lot of line out. I hope we don't get cut off by sharks. There must be dozens of big sharks here with all of these tuna. Fishing lust has taken over and we don't want to lose it. Bonnie, Josh and I are thinking about the sharks. Katya is working very hard. Sweating and hauling back. If the sharks hit, all she'll bring up will be lips and gills. It is amazing how fast they devour a big tuna.

The birds are everywhere. Yapping, flapping around the outriggers, diving into the water on both sides of the boat. Katya is pulling. The physicality intrigues her and she just goes for it, hauls back against the fish, her legs straining, reels down with both hands. She flat out brings it. Josh grouses a little but he is proud of his sister. The tuna are jumping on all sides of us, big fish, hundred-pounders. After a thousand miles of empty ocean you could dive in and grab one.

Bonnie is standing in the stern holding a long gaff. She's hooked also, pagan, wants big tuna in the boat. I'm backing down. Josh is standing hip to hip with his mother, getting set to grab the leader wire. A big tuna like this pulls hard, twice as hard as a marlin the same size. I know he's a little nervous. He's been playing chess, not taking double wraps on big tuna. Katya has the double line on the reel and pushes the drag up all the way. Don't break the line, I say to myself. Katya is pulling with all of her strength, not letting line slip off the reel. And then I see the sharks. Big sharks. Three of them, each about twelve feet long. They are closing on the tuna.

"We got to take it now, guys. They are coming. Right now."

I am sick about the sharks. Josh reaches out as far as he can and grabs the wire. I ease the boat ahead so we don't lose the fish in the props. Josh is pulling on the wire with both arms, his legs flexed and straining and the sharks are coming hard, maybe twenty feet behind the tuna, which has its head down, pulling for the bottom against Josh's strength. An arm wrestle is what it is.

"Take him now, Josh, or break him off."

Josh pulls with all his strength and the tuna yields, rises into the wash, right alongside. I can't see the sharks in the white water, but they are right below, a few feet away.

Bonnie strikes with the gaff—no cork on the end of this one. She's got the tuna—or it has her. She can't lift it an inch and grabs for the gunwale with one hand to stay in the boat. Josh grabs his mother's wrist and then reaches for the gaff and hauls the tuna half out. Then he lifts with everything he's got, gets the head over the transom and then Bonnie and Josh pull once together and it falls into the boat. It's a big yellowfin tuna, a hundred fifty pounds or more, the largest we have ever caught.

From the bridge I can see the sharks lingering behind the transom. No more menace, just big creatures. The tuna is beating on the white fiberglass deck, blood splattering everywhere, all over Katya's legs and Bonnie's white shirt. Josh tackles the tuna and covers its eyes with his hands, leans against it. Almost immediately the fish is quiet and Josh holds this pose until the little yellow dorsal fins stop quivering.

We are drifting in a soft, oily swell and all around the boat the birds are wheeling and flying through the riggers, the tuna are jumping. A few years ago we would have put the lines right out and caught another fish or trolled around the edge of the school for a marlin; but this isn't even an issue. One tuna is enough. The rules have changed.

Bonnie unclips the leader wires and then coils them while Josh finishes "bleeding" the tuna, so it will be fit to eat, and then he starts hosing the deck. Katya announces that her back is killing her, where are the Tylenol, she'd like to help with the cleanup but isn't up to it. In a minute Katya is below blasting Fiona Apple, her eyes closed, her leg pumping to the rhythm.

By the time we get the anchor set in the lagoon, it is dark with just a trace of rosiness to the west. We are the only boat here, as I had expected. I am on the bridge, sipping a beer, looking at the blinking light on the southern tip of Eleuthera, fifteen miles away. Between our anchored boat and the lighthouse is a terrific stretch of deep water that piles up against a long, shallow bank called "the bridge." In the past we have caught marlin, tuna and sailfish trolling this ridge and in the shallow water we have chummed up yellowtail snapper the size of big bluefish. We almost never see another boat fishing here, occasionally a sailboat passing in the distance. It's our ocean. We'll troll the bridge tomorrow. I always feel good to have a fishing plan. One more night anchored here and then it's time to head back. We'll troll the Exuma Sound and the Tongue of the Ocean and spend two nights on Bimini visiting friends before crossing the Gulf Stream to Florida.

One of my kids turns on the stereo and Errol Garner's voluptuous piano rolls out across the calm water toward Eleuthera and all the big fish. I am beside myself with this gentle night and his grunting over the chords, the lapping of the waves, the soft breeze coming across the island. Down below, Josh and Katya are cutting thin slices of tuna for sashimi and Bonnie is cooking rice and vegetables. It simply cannot be better than this. In the morning we'll sleep late and then take off our clothes and swim around the boat. Before breakfast Bonnie and Katya will snorkel into shore and wander the beach looking for shells.

I'm hungry but I'm also very tired. I don't know if I'm gonna make it until dinner. My mind drifts to the Tartar Bank sixty miles south of here off the southern coast of Cat Island. The Tartar Bank is a mesa that rises from the deep ocean to a depth of eighty feet. There are always big seas and working birds above wahoo and tuna, sometimes marlin. A big population of tiger sharks feeds under the tuna— you must take a fish very quickly. No other boats around. Next summer we'll troll the Tartar Bank.

Something is slamming in my head. I have never heard such a racket before. A terrible crash, and the chug of a big engine. A rhythm to it: CRASH, CHUG, CRASH, CHUG, CRASH, CHUG. I have heard this sound before. A pile driver. Also the straining lifting hauling sounds of huge derricks and tractors. When I was a kid Dad and I would stand next to building sites in the city, watch the heavy equipment work.

I climb out of my bunk and walk outside into the cockpit in my underwear. Thirty feet from our bow is an enormous barge with a pile driver working on one end. On the shore, fifty yards away, there are derricks lifting rocks and tractors pushing sand. We must have dropped anchor in front of the wrong island. There are a dozen dormitory-like buildings on shore, a church going up, many stores, a straw market, men in hard hats rushing up and down the white beach in jeeps. Workers in a skiff are hanging a "predator net" with designer floats right in front of my bow. Everything on the land is painted in playful zesty colors.

Almost immediately a man comes by the *Ebb Tide* in a Boston Whaler, a British fellow, the construction manager. He is a pleasant guy. He explains that Holland America lines has leased Little San Salvador from the Bahamian government and they are putting up a replica of a Bahamian village. Within two months thousands of tourists will be walking the beaches, visiting the imitation straw market and Bahamian church, eating surf and turf onshore—they can cook for two thousand at a sitting. A big attraction will be the game fishing. In the afternoon, before returning to the ship anchored off the reef, vacationers can board a fleet of swift fishing boats and troll the virginal stretch of ocean between here and Eleuthera.

I am bemused by all this activity. I smile and accept his invitation to have a tour of the new facility. He seems like a good guy, genuinely enthusiastic about the transformation of the island, as though he has groomed a savage land. But I can't help myself and I mention to the Englishman there is perhaps one problem. With many boats trolling and chumming the area, the fish will soon be gone—the Holland America line will have the white beach and colorful village but the surrounding water will be dead. "Do you think so?" he asks mildly. And already I sense the weakness in my thinking. Putting up an imitation Bahamian village is fast, relatively inexpensive work, a lot of plywood. There are many more islands.

It is about five in the afternoon and we are running across the Shallow Sea between the Berry Islands and the Bimini chain at sixteen knots approaching the Gun Cay Passage—the same narrow cut where we almost died in the night with Abe three decades earlier. At low tide we have only four and a half feet under the hull, but I've been through this area many times and I know that we won't hit bottom. The surface is perfectly calm, without a ripple, which magnifies the ledges, starfish, a crawfish walking on the bottom, cudas here and there. Watching the passing bottom is mesmerizing but also a little disorienting, the bottom seems too close. When we enter the passage I run near the Gun Cay side and pass the island twenty feet away, where the water is deepest. I notice the flock of birds working a mile offshore. Josh is on the bow watching the reef below. He signals for me to slow down, but I keep steaming at sixteen knots, about as hard as I dare push the old Hatteras. For some reason he doesn't trust my eyes, which I find annoying. Josh shouts for me to slow down but I ignore him. He doesn't realize that I have been through this area of reefs and ledges hundreds of times with Bonnie in the twenty-footer.

When the depth recorder marks eighty feet I turn north and Bimini comes into view, just another nine miles to go. I can't wait. I'm rushing back to the island where we were kids. I wonder if the South Bimini house is still standing. Probably someone filled it up with marijuana, funny idea. After hurricanes and drug wars, Bimini persists, dead ahead, beautiful as the first day I saw it emerging from the sea. So much promise.

Look at the Big Game Fishing Club. They've put in staunch concrete pilings. The hotel is all painted, the palm trees groomed and swaying in the evening breeze by the pool. Isaac is serving piña coladas in the Gulf Stream Bar and Restaurant. He used to serve drinks to Abe. My mother always hated these bourgeois places by the sea where Abe ordered lavishly and gave big tips. I love them.

The following morning there is a light breeze and a vibrant blue sky overhead, a perfect fishing day. At the Big Game Club the bonefishermen are sitting on the wall waiting for their charters to finish breakfast in the chilly dining room. Bonefish Rudy, Action Jackson and Cordell are itchy to get going. I'm half-asleep in the stern of my boat, sipping a cup of tea. I can see Ansil Saunders walk down the dock, climb into his skiff, arrange his two chairs in the bow, check the condition of his shrimp. He tosses some dead ones over the side.

Ansil is still beautiful to look at, lithe and strong, though he is almost seventy. No one can find them like Ansil.

Up and down the dock, the mates are finished rigging baits and putting the big coolers on board. Maybe someone will hook a marlin today. One after the next the enormous diesels come alive with a roar. Same sound as when I was a kid. My father shakes me gently, "Wake up, boy." I am trying to sleep late after pounding on the conga drums for Sexy Mama until three A.M. at the Calypso Club. I had them standing and cheering. I was Armando Peraza. But I couldn't tell my dad. I hope he slept through the night and didn't notice my bunk was empty. "It's time to go fishing, boy." I smile at him. We are in this fish hunt together. I'll climb the tower and find the birds, we'll raise one. There is still hope, and fishing is another name for hope.